50 LICKS

ALSO BY PETE FORNATALE

Back to the Garden

Simon and Garfunkel's Bookends

Elfis

All You Need Is Love

Wackronyms

The Story of Rock 'n' Roll

Radio in the Television Age

The Rock Music Source Book

50 LICKS

Myths and Stories from Half a Century of the Rolling Stones

Pete Fornatale
with Bernard M. Corbett
and Peter Thomas Fornatale

BLOOMSBURY

NEW YORK • LONDON • NEW DELHI • SYDNEY

Bloomsbury USA, 175 Fifth Avenue, New York, NY 10010
Bloomsbury Publishing, Plc, 50 Bedford Square, London, WC1B 3DP

All papers used by Bloomsbury Publishing are natural, recyclable products made from wood grown in well-managed forests. The manufacturing processes conform to the environmental regulations of the country of origin.

LIBRARY OF CONGRESS CATALOGING-IN-PUBLICATION DATA HAS BEEN APPLIED FOR.

US ISBN: 978-1-60819-921-1
UK ISBN: 978-1-40883-382-7

First published in Great Britain and the USA in 2013

1 3 5 7 9 10 8 6 4 2

Designed by Lawrence Kim
Printed in China by C&C Offset Printing Co., Ltd.

Peter Thomas Fornatale:
For my father and my daughter;
it's a damn shame you never got to meet.

Bernard M. Corbett:
To my Aunt Canu. The hand-me-downs
(Aftermath, Between the Buttons,
December's Children) *were a perfect fit.*

CONTENTS

Introduction 1

1. Start Me Up 3

2. 2120 South Michigan Avenue 10

3. Come On 17

4. I Wanna Be Your Man 23

5. Street Fighting Man 28

6. Sing This All Together 37

7. Rip This Joint 42

8. (I Can't Get No) Satisfaction 47

9. Get Off of My Cloud 49

10. Paint It Black 51

11. Little T & A 53

12. Waiting on a Friend 59

13. Let's Spend Some Time Together 63

14. Ruby Tuesday 67

15. 2000 Light Years from Home 69

16. Mother's Little Helper 75

17. Jigsaw Puzzle 77

18. Rock and Roll Circus 86

19. Let It Bleed 92

20. Gimme Shelter 103

21. Honky Tonk Women 105

22. You Can't Always Get What You Want 108

23. Sympathy for the Devil 114

24. Brown Sugar 121

25. Like a Rolling Stone 123

26. Sticky Fingers 128

27. Wang Dang Doodle 136

28. Tumbling Dice 141

29. Let It Loose 153

30. On with the Show 161

31. Dancing with Mr. D 165

32. Angie 167

33. Time Waits for No One 170
34. It's Only Rock 'n' Roll 174
35. All Down the Line 177
36. Around and Around 181
37. Before They Make Me Run 184
38. Some Girls 187
39. Miss You 193
40. Send It to Me 197
41. Hang Fire 200
42. Black Limousine 204
43. Had It with You 210
44. Not Fade Away 218
45. Mixed Emotions 222
46. In Another Land 232
47. New Faces 237
48. Don't Stop 245
49. Rough Justice 249
50. Shine a Light 255
Epilogue: Memory Motel 259

Acknowledgments 262
Cast of Characters 264
Source Notes 269
Image Credits 273

INTRODUCTION

BACK IN 1977, when *Love You Live* came out, the question on the table for Charlie Watts was, "Do you still see a real long future ahead for the Rolling Stones?" His answer was as prescient as it gets:

CHARLIE WATTS: It's really funny because I just said to some guy, and he must be about twenty-four, and he said, "You've been going a long time." And I said, "Yeah, but you know Duke Ellington had a band with the same personnel virtually for fifty years."

And now it has come to this: somewhere near the end of the twenty-first century, some pop cultural music superstar will be asked how long they can keep doing what they're doing, and the answer will be, "Hey, the Rolling Stones were a band with the same personnel virtually for fifty years!" Fifty years. Half a century.

How ironic that rock 'n' roll—whose imminent demise was predicted as early as the mid-1950s—has produced a band whose longevity has defied all odds and given it a stature unmatched by any of its peers, including its sometimes rival/sometimes doppelganger—the Beatles.

The first record I ever played on my debut program at WNEW-FM in July of 1969 was a Stones tune, "Sing This All Together," from *Their Satanic Majesties Request*. I wanted something upbeat and memorable that made the case for the role progressive FM radio was playing in people's lives at the end of the '60s. Who better than the Rolling Stones?

Fifty years ago, in the early days of the British Invasion, the Stones played devil's advocate to the sainted Beatles. Their brand of rock 'n' roll was always a bit blacker, a bit bluer than the Fab Four's, and had more of a jagged (Jaggered?) edge to it.

50 Licks will be a raucous, rollicking celebration of the rock 'n' roll roller-coaster ride that is the Rolling Stones. We will take you on a thrilling journey *Through the Past, Darkly*, with all of the highest highs and lowest lows, all of the hairpin turns and screeching *Steel Wheels* befitting the still aptly described "Greatest Rock 'n' Roll Band in the World." We'll look *Between* all *the Buttons*, put the *Ya-Ya's* under a microscope, and, finally, place the *Aftermath* in historical perspective. Consider this observation by a certain Academy Award–winning director:

MARTIN SCORSESE: For me, their music is part of my life, particularly during the '60s. I'd never seen the band perform until maybe the early '70s. I experienced this music by seeing it in my head, by listening to the records . . . the chords, the vocals, the entire feel of their music inspired me greatly. It became a basis for most of the work I've done in my movies, going from *Mean Streets* on through *Raging Bull*, all the way up through *Casino* to *The Departed*.

Mick and Keith were born in 1943; Charlie in 1941; and Ron, a mere pup, in 1947. So far the band has always managed to overcome any and all obstacles placed in its path, and come back bigger and stronger than ever. And there is always a ready and waiting audience for whatever it is the Stones choose to do. Amazingly, in this fickle world, they have held on to their fans from the early days, and just continue adding new ones.

There are very good reasons for this. First and foremost, there is the music—a gutsy, guitar-based, blues-drenched raunch 'n' roll that is uniquely their own. Then there is the legendary Mick Jagger persona—the pouting, prancing, posturing prototype for every young vocalist who dares to dream about becoming lead singer in a rock 'n' roll band. Finally, they are almost more defiant on the precipice of old age than they were in middle age and as young adults, albeit in different ways. They do not bow to trends or hot new acts but instead turn out worthy albums and memorable performances that remind people of exactly what it was that made them fall in love with the group in the first place.

The proof that the Stones still matter is everywhere. Contemporary artists mine their catalog for great gems to cover and record. Advertisers scramble to use memorable Stones classics to sell cars, financial services, and candy bars. And when it's time to put up or shut up, the Stones routinely deliver. Mick Jagger's first appearance at the Grammys was in 2011, and it was a command performance. Right there in the Land of Gaga and the Kingdom of Bieber, Mick the Magic Jagger stole the show singing his tribute to the late Solomon Burke—"Everybody Needs Somebody to Love."

We began this prologue with Charlie Watts's observation in 1977 about the potential longevity of the Rolling Stones. I wrote about it and made my own prediction in my 1986 book *The Story of Rock 'n' Roll*: "(Charlie) once marveled in an interview at the continuing vitality and energy of musicians from the big band era who still make relevant and vibrant music well into their sixties and seventies, often with their original bandmates. I'm betting the Stones will do likewise."

And as this book will attest, the Stones keep rolling on.

CHAPTER 1

START ME UP

EVERY GREAT STORY has to start somewhere. So where does this great story start?

July 12, 1962, was the first time that an entity publicly described as "Mick Jagger and the Rolling Stones" took the stage. It happened at the fabled Marquee Club in London, opening for the late, great Long John Baldry (known for a tune that went, "Don't try to lay no 'boo-jee woo-jee' on the king of rock 'n' roll!").

Wait a minute. "Mick Jagger and the Rolling Stones"? In the early days, the Rolling Stones were very much Brian Jones's band.

DICK TAYLOR: Brian Jones pulled Mick and Keith and then myself into the band. We were definitely Stones at that point. All the elements were there, apart from Bill Wyman, because at various rehearsals Charlie played.

Brian's head must have exploded when he saw that billing, but it is explainable.

BILL WYMAN: Brian was the leader of the Rolling Stones for a year and a half. He formed the Rolling Stones.

CHARLIE WATTS: He worked very hard, Brian.

BILL WYMAN: He organized the whole thing when nobody would accept us, nobody would book us in clubs, nobody. He used to write letters to the magazines and things.

HOW LITTLE BOY BLUE AND THE BLUE BOYS BECAME THE ROLLIN' STONES

DICK TAYLOR: Mick and I first met when I was eleven. Myself and another guy, Robert Beckwith, were both into rock 'n' roll and rhythm and blues. We met Mick and we had a mutual liking of such music. When we got to be about thirteen, we were all very much into that. Eventually, we started a little band where Mick sang and Robert and I played guitar, and a guy called Allen Etherington had a little drum kit. We had a little band that didn't really have a name.

Keith knew that I was doing this band and he was too shy to ask if he could come to rehearsal. Then, he met Mick again at Dartford station—they had known each other when they were very young. And one of them had a Chuck Berry record. They started talking and Keith came up to our next rehearsal. So we then had Keith, Mick, myself, occasionally Allen Etherington, and Robert Beckwith, and we were all playing together.

One night we all piled in Mick's father's car to watch Alexis Korner and Blues Incorporated play the Muddy Waters–type stuff. We thought we could do at least as well as that. Prior to that, we recorded stuff and we needed a name so we just decided on Little Boy Blue and the Blue Boys.

What happened next was we met up with Brian Jones. Mick went along to Brian's band. Brian, at that time, had a guy called Brian Knight singing, Geoff Bradford on guitar, and Ian Stewart on piano. Mick dragged Keith along. Brian asked me about playing bass. We needed a name. Someone said, "How about Rollin' Stones?" I think it was Brian. I can't really swear who it was. I think it may well have been Brian.

CHARLIE WATTS: I was in this very strange situation with the Rolling Stones because I used to play in a band that the Rolling Stones used to knock because they had all the gigs: Alexis Korner. We had somewhere to play. It was a bum jazz night, which was Thursday, a no-money night, and Alexis turned it into the biggest night of the week financially for the club, which was a big thing in London. And there was a helluva lot of animosity about it all. And Brian thought that the Rolling Stones were as good as Alexis's band and he wanted the club owners to give his band a chance. Alexis got all these people together really. He gave you a stage to play on. I didn't know what the hell he was talking about when I used to play with him. It was a really good band at one time, but you're talking about real history now. That's when Brian was really fighting.

As Charlie points out above, actual Thursday night residency at the Marquee belonged to Alexis Korner's Blues Incorporated, but on this particular July Thursday the group was booked for a very high-profile appearance on the BBC *Jazz Club* broadcast. So Baldry was bumped up to headline at the club, and an opportunity was thus created for this shiny new ensemble revolving around Brian Jones, Mick Jagger, Keith Richards, Ian Stewart, Dick Taylor, and Tony Chapman. But still, shouldn't it have been "Brian Jones and the Rolling

THE GREAT DRUMMER MYSTERY

We can pinpoint five of the musicians who took the stage at the Marquee Club on July 12, 1962:

Mick Jagger—vocals, harmonica
Elmo Lewis, aka Brian Jones—guitar
Keith Richards—guitar
Ian Stewart—piano
Dick Taylor—bass

There was a sixth musician on that stage, sitting right behind the drum kit. Before we get to who it was, a little background:

ALAN CLAYSON: A drummer was a very prized commodity in early '60s beat groups in Britain. Partly because the amount of money you had to spend on a drum kit was considerable. And often, drummers were taken on regardless of their skills simply because of their ownership of the right equipment.

Who drummed for the Stones in the early days?

ALAN CLAYSON: The Stones had a very movable feast of drummers. Tony Chapman was a traveling salesman and often absent. Carlo Little was straight out of the army and playing with Screaming Lord Sutch and the Savages.* Carlo tended to be a Rollin' Stone when his commitment to Lord Sutch was not pending. Mick Avory, a rising sap of puberty, came from South London, looking for an opening in a pop group. The drummer the Stones most wanted to recruit was Charlie Watts. He was very reluctant to commit to being anything more than a semi-professional musician. He was a draftsman and he thought the late nights would affect the steadiness of his hand.

*A band that at various times included Jimmy Page, Jeff Beck, and Keith Moon!

As for our mystery man, even though Keith Richards (and an ad from that week's *Jazz News*) claim it was Mick Avory, later of the Kinks, in doing our research, we received word from Mick Avory himself that it wasn't him. Both Dick Taylor and Alan Clayson told us it was possibly Charlie Watts—surmising that he might have been excluded from the Alex Korner BBC session. But Charlie himself has confirmed that he was at the Beeb that night. Here's how we handicap this particular horse race: 90 percent it was Tony Chapman; 10 percent it was none of the above.

Stones"? Or rather "Elmo Lewis and the Rolling Stones," since Jones was still using his pseudonym at the time?

Since earlier in the year, Mick had been a regular vocalist with Korner's ensemble band. But the BBC budget only allowed for a total of six musicians, and Mick was the odd man out for *Jazz Club* and didn't make the trip. Since his name was already known to the Marquee Club regulars, it was slapped onto the blurb about the gig. It signaled some sense of Thursday night continuity: in Korner's absence, the club would be serving up business as usual. Needless to say, it was anything but "business as usual."

So how does a band get from one good gig to the biggest stages in the world—for half a century? Well, it's a process of mix and match, trial and error, charisma and chemistry. Let's not forget addition and subtraction. For instance, subtract Chapman and Taylor; add Charlie Watts and Bill Wyman.

DICK TAYLOR: There were various little things which nudged me towards not continuing. Basically, the bass thing was one of them, because I felt I always wanted to play guitar. I think if I had been the guitarist in the Stones . . . But I must say, there was no personality clashes or anything like that. We all got on very well. That's one of the things that I think everybody should know, that while I know that they had their problems later between Brian and Keith, in that time everybody got on very, very well.

The early days were not easy. Keith Richards tells a story about collecting cans for their deposits so he could buy guitar strings.

BILL WYMAN: Those first six or nine months it was really hard to get gigs.

CHARLIE WATTS: Then you joined, then I joined and we had nothing, man.

Brian, Mick, and Keith lived together in a flat in Edith Grove (along with another roommate, James Phelge, who would go on to provide half of the Stones' nom de plume in the early days, Nanker Phelge). The place was a notorious dump.

DICK TAYLOR: I couldn't believe it. I'd been to a few places that were a bit squalid. I think Edith Grove really took the biscuit.

BILL WYMAN: Nobody would book us, they were all into traditional jazz. And some blues groups. Brian used to write to the BBC to ask for auditions. And we went down for an audition, to play, and afterwards they rejected us. They said the band is OK, we could use them for American musicians that come over, blues musicians, but the singer's no good, he sounds too colored. That was the reason they rejected us. And Brian would write to the music papers letters saying what he thought blues was, and he was in a band that played a Chicago form of blues, and he would really get involved in all that when everybody else was almost giving up. And nobody had any money. The band was almost breaking up at different points. There were people coming and going, different musicians.

CHARLIE WATTS: I was out of work at the time. Because me and him are the only two people who actually had jobs. And I was out of work and I used to hang around with Brian and Keith, and their days used to be mad. They'd just sit around all day, actually they'd sleep all day, and sit around all night listening to Jimmy Reed, the same record. I can remember listening to these records. And I'd never heard of Jimmy Reed at that time. Well, I had but it was very new to me. They showed me how good those people were.

A picture of the Stones circa 1963, note Ian Stewart on the upper right.

BILL WYMAN: I used to borrow records, learn them by heart, and sell them for breakfast.

The hard work and blues obsession eventually started to pay off as the new lineup, including Charlie and Bill, started to build a following.

JOHN MAYALL: I heard them first on a Sunday afternoon at a club where they had a residency. It was very professional. They had a really good repertoire. They were a really exciting band and they had it all together. The thing that struck me was the reaction of the audience. They were really getting off on it and everybody knew there was something happening.

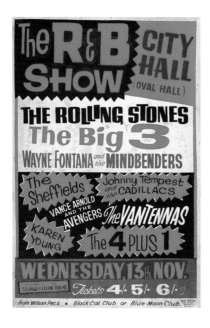

Let's not get too far ahead of ourselves, though. On this first night of going out publicly in front of approximately 150 people, most of whom could be described as middle class bohemian blues purists, stick to the basics. Build on the shoulders of the masters who got you here in the first place. No one expects any original compositions from a fledgling entry on the R&B circuit. No one wants attempts by someone with future songwriting potential to slow down another blues-drenched Thursday. In fact, quite the contrary. They want tried-and-true classics to propel them into the last workday of the week, so they can pick up their paychecks and make their plans to party for the entire weekend ahead. That means selecting a repertoire that leans heavily on those acknowledged masters, and covering the hell out of them for your entire time on stage.

The Stones took the stage, and opened up with an internationally known rock 'n' roll hit written in 1952 by the seminal songwriting team of Jerry Leiber and Mike Stoller. Originally called "K.C. Loving" by Little Willie Littlefield, the title was changed seven years later to "Kansas City," and a new version by Wilbert Harrison made it all the way to number one on the popularity charts. The Stones (and for that matter the Beatles) probably became aware of it from a cover version by Little Richard that became a hit in the United Kingdom in 1959. Mr. Penniman performed it in a medley with his own song "Hey, Hey, Hey," which is exactly how the Fab Four recorded it on their *Beatles for Sale* album at the end of 1964.

Not surprisingly, the Stones also covered selections from the sacred blues canon, by Robert Johnson, Muddy Waters, Elmore James, and no fewer than six songs (fully one third of their entire set) by Jimmy Reed: "Honey What's Wrong," "Bright Lights, Big City," "Hush, Hush," "Ride 'Em on Down," "Kind of Lonesome," and "Big Boss Man." Also not surprisingly, they did the Chuck Berry hit "Back in the USA." But *very* surprisingly, Mick Jagger and the Rolling Stones covered a song called "Tell Me That You Love Me" that was written by Canadian teen heartthrob Paul Anka. (As he proved once again on a recent PBS tribute to the late Buddy Holly, Anka earned his street cred in the formative days of rock 'n' roll music. The Stones' decision to cover him in their debut is a testament to it.)

In summation, a quartet of musicians that music historians regard as four sixths of the original Rolling Stones came together under that name on that sweaty July night in 1962.

We began this chapter with a question, so let's end it with two more:

Was this the night that changed the music world forever?

No.

Was this the night that would be worth celebrating as the fiftieth anniversary of the Rolling Stones in 2012?

Absolutely.

CHAPTER 2

2120 SOUTH MICHIGAN AVENUE

ONE OF THE MOST famous addresses in rock 'n' roll history, 2120 South Michigan Avenue, Chicago, Illinois, was the home of Chess Records from about 1956 to 1965. The label was run by brothers Leonard and Phil Chess, who knew how to find, record, distribute, and promote the finest American practitioners of Delta blues, one of the earliest styles of blues music in the United States. Thanks to recording and broadcasting technology, the sounds created by these unique individuals reverberated all over the globe, finding a particularly receptive audience in post–World War II England in the '50s and '60s.

JOHN MAYALL: It was a very special time, obviously. And there was a great feeling of enthusiasm for the music. It all happened very, very quickly. One minute all the clubs were featuring traditional New Orleans jazz, and then all of a sudden Alexis Korner and Cyril Davies kicked this new thing off, which was an offshoot of the folk clubs I guess. It was a Chicago blues thing, with amplifiers.

I'd been playing blues for myself, without an audience, for many years before that, but this was the opportunity I needed to come down to London and join in. And I think that was the case with a lot of people from the north. The Animals came down from Newcastle, and the Spencer Davis Group with Steve Winwood came down from Birmingham, and the whole thing mushroomed very quickly. The Flamingo Club and the Marquee Club, those were the mainstays. They were really booming. I had started record collecting ten or fifteen years before. There's lots of talk about how suddenly this stuff was available, but there had been access on seventy-eights and various other forms, a lot of access to blues before that. But for the younger guard, it was new stuff for them.

RON WOOD: England is so small. [It was] the hub of what was going on when the Stones were first born. My elder brother Art, he used to be in a band with Charlie, Cyril Davies. Through my elder brothers they used to take me along to the little clubs to see these bands playing Chuck Berry songs at the time when there was nothing going in England other than Petula Clark and things, and we used to go down to these little clubs and I was still very young and I used to think, wow, this music's really quite amazing. It used to blow me away. I was at art school trying to make a thing of being an artist at the time.

Why was Chess Records so special?

MARSHALL CHESS: It was the artists. We had Beethoven, Bach, and Mozart on the same label. That's Muddy Waters, Chuck Berry, and Howlin' Wolf. But it was also down to the feel for music that my father and uncle had. It goes back to their roots in this small village in Poland where one man had a wind-up Victrola. When he wound that thing up the whole fucking village would stand under the window to hear some music. When they moved to Chicago, their father (my grandfather) ran a scrap metal yard in the black neighborhood. There was a black gospel church across the street, the kind with an upright piano, tambourine, and drum. My grandfather used to take a strap to the boys because they were always late from listening to the music coming from the church. That would have been their first experience of black music. During the war my father wanted his own business and the cheapest rent was in black neighborhoods. So he opened a liquor store. There was a huge influx of black workers who came up from the South where they were earning next to nothing. Suddenly they were making good money in the Chicago factories and wanted to party on the weekend, so they bought plenty of alcohol. Then my daddy had a tavern with a jukebox. They kept feeding that jukebox with nickels and my dad had the first inkling of what made a hit record.

One thing that made American R&B so attractive to that generation of Brits was probably the very fact that it was American. A majority of these young Brits were "war babies" who were fascinated by their newly significant allies. It made an impression on everyone, including Keef himself.

KEITH RICHARDS: We lived with the war, and in the ruins of it. We were still on rationing until well into the '50s. Especially with cane sugar—that was the last thing to come off rationing, which is probably why a lot of us are still skinny.

Slenderness aside, what *wasn't* there to like about America? The cars, the bars, the stars—all of it! Just ask another rock superstar:

ERIC CLAPTON: The first books I bought were about America. The first records were American. I was just devoted to the American way of life without ever having been there. I was ready for it all. I wanted to learn about red Indians and the blues and everything. I was really an American fan.

And what about those boys from Dartford, Kent, England? Where and how do they enter into the equation? That's the story Alan Clayson referred to in the previous chapter, a story of a chance meeting on a train. Mick and Keith had known each other since grammar school as classmates and neighbors, but didn't really travel in the same circles—until a fateful encounter at the Dartford train station in October of 1960.

KEITH RICHARDS: So I get on the train one morning and there's Jagger, and under his arm he has four or five albums . . . We recognized each other straight off. "Hi man," I say. "Where ya going?" he says. And under his arm he's got Chuck Berry (*Rockin' at the Hops*) and Little Walter, Muddy Waters (*The Best of Muddy Waters*). I say, "You're into Chuck Berry, man, really? That's a coincidence. I can play that shit. I didn't know you were into that." He says, "Yeah, I've even got a little band. And I got a few more albums. Been writin' away to this, uh, Chess Records in Chicago and got a mailing list thing and got it together, ya know?"

Chess Records. Of course. And how's this for delicious happenstance? The person who most likely fulfilled Mick Jagger's mail order request for those albums was Leonard Chess's eighteen-year-old son, Marshall, who helped out his dad in the Chess stockroom in Chicago.

The musical scene in Britain was stagnant in those days; the time was ripe for anyone peddling a new sound. Rhythm and blues became a dominant subculture, out of which rose that core group of English musicians and bands spearheading the Great Blues Revival of the early '60s, at the forefront of which were the Rolling Stones.

More than any other band (the Beatles included), the Stones were the bridge from the narrower "Isle of Blues" to the much broader "Mainland of Rock 'n' Roll"—a transition that began on that stage in 1962. The Rolling Stones were and are the bedrock of the movement by the best and brightest Brits who reintroduced American rhythm and blues to the whole wide world on a grand scale in the 1960s.

Blues guitar legend (and Chess recording artist) Hubert Sumlin was grateful for the attention his music attracted from overseas.

HUBERT SUMLIN: They did a good job. They put us on the map. We were already, but now were around the world. I saw them play and I liked them all, the Rolling Stones, all of them. Nineteen sixty-four I think it was in England and we was playing this club, Wolf and I, and we met the Rolling Stones and they said, "Mr. Wolf, you didn't mind us recording 'Little Red Rooster'"? And he said, "No, no. I didn't mind." And one of them asked me, "Are you Hubert Sumlin?" And I said yes. And he said, "We heard your playing with Wolf and we like it very much."

MARSHALL CHESS: Well, to our surprise, by osmosis somehow that great early Chess stuff got into the UK. And so, very early on, we found a couple of scruffy Englishmen knocking at the Chess Records' door in Chicago saying, "We're the Chess Records Appreciation Society from England"! . . . I mean we didn't even know what they were TALKING about! But anyway, I took them and I showed them the Chess Master Book, which was like a big black book with everything written in script—this was before the days of typewriters and computers in the office—and they put their hands on that book like it was the Holy Grail! . . . And that was our first inkling of what was happening in England! But then, as you know, shortly after that groups like the Rolling Stones, the Yardbirds, and the Kinks all started doing Chess material and talking about Chess artists. The Stones were pushing Bo Diddley and Howlin' Wolf; the Yardbirds were pushing Sonny Boy Williamson . . . Plus there were shows like *Ready Steady Go!* who'd bring the Chess artists over and put them on television in England . . . So yeah, I definitely credit the English with really helping break the legacy of Chess to a whole new audience.

The Stones record at legendary Chess Studios in Chicago in June of 1964

Flash forward to the Stones' first tour of America, when they got a chance to visit Chess Studios. They were in need of a boost. Their tour wasn't going exceptionally well (more on that in chapter 5). They recorded fourteen tracks in two days, including "It's All Over Now."

BUDDY GUY: I was in Chess Studios when they came to Chess to record. I was at the studio doing a cut called "My Time After Awhile" and I had never saw a white man with their hair that long before. And Leonard Chess brought them in the studio and lined them up against the wall while I was doing the session. And I didn't know who the hell they was. I was saying, "Is these women or men?"

Mick and Brian onstage during their first English tour in October of 1963

Famously, Keith Richards insists he saw none other than Muddy Waters himself up on a ladder painting the ceiling!

MARSHALL CHESS: I've laughed in [Keith's] face many times as he's insisted he saw Muddy up a ladder with a paint brush in hand. I guess people want to believe that it's true.

KEITH RICHARDS: Marshall was a boy then; he was working in the basement. And also Bill Wyman told me he actually remembers Muddy Waters taking our amplifiers from the car into the studio . . . I know what the Chess brothers were bloody well like—if you want to stay on the payroll, get to work.

NORMAN DAYRON: Marshall is right, Keith is wrong. And if Muddy Waters was helping carry anybody's amplifiers, he was doing it out of courtesy.

BUDDY GUY: Muddy Waters had helped them bring their instruments up the stairs and they were so ecstatic about that because they was saying, "We was supposed to be bringing Muddy's stuff upstairs, not the other way round."

MARSHALL CHESS: It says something about how unfashionable the blues had become at that time. By '64 nobody really wanted to know. White people had never bought blues records. The audience had always been black. A new generation of black people looked down on the blues. They saw it as slavery music. Instead they were listening to Motown and Stax. It was bands like the Stones and the Yardbirds who introduced the blues to a white market.

BUDDY GUY: I was unaware how famous they was becoming but a lot of white audiences started listening to the blues. I didn't have the slightest idea that the British was listening to the blues, but they had more information than we had on the blues players—the blues players before me—than I did. They knew when you recorded, where you recorded, and who you recorded with. We didn't keep track of that. These guys came in and opened not only my eyes, but America's eyes that the blues was being recognized by the British as a music that should be heard. I went to play in England, February 1965. There was nothing but white people and they was eating it up. I didn't think nobody other than the south side of Chicago and the west side know who the hell I was. But the Stones guys helped open up the doors. Thank you guys.

BILL GERMAN: The very first time I picked up *Get Yer Ya-Ya's Out!*, I was like, what are these names in the parentheses? The beauty of the Stones is that they lead you down this investigative path. They turn you on to Muddy Waters, Buddy Guy, Bo Diddley, and Howlin' Wolf . . .

But we're getting ahead of ourselves again. Before we leave 2120 South Michigan Ave., I'd like to offer one final piece of evidence for why the Stones sparked the American blues revival. When it came time to unleash *The Rolling Stones*, their first full-length long-playing album on the ears of the world in April of 1964, here is the song selection that they chose. (The American edition on London Records added the phrase "England's Newest Hitmakers.")

"Route 66" written by Bobby Troup
"I Just Want to Make Love to You" written by Willie Dixon
"Honest I Do" written by Jimmy Reed
"Mona (I Need You Baby)" written by Ellas McDaniel (Bo Diddley)
"Now I've Got a Witness (Like Uncle Phil and Uncle Gene)" credited to Nanker Phelge (the pseudonym created when all group members participated in the composition)
"Little by Little" credited to Nanker Phelge/Phil Spector
"I'm a King Bee" written by Slim Harpo
"Carol" written by Chuck Berry
"Tell Me (You're Coming Back)" written by Mick Jagger and Keith Richards
"Can I Get a Witness" written by Brian Holland, Lamont Dozier, and Eddie Holland

"You Can Make It if You Try" written by Ted Jarrett
"Walking the Dog" written by Rufus Thomas

It was a full serving of nine R&B and blues covers, coupled with three fledgling attempts at original songwriting. And by April of 1964, it is quite apparent that the Rolling Stones mythmaking machinery was already in overdrive. Here is a quote from the original liner notes prepared for that debut album:

The Rolling Stones are more than just a group—they are a way of life. A way of life that has captured the imagination of England's teenagers, and made them one of the most sought after groups in Beatdom . . . They have emerged as five well rounded intelligent talents, who will journey successfully far beyond the realms of pop music. And in this album there are twelve good reasons why.

You've already seen the twelve "reasons" above, but who lays claim to the powerful hyperbolic words written on the cover of that debut recording? None other than the man who would loom large in the formation, creation, and dissemination of all things Stones in the early days—and the subject of our next chapter—Andrew Loog Oldham.

CHAPTER 3

COME ON

THERE PROBABLY WOULDN'T have been an Elvis Presley without Colonel Tom Parker. And there probably wouldn't have been a Beatles without Brian Epstein. And we could say with some certainty that there wouldn't be a Rolling Stones as we know them without Andrew Loog Oldham.

Managers, producers, image makers, cheerleaders, and hand-holders all play a significant role in the rise of a pop phenomenon from obscurity to international acclaim. In the early days, Andrew Loog Oldham provided all five of those necessary services for the Rolling Stones. Less than a year after the group's first gig, Oldham was made aware of them by journalist Peter Jones of the *Record Mirror*. He went to see and hear them at the Station Hotel in Richmond.

ANDREW LOOG OLDHAM: I was a press agent in London doing the publicity for people from the Beatles, to Sam Cooke, to Gene Pitney, and a journalist told me to go and see this group in a pub and that group was the Rolling Stones. So I immediately became a manager and a producer. It was the Station Hotel, Richmond, just outside the center of London with these blues evenings run by Giorgio Gomelsky. They were playing all blues circuits, which I think was the Marquee, Station Hotel, Crawdaddy, Eel Pie Island, and that circuit, and there were six including Stu (Ian Stewart) the first time I saw them.

I asked him how and why he became involved with the group, and, without hesitating, he offered four words and an explanation:

ANDREW LOOG OLDHAM: I fell in love. We had a lot of things in common: age, ambition, lack of knowledge. In reality, how it progressed, how I became the producer was, number one, I wanted to be a producer; and number two, because of the type of music we all liked, especially them, they felt more protected by a situation in the studio I could give them. In England then, the A&R thing was rather like your Mitch Miller thing was here: twenty-five pounds a week, suits, nine to five.

I asked him if, at that point, the group had done any recordings at all.

ANDREW LOOG OLDHAM: They had tried. They had done a few things on home tape recorders but not really much had come of it. This was really the first time at this stage. Their material was all the blues and R&B things they were weaned on. Because this thing was put together—I mean I was twenty-four hours ahead of the rest of the world!—it was as close a margin as that. It was sped up by the fact that we went to the record company that turned the Beatles down, so we knew that they probably would not make the same mistake twice, regardless of what they were looking at.

MICK JAGGER: Andrew was a publicist for Brian Epstein, although we didn't know that. He probably said, "I am the Beatles' publicist"—how about that as a line? Everything to do with the Beatles was sort of gold and glittery, and Andrew seemed to know what he was doing.

KEITH RICHARDS: Andrew pulled together the innate talents within the band. He turned us into a gang, and he broadened our horizons. Our biggest aim at the time was to be the best blues band in London, and that would have done it for us. But Andrew said, "What are you talking about?" He had the experience—even though he was just as young as we were—but he was very precocious; a sharp fucker and a right little gangster. Also he really wanted to be one of the band. At one time he called himself "the sixth Rolling Stone," so as well as the management side, he thought of himself as part of the gang.

I asked Andrew what that first time in the studio with the Stones was like.

ANDREW LOOG OLDHAM: I just said, "Play me some of your things—the five that you think are the most commercial." Well, out of the five or six songs that they played me, "Come On" by Chuck Berry was the best-known song, the most "whistleable" ditty, and they actually had a slant and an arrangement for it, whereas the other things they played were more out of total respect to the way they had originally heard them. In other words, there was nothing else original. So, we went to record it on a four-track at the original Olympic Studios in London. We had about forty quid and two hours and at the end of it—about five to six—they were in a real hurry to get through it, as you can hear on the record. And five minutes to six I said, "Right, let's go." And the engineer said to me, "What about mixing it?" And I said, "What's that?" and he politely explained it to me. And, thinking that if I weren't there I wouldn't have to pay for it, I said, "Oh, you do that. I'll come back in the morning."

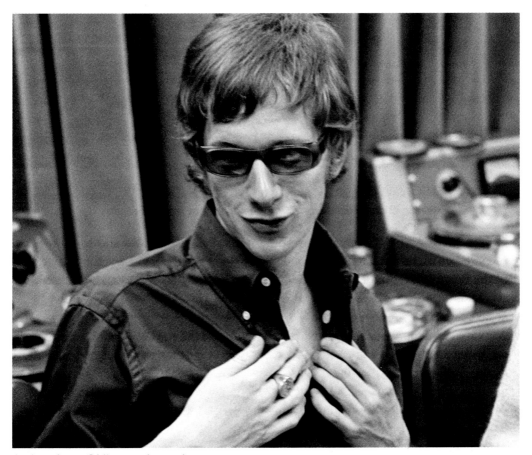

Andrew Loog Oldham in the studio

Both Andrew and the boys were quick studies.

ANDREW LOOG OLDHAM: A year and a half later we were experts. But in that year and a half we decided we'd better go to straight, cruddy mono and just deal with "what you hear is what you get." And that's how we worked right through "Not Fade Away." "Come On" had gone to number eighteen in England. It took a while before we got to the reality of what plastic was here (in the States). Plastic in England was plastic plus an "image"!

Ah, there's the word that might best capture Andrew's biggest contribution to the group: "image."

Ever the orchestrator, Oldham conducts a promo photo shoot for the Stones

CHARLIE WATTS: He always was sharp. He had great taste and style, which reflected on us, he reflected what London was like at the time. We were in the world of the Beatles because of our age, but we were a totally different band. We were a live band for a start—much better than they were live—and Andrew, compared to Brian Epstein, was younger and he looked much hipper. That doesn't mean to say he was cleverer than Brian, because no one has matched the popularity that the Beatles still maintain. Brian set all that in motion, but then in another way Andrew set up the Rolling Stones for forty years!

MICHAEL LINDSAY-HOGG: I met Andrew Oldham, who was always with the Stones. He wasn't only their manager, but he was also their influence. He was the sort of person they copied a lot to do with his kind of outlaw way of looking at the world.

Lindsay-Hogg, a director who has worked with the Stones extensively over the years, shares this memory:

MICHAEL LINDSAY-HOGG: I remember when Andrew was still their manager and after a show we're in the bar having a drink. And I noticed, over in one corner was Mick and Keith and Andrew, and Andrew was talking about something. And Mick and Keith were leaning into him like baby birds getting seed from their mother. They were very influenced by Andrew and his take on the world. I think that fed into the way they related to the audience, which was slightly antagonistic and at the same time seductive. Andrew was a very important initial role model for them. He knew that. And they were grateful for it. Brian Epstein of the Beatles was much more of a protective person . . . Andrew was saying to them, "Don't be careful."

Perhaps one of Andrew's most brilliant ideas was to position the Stones as a kind of "anti-Beatles."

KEITH RICHARDS: Andrew also realized how easily you could manipulate Fleet Street. He would call a few of the papers and say, "Watch the Stones get thrown out of the Savoy," and then he'd say to us, "We'll just go dressed as usual and try and get lunch." And of course with no ties you'd get chucked out of the Savoy and there's the press with their story: THE STONES THROWN OUT OF THE SAVOY. Just silly things like that.

Or how about "silly things" such as manufacturing the headline, WOULD YOU LET YOUR SISTER GO WITH A ROLLING STONE? Or encouraging fans to mug blind beggars for money to buy Stones records? The Beatles just wanted to hold your hand! Parents could only imagine with horror what mayhem the Stones might want to attempt.

But the strategy worked. It gave the Stones an identity that separated them from all of the other myriad British Invasion bands, especially the Beatles.

Another undeniable Oldham stamp on the Stones was his insistence that they move away from covering songs penned by other artists, and that Mick and Keith begin to write their own. He also oversaw the very mercurial shifts in the ever changing leadership roles within the group.

ANDREW LOOG OLDHAM: Yeah, well it went from variations of Brian; to Mick, Keith, and Brian; to Mick/Keith; back to Mick, Keith, and Brian again. Brian was definitely the leader up to that time.

Shepherded by Oldham, the Stones were ready to take their next step.

THE RISING STONES

MICK JAGGER: I was studying economics in college and I was just singing. After two years I was just too interested in playing, and when I finished my second-year exams I said I wasn't interested anymore in doing any more work at college on economics. We'd been playing six or nine months and we had a record out, "Come On." When it got in the charts I just quit. Well, they were very sweet to me. I was given the best of both worlds because when I went to see the registrar of the college he said, "Well, if it doesn't work you can always come back next year." So I didn't see how I had anything to lose.

After "Come On" managed to chart, the Stones played outside of London for the first time. The crowds knew who they were.

MICK JAGGER: In Liverpool, we saw girls with "Rolling Stones" on their handbags, and we realized they knew about us, which was a surprise because we were a London band. Something was happening that we weren't aware of. We had never played there, and Liverpool had the most bands in the country, so we were very surprised.

BILL WYMAN: The first time we ever had an article in an English music paper was March or April of '63, in the *New Record Mirror*. We were in town shopping one day and we bought one and there was our picture with the headline, NEW RHYTHM AND BLUES BAND IN RICHMOND DRIVING PEOPLE CRAZY, or whatever it was. So when I went home on the train that night, I neatly folded the magazine so that the picture was uppermost, and I sat there with it on my lap waiting to be recognized. That's how naïve I was! And it didn't happen (*laughs*). And then when it finally did start happening, I wished to hell it hadn't because it's so boring, with people bugging you all the time for this and that.

I guess some people in that situation would have run up and down the platform saying, "Oi!! This is me. Everybody, this is me!" And some people would have just folded it up, put it in their pocket, and looked out the window at the view, and not even thought about it. It's just in the way it gets to you.

As the band got bigger, so did the venues, and the Stones choice of material changed as well.

MICK JAGGER: When we started, we were just playing rhythm and blues because that's what we liked. We were playing it well, and nobody else seemed to be doing it. At the time, we were doing up to three-hour sets. Now when we went into the ballrooms we listened to what other bands were playing, and picked up a lot of new numbers. Things that might not have been current like "I Can Tell," "Poison Ivy," and "Fortune Teller." We knew 'em anyway but had never gotten around to actually playing them. I can remember buying Barrett Strong's "Money," which was a really big R&B hit in America, but didn't happen when it came out in England. When we saw that those things were, like, popular, we said, well—let's do that. So we did and people liked it.

CHAPTER 4
I WANNA BE YOUR MAN

PERCEPTION IS REALITY. And good marketing controls perception. In the words of one pundit, "The Beatles were thugs who were put across as nice blokes, and the Rolling Stones were gentlemen who were made into thugs by Andrew [Loog Oldham]." There is some truth in this black-and-white depiction of the rivalry, but, just as in life, there is also plenty of gray.

It is, of course, the greatest argument starter in the annals of rock 'n' roll history: the Beatles or the Rolling Stones—who's better? (If your answer is *the* Who's better, well, that's another book entirely.)

A writer named John McMillian came to a very salient conclusion in his "Beatles, Or Stones?" essay in the June/July 2007 issue of the *Believer* magazine. He states that by 1968, "the mostly good-natured rivalry between the Beatles and the Stones had been ongoing for several years. Although the Beatles were more commercially successful, the two bands competed for radio airplay and record sales throughout the 1960s, and on both sides of the Atlantic teens defined themselves by whether they preferred the Beatles or the Stones. 'If you truly loved pop music in the 1960s . . . there was no ducking the choice and no cop-out third option,' one writer remarked. 'You could dance with them both,' but there could never be any doubt about which one you'd take home."

Let's offer a bit more background. On February 9, 1964, way before Facebook, more than seventy-three million of my dearest, closest friends and I tuned in to watch the Beatles on *The Ed Sullivan Show*. It was—no exaggeration—a truly life-altering experience. If you lived it, I don't have to explain why. If you didn't, there are many credible print, audio, and visual accounts and resources to consult. Let it suffice to say that the Sullivan show rapidly became the Ellis Island of the British Invasion.

Sullivan's contract with Brian Epstein called for three appearances: the live debut on February 9; another live performance from Miami Beach on February 16; and a prerecorded third visit on February 23. As 1964 was a leap year, the next open slot for a musical guest was Sunday, March 1, and the group chosen to fill it was the Dave Clark Five—whose bombastic first big American hit "Glad All Over" was zooming up the charts. Sullivan immediately invited them back for a second appearance on Sunday, March 8. Gloria Stavers, editor of the then-influential teen magazine *16* chronicled the group's accomplishment:

GLORIA STAVERS: On the first day of March in 1964, five polite, fascinated, enthusiastic lads from Tottenham, England, deplaned at Kennedy Airport in New York City. Dave Clark, Mike Smith, Rick Huxley, Lenny Davidson, and Denny Payton had come to America to sing their first number one hit record, "Glad All Over," on *The Ed Sullivan Show*. Since that time Dave and the boys have been invited back again and again to perform on that top-rated variety show. In fact, they are the only English singing group to be invited to appear on Sullivan's show over ten times! [A record that was never toppled.]

RICK HUXLEY: Ed Sullivan was a major player in our success story in the USA. His word was law on his program and if he didn't like you then your future career could be in jeopardy. Fortunately he liked us, and after our first show he announced we would appear the next week too. Even though we had prior commitments, such was his standing and power that we were back the next week. I wonder how it would have affected us if we had not returned the following week?

The Stones' first appearance on *The Ed Sullivan Show*—note Mick's infamous sweatshirt

No question about it, the floodgate was now opened for a non-stop parade of Englishmen (and women) across the stage of CBS Studio 53 (later renamed The Ed Sullivan Theater). Firmly established as the launchpad for any and all rock 'n' roll groups with a British accent, the Sullivan show hosted every major (and minor) player from across the pond until it was canceled in 1971 after a twenty-three year run. It was inevitable and just a matter of time before the Rolling Stones would take the plunge. It happened on October 25, 1964, but with markedly different results than the Beatles debut over nine months earlier.

The Stones had already appeared on network television in the US in June. It was a somewhat disastrous visit to ABC's *The Hollywood Palace*, guest-hosted that week by a mocking, eyeball-rolling Dean Martin (see chapter 5 for more on this). So would the Sullivan show provide a friendlier opportunity for the Stones to be showcased on national television in America? Not so much.

What happened is very simple to understand and explain. The Stones were the Stones. They came off sullen, sexual, and threatening. The CBS switchboard was jammed with damning calls from angry parents about the group's performance.

ANTHONY DECURTIS: The Rolling Stones looked tough. They looked scary. And that's what made them enticing . . . I remember the first time they were on *The Ed Sullivan Show*, when Mick Jagger wore a sweatshirt. The response to that was incredible. At my Catholic school the next day, every single one of my teachers gave a lecture about the Rolling Stones and how repulsive they were. They'd pat you on the head for liking the Beatles. They got a kick out of them. They didn't get a kick out of the Rolling Stones. Liking the Rolling Stones radicalized you. It made you make a stand. Whatever my teachers had to say, that only stiffened my spine. That was the element of the Rolling Stones that was thrilling.

Here is the content of one of the actual telegrams sent to CBS on October 25, 1964: "Stop presenting crude ignorant demoralizing disgusting groups like the Rolling Stones and causing frustration to clean American youth struggling to achieve a spot on a decent show. You disturb parents and morally sicken our youth while you greedily pursue TV ratings with odoriferous arrogance towards the moral conditions you help create in this country."

Unlike his blanket endorsement and praise of the Beatles, Sullivan reverted to his "Elvis era" moral-guardian guise, and issued the following statement to the press:

ED SULLIVAN: I promise you they will never be back on our show. If things can't be handled, we'll stop the whole business. We won't book any more rock 'n' roll groups and will ban teenagers from the theater. Frankly, I didn't see the group until the day before the broadcast . . . It took me seventeen years to build this show, and I'm not going to have it destroyed in a matter of weeks.

It was all talk. Sullivan rebooked the Stones for a second appearance on his May 2, 1965, telecast. They ultimately appeared six times on the show between 1964 and 1969.

Bill Wyman once told me a funny story about the Stones appearance on Sullivan in February 1966.

BILL WYMAN: So they wanted to beep out a word in "Satisfaction" and they just wound up making everything that much worse. We were miming to the record and Mick was singing live, and when he came to the line "trying to make some girl," they beeped it so it came out, "trying to BEEP some girl," which made it so much worse because everybody's vivid imaginations were trying to figure out what he really said (*laughs*). "What did he say?" "Did he say . . . 'fuck'?" In the end it kind of helped our image in a way (*laughs*). I mean, it's still talked about now, right?

Promo ad for "I Wanna Be Your Man," the Stones' second single, given to them by Lennon and McCartney

There can really be no question or debate about the trailblazing role that the Beatles played for the Rolling Stones and every other British band. And the Stones also benefited mightily from the support (however self-serving it was) that the Liverpool quartet gave to the London quintet.

First of all, it may have been George Harrison himself who helped the Stones get their first recording contract.

GEORGE HARRISON: There was a big showcase at the Liverpool Philharmonic Hall. The Beatles had become famous . . . Anyway, I remember meeting some executives from London, one of whom must have been Dick Rowe [of Decca]. He said, "You'll tell us who the good groups are, will you?" And I said, "I don't know about that, but you want to get the Rolling Stones."

Then there's the story of the Stones recording the Lennon and McCartney–penned tune that gives this chapter its title, "I Wanna Be Your Man."

ANDREW LOOG OLDHAM: The Rolling Stones were in this rehearsal place in Leicester Square and we had nothing to record. Can we do "Poison Ivy"? No. "Fortune Teller"? No. I went out for a walk pissed off, and ran into John and Paul who were coming—being very nice—coming from a Variety Club of Great Britain. I think they'd been honored for something for the first time, and they said, "What's wrong with you?" So I told them and, out of the good old Brill Building/Liverpool training they had, they said, "Well we've got something." And they came down and finished ["I Wanna Be Your Man"] off in front of them—which was a great lesson in songwriting for Mick and Keith as well—and I felt so good about it that I went to Paris. I didn't even go to the session . . . I think "I Wanna Be Your Man" went to number nine or ten in England.

Here's another take on that same tale:

JOHN LENNON: The story on "I Wanna Be Your Man" was that they needed a record. They'd put out "Come On" by Chuck Berry and needed a quick follow-up. We met Andrew Oldham, who used to work for Epstein then had gone to the Stones and probably got them off Giorgio Gomelsky. He came to us and said, "Have you got a song for them?" And we said, "Sure," because we didn't really want it ourselves.

We went in, and I remember teaching it to them. We played it roughly and they said, "Yeah, OK, that's our style." So Paul and I just went off in a corner of the room and finished the song while they were all still there, talking. We came back and that's how Mick and Keith got inspired to write. "Jesus, look at that. They just went in the corner and wrote it and came back!" Right in front of their eyes we did it.

You could easily make the case that the Beatles were more helpful to the Stones than vice versa. So let's give this early round to the Fab Four, but the rivalry is far from over.

CHAPTER 5
STREET FIGHTING MAN

FOUR MONTHS AFTER the Beatles' triumphant arrival in America, the Stones took their own plunge, at which point another vast difference between their respective strategies revealed itself immediately. Paul McCartney swears that he (and his bandmates) had learned a valuable lesson from all of their fellow musician countrymen who had come here before them and failed.

PAUL MCCARTNEY: The thing we did—which I always think new groups should take as a bit of advice—was that we were cheeky enough to say that we wouldn't go to the States until we had a number one record there. We were offered tours, but we knew we'd be second to someone and we didn't want that. There was a lot of careful thought behind it. There were a lot of artists who'd go over and vanish . . . We always looked at it logically and thought, "Well, that's the mistake. You've got to go in as number one."

This was far from the way the Stones did it on their first visit. Of course America was just as much the big rock candy mountain for even these hardcore "anti-Beatles." (Have we mentioned that one of Keith Richards's childhood idols for both his music and his movies was the so-called King of the Cowboys—Roy Rogers? Asked about it during a press junket for one of his appearances in the *Pirates of the Caribbean* film franchise, Keith replied, "Oh, yeah, Roy was great. He could shoot, play the guitar, and ride a great horse. What more do you want?")

Keith's excitement about coming here was palpable.

KEITH RICHARDS: America was a real fantasyland. It was still Walt Disney and hamburger dates and kids going steady. We watched the presidential debates, Lyndon Johnson and Barry Goldwater, and noticed that kids were more into what was going on [politically] . . . the girls were better looking, ha-ha! It was like throwing a load of demons into heaven.

And Mick Jagger's take on the same subject?

MICK JAGGER: I was knocked out. Things seemed to be open all night and everything was so exciting and there was a lot of energy. Also a lot of things made us laugh. We were very unsuccessful at first but we still liked it. You see, we knew that we just had to make it in America. It took us two years to make it over there. There we were touring all over the place on our own and nobody seemed to know us. Touring on our own wasn't too bad in a way, but there was this total apathy building up from just about everyone. Everything was all wrong. Nobody has ever done it all in one go . . . it takes time to "conquer" America.

The Beatles might have begged to differ, but that was up to them. The Stones certainly got off on the wrong foot. They touched down in New York on June 1, and made the obligatory visit to the self-proclaimed "Fifth Beatle" disc jockey Murray the K's broadcast on radio station WINS. Not yet on Ed Sullivan's "must-book" list, the Stones soon after took off for Los Angeles, where they were scheduled to make their American network television debut on ABC's weekly variety program *The Hollywood Palace*. Hosted by a rotating list of establishment celebrities, this generational mismatch created even stranger bedfellows than the Sullivan extravaganza. For example, comedian Milton Berle was completely flummoxed by Spanky and Our Gang (though Sammy Davis Jr. fared a little bit better when he hosted a return appearance by the group); singer Tony Martin brought on Buffalo Springfield with a few corny jokes about their name. But the most notorious debacle of them all had to be the Rolling Stones debut on a show hosted by Dean Martin.

The post–Jerry Lewis Martin was enjoying all-media solo success with hit records, starring roles in major feature films, and a successful network television series of his own just a year away on NBC. And he was already established as a member in good standing of Frank Sinatra's notorious "Rat Pack"—a contingent of Hollywood elite devoted to booze, broads, and buffoonery. If ever there was a cataclysmic confrontation between old guard show business and the onslaught of "take-no-prisoners" rock 'n' rollers from the British Isles, it was best symbolized by *The Hollywood Palace*'s handling of the Rolling Stones.

BOB BONIS: Dean Martin came in and had no idea what he was dealing with. The vibe, as we call it today, was just awful. Dean and I got into an argument at one point and Keith, my newfound friend, was about to pop him one with one of those solid-body guitars.

ANTHONY DECURTIS: Dean was such an asshole. He read the writing on the wall, which was, "Goodbye, Dean Martin." The Stones, I think, scared him.

In fairness to Dean Martin, he was true to the beloved caricature of himself that he cultivated for his nightclub, movie, and television fans: the sloshed hipster who was as likely to make fun of himself as he was of anyone or anything else within striking distance, whether it be Frank Sinatra, Sammy Davis Jr., or, yes, even the Rolling Stones: "Now . . . something for the youngsters . . . five singing boys from England who sold a lot of albums. They're called the Rolling Stones. I've been rolled while I was stoned myself. I don't know what they're singing about . . . but here they are."

The Stones came on and did a blistering performance of "I Just Wanna Make Love to You," following which Dino looks a little bewildered and says: "Rolling Stones . . . aren't they great?" (Rolls his eyes.) "They're going to leave right after the show for London.

Charlie Watts

They're challenging the Beatles to a hair-pulling contest. I could swear Jackie Coogan and Skippy were in that group." (A *really* ancient old-show-business reference.) "Well I'm going to let you in on something. You know these singing groups today? You're under the impression they have long hair. Not true at all. It's an optical illusion. They just have low foreheads and high eyebrows."

And then: "So as we leave you right now, we'll have a short intermission. And we'll be back at *The Hollywood Palace* in about a minute. Now don't go away. You, you wouldn't leave me here alone with the Rolling Stones now would you?"

But the worst was yet to come. After a comical trampoline act, Dean is back on camera and says: "Larry Griswold! Isn't he wonderful? He's the father of the Rolling Stones. And ever since he heard them sing, he's been trying to kill himself."

The Stones managed to do two more songs—their cover of "Not Fade Away" as well as the Jagger/Richards composition "Tell Me." They were furious, but not as furious as they would be when the program aired on June 13, and they realized that their appearance had been whittled down to just an excerpt of "I Just Wanna Make Love to You"!

The seeming insults did not go unnoticed. In the self-composed liner notes for his album *Another Side of Bob Dylan* released in August of 1964, Bob drops in this non sequitur:

an dean martin should apologize
t the rolling stones. [sic]

(Back then, anyone sensitive to the battle between the mainstream and the underground cultural revolution that was under way could not misunderstand the source of that reference. But I wonder if readers today, without any direct knowledge of *The Hollywood Palace* fiasco, would be scratching their heads over a negative Bob Dylan quote about Dean Martin? Especially in light of the fact that Bob covered one of Dean's biggest solo hits, "Return to Me," on the second anthology of music released from the HBO hit series *The Sopranos*!)

So much for the television debut. How did that first tour of the States turn out? A mixed bag, for sure. On June 5, the Stones did their first concert in America in San Bernardino, California, just about an hour outside of LA. They were part of a touring lineup that included at various points the Chiffons, Bobby Comstock, Bobby Vee (playing with a saxophonist named Bobby Keys), and Bobby Goldsboro! (The original *Bobfest*?) The show attracted 4,500 young fans.

KEITH RICHARDS: It was a straight gas, man. They all knew the songs, and they were all bopping. It was like being back home. "Ah, love these American gigs" and "Route 66" mentioned San Bernardino, so everybody was into it.

Bobby Goldsboro traveled with the Stones that week.

BOBBY GOLDSBORO: I knew about the Stones. And when it was finally announced that they were coming over to do their first tour, and I got the call and they asked if I would open for the Stones, I thought, "Man, I'd love to do that." . . . I couldn't wait for it. We toured together on a bus for a week and ended up playing Carnegie Hall. It was just me and the Stones and a backup band on this big bus. They got the reputation of the bad boys of rock 'n' roll but all of them were really nice guys to me. They were doing just good rock 'n' roll music from the word "go."

The Stones play the State Fair of Texas; chimpanzees and elephants were among the acts on the ticket

Soon the reality of the tour set in. The next gig was in Texas for the San Antonio Teen Fair, where the group endured non-stop misguided homophobic insults and slurs from a population of crew-cutted rednecks and uptight all-American girls openly hostile to the long hair and ambiguous sexuality of this sullen British quintet.

Then it was off to Chicago for, perhaps, the highlight of the whole trip— recording a bevy of tracks at the fabled Chess Studios in the company of Muddy Waters, Willie Dixon, and Buddy Guy (see chapter 2). It was a very productive two-day session including their next single, their second EP, and a number of possible tracks for the next album. One of the songs recorded on that first day was a cover of Irma Thomas's "Time Is on My Side." Years later, Ms. Thomas recalled her initial reaction to the Stones version:

IRMA THOMAS: At the time they did it, I was about twenty-three years old, very naïve, and I was a bit miffed. My career was just starting to show some promise, and then came along the British Invasion, and at that time, it didn't necessarily have to be good, as long as it was British. We as American artists were darn good performers, and I felt my version of "Time Is on My Side" was far better than theirs, but I wasn't British, and I was black, so there were two strikes against me. Of course, over the years I've reconsidered, and I'm not so upset anymore.

A HUMAN RIFF IS BORN

In his memoir, *Life*, Keith credits Bobby Goldsboro with teaching him the Jimmy Reed lick that has been the basis for much of his repertoire since.

BOBBY GOLDSBORO: When I was in college, we were playing all the blues stuff. We learned the Jimmy Reed songs, but we couldn't quite get the sound down that he was getting and I couldn't figure why. It turned out we were playing the chord correctly—and that was the problem. When he would go up to a B chord, he left the bass note open. Actually, if you listen to that note, it's incorrect—it doesn't go with that chord. But it gives it a different sound. So I showed that to Keith on the bus. We were touring for about a week together. I was the opening act on their first tour over here. It was a simple little guitar lick. It was nice he gave me credit in his book about that. It's a good feeling this many years later to have someone like Keith Richards acknowledge something like that. But I got far too much credit because all I did was learn it off Jimmy Reed's record.

Goldsboro is a big fan of Keith's playing in general.

BOBBY GOLDSBORO: There's so many distinct riffs that he has put on some of the Stones' records. A lot of them are very simple. That's one of the things about his guitar playing. He didn't do a lot of fancy stuff, but the things he does are so cool. That's what makes him such a unique guitarist.

And how about his development as a guitar player?

BOBBY GOLDSBORO: He left guys like me in the wind. With Keith, he's saying something every time he plays. What he's doing has its own style. Every song he plays, he gets out of the guitar what he should get out of it.

The tour resumed on June 12 in Minneapolis, Minnesota, then Omaha, Nebraska, on June 13, about which Keith remembers:

KEITH RICHARDS: The next gig was Omaha, with the motorcycles and six hundred kids. Then you get deflated. That's what stopped us from turning into pop stars then; we were always having those continual complete somebody hitting you in the face, "Don't forget, boy." Then we really had to work America, and it really got the band together. We'd fallen off in playing in England 'cause nobody was listening; we'd do four numbers and be gone. Don't blink, you'll miss us.

Next up were Detroit on the fourteenth, Pittsburgh on the seventeenth, and Harrisburg, Pennsylvania, on the nineteenth—each one with mixed audience reactions, and widely varying audience numbers. The last stop on this first barnstorming mission to the United States was none other than the legendary Carnegie Hall.

ANTHONY DECURTIS: On the first tour, when they went out beyond New York, they had some problems because they were so controversial and edgy, but in New York, they were always embraced.

Promoter Sid Bernstein booked the show at Carnegie, just as he had done for the Beatles in February.

SID BERNSTEIN: Each Wednesday I would buy my British newspaper at [the international newsstand] Hotalings. I enjoyed reading the English newspapers; they reminded me of my time as a soldier in Great Britain. On one Wednesday, I happened to notice a small, one-column item of about five lines with a Liverpool dateline talking about a group called the Beatles. The use of the word "hysteria" caught my eye. The only time I could remember the word "hysteria" being used with regard to entertainment was in reference to Frank Sinatra and Elvis Presley.

But Sid wasn't content with just bringing over one English group.

SID BERNSTEIN: The Beatles breakthrough opened up the music scene for everybody in Britain. In the fall of 1963 the British music trade papers and popular daily newspapers that I was reading began reporting on a group called the Rolling Stones. They were playing to sold-out venues and creating a hysteria of their own. I decided I wanted to introduce the Rolling Stones to America too. I called information in London and got the phone number of their manager, Andrew Loog Oldham, whose name I had seen in the trade papers. A moment later a charming, soft-spoken voice came on, "Sid, this is Andrew, I was hoping you were going to call me . . ."

Murray the K was the MC and American hit makers Jay and the Americans were the opening act. Murray promoted the show heavily on his WINS radio program. The following is an actual transcript of one of his on-air pronouncements: "Hey, everybody, this is Murray the K and I've got big news for you. Now you know that we are very close to the Beatles and it's nothing that's gonna get you upset—all of you Beatle fans—but John Lennon, as a personal favor, asked me to bring over a group that is really turning England upside down. Now, you may not have heard of them. Their name is the Rolling Stones. They've got hair longer than the Beatles and we're gonna present them in their very first US appearance at Carnegie Hall!"

The date was Saturday, June 20, for two shows. The first show proceeded normally with a very professional and somewhat buttoned-down set by Jay and the Americans. Then all hell broke loose when the Stones took to the stage. Screaming teenage girls jumped out of their seats and ran to the front. It took a phalanx of cops to quiet things down and allow the group to continue their performance.

Two interesting footnotes in rock 'n' roll history took place during the intermission between shows. The first is that Jay and the Americans co-founder Kenny Vance was sitting in his dressing room applying tanning cream to his face—a trick the group learned after they appeared on the black-and-white Clay Cole television show on WPIX in New York. Kenny told me the story on one of his visits to my radio show:

KENNY VANCE: Brian Jones walked in on me and said, "What on earth are you doing, mate?" I replied, "Stage makeup. It looks a lot better under the lights." Jones poured a gob into his hands and began applying some to his face. "Keith," he called out, "come and take a look at this!" Richards walked in and became hysterical when he saw Jones working on his face. He then followed suit, and before I knew what was happening, the Rolling Stones had descended on the dressing room, taken my makeup, and began playing with their new toys.

Based on this chance encounter, Kenny claims credit to this day for the barrels and barrels of cosmetics, creams, and makeup that the Stones would use over the course of their fifty-year career.

The second footnote occurred when Murray the K burst into the dressing room to say that the police were insisting that the Stones open the second show so that they could be safely escorted out of the theater during the intermission.

SID BERNSTEIN: I offered to take them next door where there was a German-style beer-and-sandwich pub, but only Brian Jones seemed interested. Brian and I exited Carnegie Hall through a backstage door that was only a few feet from the pub. We sat in the most out-of-the-way booth we could find. After just a few minutes I could see several young faces pressed up against the front windowpanes of the pub. In no time at all, the number of faces multiplied. I motioned for Brian to follow me and we made a mad dash across Seventh Avenue. A mob of kids ran after us. They were all grabbing at Brian's beautiful strawberry blond hair.

The plan to have the Stones open the show had one fatal flaw: the audience got up and left en masse to catch them at the stage door, leaving Jay and the Americans to close the show in a nearly deserted Carnegie. Kenny Vance took some consolation from the fact that at least the Stones looked better under the lights at the second show than they had at the first . . .

SID BERNSTEIN: After the show ended, some members of the press were interviewing me when [head booker] Mrs. Satescu came over. "Mr. Bernstein, the pictures on the walls were shaking. The kids were jumping on our plush seats and the armrests. They were rude and disobedient to the ushers. And you are lucky, Mr. Bernstein, that no one was hurt here today. Please, do not bring any of your presentations here again!"

Two days later, the Stones were back home in England, a little bit battered, a little bit bruised, from their first adventures in America, but ready to regroup and take the next steps toward nothing less than total world domination.

CHAPTER 6

SING THIS ALL TOGETHER

T.A.M.I. SHOW (TEENAGE Awards Music International) was the first rock 'n' roll concert film. It featured a host of popular acts from many genres including the Beach Boys, Chuck Berry, James Brown, Lesley Gore, Marvin Gaye, the Supremes, and . . . the Rolling Stones. Directed by Steve Binder, who would go on to work with Elvis on the '68 comeback special, and produced by Bill Sargent using a new technology known as Electronovision (a precursor to both digital and closed-circuit/pay-per-view broadcasts), the show was filmed over October 28 and 29, 1964, at the Santa Monica Civic Auditorium.

JOHN LANDIS: I went to Emerson Junior High and one of the girls-in-my-class's father produced this so the entire seventh grade went. David Cassidy was in my class. He was there. One of the go-go dancers was Teri Garr. It was hosted by Jan and Dean.

DEAN TORRENCE: Once we had an opportunity to review the whole concept, we thought, "Why wouldn't we do this?" It had never been done before. This was kind of a forerunner to something like Woodstock.

JOHN LANDIS: It showed how this time in music was extraordinary in its diversity; you have surf music, British music, pop music, soul music, Motown.

BILL WYMAN: There were an awful lot of black artists, which was great for us, but it wasn't the accepted thing at the time.

Steve Binder made a curious decision. Despite the dazzling array of more-established talent on hand, he wanted to close the show (and film) with the Rolling Stones.

BILL WYMAN: We were hardly known in America at that time—we'd never had a big hit—and they put us on top of the bill and in front of people like Chuck Berry, Marvin Gaye, the Supremes, James Brown, the Miracles.

Were the Stones happy about the opportunity?

BILL WYMAN: No! We wanted James Brown to top it. Especially after we saw him (*laughs*). But they *insisted* that we top it, and before he went on, James Brown came over to us and said, "I'm going to make you Rolling Stones wish that you'd never, ever come here to America!"

The Stones rehearse for T.A.M.I. Show

DEAN TORRENCE: A lot of groups probably thought they were strong enough to close the show until they saw James Brown. We had played with James Brown before, so we knew what to expect. There was no way we would have wanted to follow him.

STEVE BINDER: I mean, to be really honest with you, I remember saying that I wanted the Rolling Stones to be on after James Brown, and I remember Mick coming to me and saying, "We can't." Because James Brown was obviously the king, and James and I, when we met, we hit it off really well; we've been friends ever since, and his manager had sorta come to me and said, "Nobody can follow James." And I, for whatever my instincts were, whatever my feelings were, I just felt that we should put the Stones on to close the show.

Considering the audience, the choice made some sense.

DEAN TORRENCE: The audience was 99 percent white and of course they were going to scream like crazy for any group that came from England. I'm sure some of those screaming fourteen-year-old girls looked at James Brown and really liked it. On the other hand, they had no idea what was coming. They were there to scream at the teen idol types. An English band was safe.

Many consider Brown's performance that night the finest one of his ever captured on film.

BILL WYMAN: Then he went on and did this *incredible* twenty-minute set and scared the shit out of us. We were literally shaking in our boots; we couldn't face it.

JOHN LANDIS: The guy who blew me away though was James Brown. I'd never seen anything like that before.

BILL WYMAN: Marvin Gaye said to us backstage, "People love you because of what you do on stage. So just go out there and do it, and forget about James Brown. Go do your thing. That's what I do."

There are a variety of opinions on how the Stones played that night, even within the band itself.

KEITH RICHARDS: It was the biggest mistake of our career.

JOHN LANDIS: It was one of the first US performances of the Rolling Stones, who were kind of boring after James Brown. We just thought, "Who is this English twerp?" Bring James Brown back on the stage.

Weekly Variety tended to agree with Landis: "What must surely be England's revenge for losing the 1776 Revolution, the Rolling Stones."

But the reality is the Stones were excellent. They played a terrific five-song set, opening with Chuck Berry's "Around and Around," and ending with their version of Bo Diddley's "I'm All Right," which segued into *all* the acts dancing and playing with the Stones on an ensemble version of "Let's Get Together." It's a great window into the early Stones performances and a fascinating cultural moment.

James Brown chats with Brian, Keith, and Mick at T.A.M.I.

THE STONES MEET THE MASTER

The Stones at the foot of the master, Howlin' Wolf

When the Rolling Stones were slated to appear on *Shindig* in December of 1964, producer Jack Good wanted Howlin' Wolf on the show, but someone at the network didn't like the idea. The Stones put their foot down: if Wolf wasn't going to appear, neither would they.

In their wonderful book *Moanin' at Midnight*, authors Mark Hoffman and James Segrest describe the scene:

MARK HOFFMAN AND JAMES SEGREST: A top-notch studio band—Billy Preston on piano, James Burton on guitar, Larry Knechtel on bass, and Mickey Conway on drums—recorded tracks for the taping. Dressed in a dark suit the next day, Wolf strode majestically onstage, and with the Stones and a bevy of go-go dancers sitting at his feet, launched into an incandescent version of "How Many More Years." As the band play-synched behind him, Wolf sang and played live, stabbing his massive finger at the camera, shaking his gargantuan rear end, and blasting blues out into prime-time America.

KEITH RICHARDS: Here was this enormous man who looked like an elephant without a trunk, and very polite. Then he starts playing the shit. Oh, man—here comes another education! I was incredibly impressed by him. It was that voice, man, and the attitude. All you had to do was put a microphone in front of him and he did the stuff. There was no tricks involved.

The sight of this literal giant of a bluesman offering up this almost feral performance on a show normally associated with teeny-boppers was arresting. In fact, music critic Peter Guralnick has described it as one of the great cultural moments of the twentieth century.

PETER GURALNICK: What was so great about seeing Wolf on *Shindig* was it was in a sense reality imposing itself on this totally artificial setting. While I was a big fan of the Stones, it was altogether appropriate that they would be sitting at Wolf's feet. And that's what it represented. His music was not simply the foundation or the cornerstone; it was the most vital thing you could ever imagine.

Years later, in 1981, Wolf would appear with the Stones once again, at the Rosemont Horizon in Chicago. Mick acknowledged Wolf's importance to the Stones' musical heritage.

STEVE BINDER: And, as it turns out, to this day, I think it is one of the great performances of the Stones. Because I think, at the time that they went on, either they were so stoned-out or whatever, they just literally . . . Mick was impersonating James, almost, with all the dancing and the shenanigans and so forth, and that performance would've never happened if I had them on before James.

BILL WYMAN: We went out there and somehow or other it worked, everybody gave everything they had—Keith and Mick were fantastic. They really tried. Then afterwards James Brown came over and congratulated us, and we were all mates after that. We saw quite a bit of him over the next two years. But anyway, that show captured, all in one shot, where music was at in '63–'64, and you can always go back and see those acts doing their hits and get an idea of how exciting it all was. Since then, I don't think I've really seen anything comparable to that—where you've had fifteen top acts on the same show, and it's come off as well as that.

CHAPTER 7

RIP THIS JOINT

REMEMBER MICK'S OBSERVATION about the Stones' first trip to the States in 1964? "It takes time to conquer America." Well, later that same year, the second trip to America was quite a different story. This time, the Stones were more than just a blip on the radar of American media. This time their songs "Tell Me" (a Jagger/Richards original) and "It's All Over Now" (a cover of the Bobby and Shirley Womack song Murray the K suggested they record) had both spent time on the US Top 40 charts and "Time Is on My Side" (written by Jerry Ragovoy under the pseudonym of Norman Meade) was on its way to becoming the group's first Top 10 hit in America. And this time, the band was visible enough and important enough to be invited on *The Ed Sullivan Show* (described in chapter 4), and also important enough to headline and close the T.A.M.I. Show (see chapter 6).

But something else was happening as well. The group was transforming and reinventing itself right before our eyes and ears. No longer content with being the top-tier British interpreters of American rhythm and blues music, the Stones were forging a new identity that relied heavily on the burgeoning songwriting talents of Mick Jagger and Keith Richards.

There's a famous quote from the John Wayne/Jimmy Stewart cowboy movie *The Man Who Shot Liberty Valance* that came out the same year that the Stones got started: "When the legend becomes fact, print the legend."

Following that bit of wisdom, here's the legend. Andrew Loog Oldham figured out that the only true way the Rolling Stones could realistically compete with the Beatles was to slightly change course and move in a different direction. They had already loaded their first three albums with amazing American R&B covers, but that process could not possibly continue indefinitely. The group had to follow the Beatles' lead and begin incorporating much more new, exciting, and original material into their repertoire. Bill complained the most about not being able to get more of his original songs on a Stones album. Brian was always more interested in covering the masters. And Charlie had no desire to write.

Mick and Keith were quite a different story. Early on, Andrew determined that they had the potential to rival Lennon and McCartney, or, at the very least, take the Stones to the next level of success. To accomplish this (Look out! Here comes the legend!), he supposedly "locked" Mick and Keith in the kitchen of his flat and told them not to come out until they had an original song finished.

Keith is the one who relishes telling the "locked-in-the-kitchen" story:

KEITH RICHARDS: With the pressure of the game, Andrew Oldham boxed Mick and me in a kitchen and said, "Come out with a song." I said, "Well, we've got some food, so I guess we can last for a while." Eventually, we did come out of the kitchen, with "As Tears Go By," which within six weeks was in the Top 10 by Marianne Faithfull. Before that I thought of songwriting as a totally separate job—like there's the blacksmith, and there's the stonemason, and you did this, and I did that. So at that point I integrated that I was not only a guitar player, but that I could write what I was going to play, instead of just revamping all the time. It was an eye-opener.

Mick demurs:

MICK JAGGER: Keith likes to tell the story about the kitchen, God bless him. I think Andrew may have said something at some point along the lines of "I should lock you in a room until you've written a song," and in that way mentally he did lock us in a room, but he didn't literally lock us in.

They were ALL making it up as they went along. That goes for all four of the Beatles, all one of Bob Dylan (although it took five actors and one actress to portray him in the 2007 biopic *I'm Not There*!), and all five Rolling Stones. But myths and legends aside, the new formidable songwriting team of Mick Jagger and Keith Richards was poised to take its place in the pantheon of great rock writers.

There were other factors that were contributing to the redefinition and redirection of the Rolling Stones in 1965. The balance of power in the group was changing dramatically and swiftly. What began as Brian Jones's band of purist blues interpreters was morphing into Mick and Keith's band of pop prophets and profiteers. Brian's growing frustration with his change of status was undeniable.

BILL WYMAN: There came a time when he wanted to write for the band but he couldn't. He was just not able to produce a song for the Rolling Stones, which frustrated him. Remember, he was the leader of the band in the beginning. Brian Jones formed the Rolling Stones, not Mick Jagger. And Brian got more fan mail during the first year and a half than anybody else. When the limelight went away from him, and Mick started getting the attention, Brian found it difficult to deal with.

Simultaneously, Mick and Keith, even more than the Beatles, had their fingers on the pulse of US culture. The romantic notion of America as some sort of dreamlike fantasy world was giving way to a much more realistic, harsher view of the colonies. As they crisscrossed the country for the third time in twelve months, they witnessed firsthand the commercialism, racism, and materialism in abundance in the land of the free and the home of the brave.

There is no formula for tuning into the zeitgeist of a country—the cultural, ethical, intellectual, political, or spiritual climate of an era. It is not something that can be conjured or willed. It is a multiplicity of circumstances and events usually resulting in the rise of a force that is unstoppable. Such a vacuum was created in the 1960s and the Stones were primed to fill it. Building on an image that was partly truth and partly fiction, they

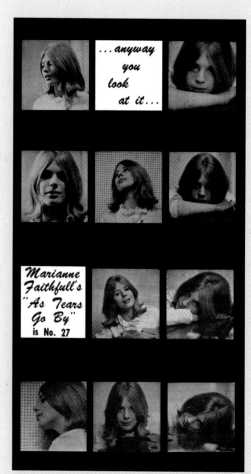

"As Tears Go By" was among the first Jagger/Richards compositions

AS TEARS GO BY

Marianne Faithfull became involved with Mick from 1966 to 1970 and must be counted as one of the great muses in rock history, as well as a legendary singer and performer in her own right. She spoke to us for the book (briefly). Here's what she had to say about "As Tears Go By."

MARIANNE FAITHFULL: This is a song I first sung when I was little. I was seventeen years old. My friends Mick and Keith wrote it for me. Last night even, as I sing it, I feel it. What a beautiful song. And how wonderful it is for the audience. There are moments I can tell you where I'd like to retire it. But there are certain songs that I have to sing and "As Tears Go By" is definitely one of them . . . If you are going to have a song slung around your neck for life, you could do a lot worse . . . What if my hit song was "Wooly Bully"?

ultimately found a voice and gave a voice to a burgeoning global youth culture. They became the conduit to express the angst, frustration, rage, and uncertainty of the times for a generation aching to express itself artistically, sexually, and socially.

The Stones' rebellion against the establishment finally came together with a single declaration, one that completely changed their future as a band: "(I Can't Get No) Satisfaction." That line said it all: who they were, what they wanted, where they were headed. It screamed non-stop, 24/7, from the phonographs and radios, first in the United States, and soon thereafter all over the world. Dylan liberated songwriting, the Beatles redefined pop stardom, and both

Another side of Mick Jagger

gave the Stones a launchpad for their unique brand of insolence, rebellion, and decadence.

Tom Wolfe once brazenly suggested: "The Beatles just want to hold your hand. The Rolling Stones want to burn your town down." "Satisfaction" gave them the match to do it with.

MICK JAGGER: It was the song that really made the Rolling Stones, changed us from just another band into a huge, monster band. You always need one song. We weren't American, and America was a big thing, and we always wanted to make it here. It was very impressive the way that song and the popularity of the band became a worldwide thing. It's a signature tune, really . . . a kind of signature that everyone knows. It has a very catchy title. It has a very catchy guitar riff. It has a great guitar sound, which was original at that time. And it captures a spirit of the times, which is very important in those kinds of songs . . . Which was alienation. Or it's a bit more than that, maybe, but a kind of sexual alienation. Alienation's not quite the right word, but it's one word that would do.

The French have a phrase for it (Don't they have a phrase for everything?!?): "succès fou"—crazy success. There is "success," then there is "unimaginable, wild success." That is what the Stones achieved first in America, then all over the globe in 1965. Some of it was sheer luck; some of it was sheer timing; but all of it put them on the path unlike any other in music history.

CHAPTER 8
(I CAN'T GET NO) SATISFACTION

As MICK AND KEITH's partnership matured and jelled, their strength as great rock 'n' roll writers dovetailed beautifully with the image that Oldham had manufactured for them. Finally, by late 1964, early 1965, even the States began to notice. When their song "The Last Time" reached the Top 10 in April of 1965, they were poised and ready for the kind of explosion that catapults a semi-successful group into the stratosphere. It's ironic, considering the message of the song, that it was "(I Can't Get No) Satisfaction" that did the trick.

ANDREW LOOG OLDHAM: We'd gone from the point of arranging somebody else's song to the top of the mountain with "Satisfaction." The rest of that run was almost too easy. They knew what they were doing. They knew the distances from it. We knew we were there. The one before we were in California—"The Last Time"—I called up Phil Spector to come down to the studio. "Listen to this. Tell me how high it will go." I love him but I didn't need him to tell me how far "Satisfaction" would go . . . All the way to the top!

But let's back up a second. One of the best Keith Richards lyrics cropped up in 1967's "Ruby Tuesday": "Catch your dreams before they slip away." He may just have stumbled upon that advice when the Stones were on their third tour of North America in the spring of 1965. During a stay at the Gulf Motel in Clearwater, Florida, Keith woke up in the middle of the night.

KEITH RICHARDS: It was one of the things where most songs I don't remember where they came from. But I woke up in the middle of the night to this one, and for some reason I just grabbed a guitar and turned the tape machine on and said I can't get no satisfaction; that's what I had plus the melody, the chord changes. I woke up in the middle of a dream. Songs come at the weirdest time and you've got no control over it. You can be doing the most unlikely things when songs come to you and the only thing you hope is that you've got a cassette machine with you at the time. From there on I gave it to Mick.

Continuing our theme about standing on the shoulders of giants, Chuck Berry has a lyric in his song "Thirty Days" that goes, "If I don't get no satisfaction from the judge." Keith also later acknowledged that the riff itself was a reworking of the backing track for Martha and the Vandellas' huge Motown hit—"Dancing in the Streets." Such borrowing used to be called "the folk process," but now and forever it could also be called "the rock process." But here is the real punch line to the Stones' first number one single and best-known signature song: Keith himself did not think it was a hit single. Here's his story:

KEITH RICHARDS: The first time I ever, you know, sort of flexed a muscle about what record should go out [was "Satisfaction"]. I didn't think it was a single. I mean it went right by me, you know. I just sort of wrote it down, put it on a tape. We cut it in two or three takes and I thought, "Oh well, there you go. That's a nice track for the album, but that's about all." I thought if we were going to make a single of it, that we were gonna record it and sort of work on it . . . It just sticks out—that box that some bloke had given me made a nice fuzz . . . [and I went] "Wow! Oh that's nice—Deet-Dee, Dee-Dee-Dee-Dee-Deet-Dee, Deet-Dee . . ."

Thank God no one paid any attention to him!

The reference track was recorded at Chess Studios in Chicago on May 10, but then the group decided to finish it in Los Angeles, where they had an established working relationship with engineer Dave Hassinger and the Phil Spector–tutored arranger Jack Nitzsche (who had been the musical director of the T.A.M.I. Show). The track rocked! The song put aside any notions of the Rolling Stones as merely a blues covers band. It synthesized all of the diverse styles that the group had been perfecting since 1962: blues, rhythm and blues, soul, folk, and their own unique brand of hard rock. Plus, they addressed all of their primary themes for the rest of the decade in the lyrics of that one song: frustration, hypocrisy, corruption, alienation, sexuality, boredom, aggression, suspicion, rage, and cynical mass-media manipulation.

CHAPTER 9
GET OFF OF MY CLOUD

THE FIRST NUMBER ONE single of the rock 'n' roll era was "Rock Around the Clock" by Bill Haley and the Comets. What could be more appealing than a number one hit? Every aspiring musician dreams of it.

Some of the biggest names in pop music history have never scored a number one single. Bob Dylan, for instance. Or Van Morrison. Or, believe it or not, Creedence Clearwater Revival. That's right. One of the biggest hit-making machines of the late '60s and early '70s never had a number one single.

Then too, there are the so-called super one hit wonders whose fifteen minutes of fame rest entirely on putting one single song at the top of the Top 40.

These harsh realities just magnify the accomplishments of that rare and select group of artists who manage to score multiple number one hits over the course of their career. Count the Rolling Stones in that hallowed group.

After the meteoric success of "Satisfaction," the Stones found themselves with a new problem.

KEITH RICHARDS: I remember after "Satisfaction" got to number one—bang, bang at the door. "Where's the follow-up?" I mean, every twelve weeks you had to have another one ready. The minute you put out a single, you had to start working your butt off on the next one, and the bigger the hit, the more pressure there was on the follow-up. But it was an incredibly good school for songwriting in that you couldn't piss around for months and months agonizing about the deeper meaning of this or that. No matter what else you were doing, you had to make damn sure you didn't let up on the writing. It made you search around and listen for ideas. It made you very aware of what was going on around you, because you were looking for that song. It might come in a coffee shop, or it might come on the street or in a cab. You might hear a phrase at a bus stop. You're listening for it every moment, and anything could be a song, and if you don't have one you're up the creek without a paddle.

Richards's next act after "Satisfaction" turned out to be "Get Off of My Cloud"—a blistering, primal scream about the pressures attached to manufacturing that next big hit single. Another delicious irony about "Get Off of My Cloud" is that it toppled the Beatles' vise-like, four-week grip at number one with "Yesterday." "Hey you! Get off of my cloud," indeed!

CHAPTER 10

PAINT IT BLACK

"PAINT IT BLACK" is one of the Rolling Stones' most enduring songs, and has been invoked in various bleak and scary movies, including Kubrick's *Full Metal Jacket*, and the horror flicks *The Devil's Advocate* and *Stir of Echoes*. In its earliest incarnation, it was nothing more than a send-up of an early Stones associate—Eric Easton (the man who co-managed the group with Andrew Loog Oldham from 1963 to 1965).

KEITH RICHARDS: What's amazing about that one for me is the sitar. Also, the fact that we cut it as a comedy track. Bill was playing an organ, doing a takeoff of our first manager who started his career in show business as an organist in a cinema pit. We'd been doing it with funky rhythms and it hadn't worked, and he started playing like this and everybody got behind it. It's a two-beat, very strange. Brian playing the sitar makes it a whole other thing.

There's no mystery about how and where Brian picked up the sitar.

GEORGE HARRISON: I always used to see Brian in the clubs and hang out with him. In the mid-sixties he used to come out to my house—particularly when he'd got "the fear," when he'd mixed too many weird things together. I'd hear his voice shouting to me from out in the garden: "George, George . . ." I'd let him in—he was a good mate. He would always come round to my house in the sitar period. We talked about "Paint It Black" and he picked up my sitar and tried to play it—and the next thing was he did that track.

Paint It, Black (sic)

So that's how it went from being an inside joke to a somber, deeply dark, nihilistic rant.

And although certainly not intended, the song has always had a strong connection to the war in Vietnam. At the end of *Full Metal Jacket*, it plays over the credits to illustrate the literal and emotional deaths of all men engaged in war. It was also the theme song of a short-lived CBS television series (*Tour of Duty*) about Vietnam that ran from 1987 to 1990. And Thomas Bird, founder of the Vietnam Veterans Ensemble Theater Company (VETCo), told me that it was the most compelling and relatable song that he listened to during his entire time in Southeast Asia. Then too there is this powerful recollection from www.songfacts.com of a Vietnam vet from Queens, New York:

BILL FROM QUEENS: While the Rolling Stones' song "Paint It Black" was not written about the Vietnam War, it has great meaning for many combat veterans from that war. The depression, the aura of premature death, loss of innocence, abandonment of all hope, are perfectly expressed in the song. When you walk off the killing fields, still alive, physically intact, you want everything painted black, like your heart, your soul, your mind, your life.

This is a clear-cut case of life imitating art rather than art imitating life. The Stones had their fingers on the pulse of the mid-sixties international turmoil even when that was not their primary artistic intention.

CHAPTER 11

LITTLE T & A

SHALL WE TALK about sex? Don't we have to? It's a Rolling Stones book, after all.

The phrase itself—"rock 'n' roll"—is a euphemism for sexual intercourse. "I'm gonna rock my baby with a steady roll" isn't about dancing. "Rock me baby, rock me baby, all night long" isn't a lullaby. And "Little T & A" isn't about Shakespeare's Titus Andronicus.

The early uproar about rock 'n' roll being the devil's music was elevated to iconic status in this 1950s sermon by the Reverend Jimmy Snow that you've seen and heard in countless documentaries about the evils of Elvis: "Rock 'n' roll music and why I preach against it. I believe that it is a contributing factor to our juvenile delinquency of today. I know what it does to you. And I know of the evil feeling that you feel when you sing it. And I know the . . . the . . . lost position that you get into . . . and the beat . . . well . . . uhmm . . . if you talk to the average teenager of today and you ask them what it is about rock 'n' roll music that they like, and the first thing that they'll say is the beat, the beat, THE BEAT!"

A less hysterical, much more measured analysis of the same phenomenon was offered by television journalist and commentator Jeff Greenfield:

JEFF GREENFIELD: It began with the Music. Nothing we see in the counterculture—not the clothes, the hair, the sexuality, the drugs, the rejection of reason, the resort to symbols and magic—none of it is separable from the coming to power in the 1950s of rock 'n' roll music. Brewed in the hidden corners of black America's cities, its rhythms infected white Americans, seducing them out of the kind of temperate bobby-sox passions out of which Andy Hardy films are spun. Rock 'n' roll was elemental, savage, dripping with sex; it was just as our parents feared. Not in the conspiracy theories of moral guardians, not that we dropped our books and molested children, but in the more subtle sense of what the music did, unleashing with its power knowledge that our bodies were our own Joy Machines. It would take years for successive generations of young Americans to work the equation out fully; it would take a disillusioning that included a wretched war, a wave of violence, and a brace of public murders of great men to spur on the rejection of reason as a tool of death, and the embrace of rock 'n' roll not as pleasure but as salvation. But in rock 'n' roll it began; the first tremors along the generational fault.

Doctor Fred Newman offers this explanation of the connection between music and sexuality: "Psychiatrists have long known that the source of mass hysteria springs from repressed sexual urges, composed of both sadistic and aggressive elements. The number of occasions on which pop singers are physically assaulted by their fans—Jagger himself was recently pulled off a twenty-foot platform in a Zurich stadium and almost torn to pieces— confirms the nature of the emotions involved. Essentially therefore the concert hall hysteria represents a sudden escape of the kind of emotions which the forces of Puritanism, morality, and authority—both social and parental—normally seek to contain. When a pop audience blows its top, it is in fact indulging in a communal act of defiance against a set of values which it feels to be unnecessarily and intolerably restrictive. It is a group protest against a society which it regards as impersonal, mechanistic, and money-bound. Undoubtedly Mick Jagger, purveying as he does his own brand of untamed rebelliousness, is at once a symbol and focal point of this seething insurrection."

There was nothing new about all this, of course. The same dynamic could certainly be offered up to explain Frank Sinatra's "bobby-soxer" hysteria in the 1940s. Witness this article from the January 10, 1945, issue of Britain's the *Guardian*: "The United States is now in the midst of one of those remarkable phenomena of mass hysteria which occur from time to time on this side of the Atlantic. Mr. Frank Sinatra, an amiable young singer of popular songs, is inspiring extraordinary personal devotion on the part of many thousands of young people, and particularly young girls between the ages of, say, twelve and eighteen . . . Psychologists have written soberly about the hypnotic quality of his voice and the remarkable effect upon susceptible young women."

Even the Beatles have to be viewed through the lens of sexual awakening. In 1978, famed director Robert Zemeckis (*Back to the Future*, *Forrest Gump*) made his directorial debut with a film executive produced by no less a cinema luminary than Steven Spielberg. The movie was called *I Wanna Hold Your Hand*, and it was the fictional account of that Sunday in 1964 when the Beatles debuted in America on Ed Sullivan. Six teens from New Jersey make their way to Broadway and Fifty-third Street in New York City determined to see their idols up close and personal even though none of them has a ticket to the broadcast.

One of the tag lines describing the film sets the stage: "These youngsters are suffering from a highly contagious disease called 'Beatlemania.' The symptoms are . . . screaming, hysteria, hyperventilation, fainting fits, seizures, and spasmodic convulsions. It isn't fatal but it sure is fun." It is also very sexy.

FILM CRITIC MIKE WHITE: The most dynamic of the group is [actress Nancy] Allen who plays Pam Mitchell, the frantic fiancée of Eddie. She's being forced to grow up too fast and be overly responsible. Cutting loose and enjoying a Beatles song or two isn't an option in her little world. Ironically . . . Allen's character lucks into a trip into the Beatles' hotel room where her world and her legs open up at the sight of Paul McCartney's bass. Witnessing a character's sexual awakening while moaning and licking the long, hard neck of a guitar is not standard fare in lighthearted teen romps. Without a doubt, Allen's character's transformation is remarkable. The once-uptight teen sheds the chains of her premarital oppression, announcing her triumph with screams of orgasmic delight at the sight of the group of crooning British youths.

There was, however, a difference between the way the Beatles aroused teenage girls' sexuality, and the way the Stones did.

CHRISSIE HYNDE: I listened to the Stones a lot when I was between fourteen and nineteen. Somehow rock 'n' roll music sounds different when you're just discovering the opposite sex and all that.

Let me illustrate with two extreme examples.

Do you remember Joyce Maynard? She was the teen wunderkind who made a name for herself when the *New York Times* published an article she had written called *An 18-Year-Old Looks Back on Life* on April 23, 1972. She was back in the headlines in 1998 when she revealed intimate details of her relationship with author J.D. Salinger when he was fifty-three and she was eighteen.

When the Rolling Stones came to perform at Madison Square Garden in New York City during their 1975 Tour of the Americas, Maynard wrote, again for the *New York Times*:

JOYCE MAYNARD: The first time I heard the Rolling Stones was in 1965, when I was 12. I had seen and loved the Beatles but this was entirely different. The Beatles were round-faced and bouncy, and if they wanted to hug or kiss you, it was in a friendly way. The Rolling Stones were never cuddly, even on Sunday night TV, and in the company of Ed Sullivan, hollow-eyed, cold, looking a bit evil, they were leopards to the Beatles' springer spaniels, and I thought they were marvelous.

The Stones touched off what were, I think, my first adult sexual rumblings. There was nothing teeny-bopperish in my feelings for the Rolling Stones. I didn't scream at the sight of them or paste their pictures on my walls. I don't suppose I understood what I felt when I put on "Satisfaction" and danced in front of the mirror or lay in bed at night as Mick Jagger pleaded, "Come on baby, cry to me" . . .

It is a problem for most 12-year-old girls—and certainly it was for me—that their bodies rarely match their minds. So while the young girl lies in the dark and dreams of being the one who will, at last, give Mick Jagger his Satisfaction, the next morning she must go to school and give an oral report on Bolivia.

If that's the "good girl" version of teenage sexual awakening, then the "bad girl" version has to be this steamy recollection that rock chanteuse Patti Smith penned for *Creem* magazine in January of 1973:

PATTI SMITH: Look back. it was 1965. Pa was shouting from the tv room. "jesus christ! jesus christ!" . . . I ran in panting. I was scared silly. There was pa glued to the tv screen cussing his brains out. A rock 'n' roll band was doing it right on the ed sullivan show. pa was frothing like a dog. I never seen him so mad. but I lost contact with him quick. that band was as relentless as murder. I was trapped in a field of hot dots. the guitar player had pimples. the blonde kneeling down had circles ringing his eyes. one had greasy hair. the other didn't care. and the singer was showing his second layer of skin and more than a little milk. I felt thru his pants with optic x-ray. this was some hard meat. this was a bitch. five white boys sexy as any spade. their nerves were wired and their third leg was rising. in six minutes five lusty images gave me my first glob of gooie in my virgin panties.

That was my introduction to the Rolling Stones. they did Time is on my side. my brain froze. I was doing all my thinking between my legs. I got shook. light broke. they were gone and I cliff-hanging. like jerking off without coming . . . I can tie the Stones in with every sexual release of my late blooming adolescence. The Stones were sexually freeing confused american children, a girl could feel power. lady glory, a guy could reveal his feminine side without being called a fag. masculinity was no longer measured on the football field . . . Ya never think of the Stones as fags. In full make-up and frills they still get it across. they know just how to ram a woman. they made me real proud to be female. the other half of male. they aroused in me both a feline sense of power and a longing to be held under the thumb.

You said it, Patti. Rock was sex, and the Rolling Stones were rock. And they were brazen about it as well. Let's do a quick survey of the ways that the Stones led the charge of the sexual revolution of the '60s and beyond.

In the beginning, it was through the words and music of others—cover versions of the down and dirty paeans to erotica by their American blues heroes, such as two Willie Dixon classics, "I Just Want to Make Love to You" (a hit for Muddy Waters) and "Little Red Rooster" (a hit for Howlin' Wolf). Then it was the constant flow of hits and album tracks that celebrated venery and volupté such as "The Spider and the Fly," "Back Street Girl," "Satisfaction," "Stray Cat Blues," "Parachute Women," "Let It Bleed," "Live with Me," "Brown Sugar," and "Some Girls." Or how about the ones that were so over the top and outrageous that they had to be disguised by the record company to avoid retribution ("Star Star" and "Little T & A")! What other band would allow a documentary like *Cocksucker Blues* to make its way into the public sphere?

And then what about the whole question of androgyny, unisexuality, and homoeroticism that is such a large part of the history and mystery of the Rolling Stones? From the picture sleeves for "Have You Seen Your Mother, Baby" and "Jumpin' Jack Flash" to the cover of the *Some Girls* album to the late Guy Peellaert's erotically charged depictions of the Stones in drag, with naked underaged girls, and in fishnet stockings and full Nazi regalia in his iconic art book *Rock Dreams*—the Stones have never shied away from their feminine side (They even asked Peellaert to do the cover of *It's Only Rock 'n' Roll* in 1974.)

MICK JAGGER: Elvis was very androgynous. I saw Elvis as a rock singer, and obviously you were attracted to him because he was a good-looking guy. If you look at the pictures, the eyes are done with makeup, and everything's perfect. I mean, look at Little Richard. He had a very feminine appearance, but you didn't translate that into what Little Richard's sex orientation was . . . As far as I was concerned, it was part of the whole thing from the beginning. It was very English—guys dressing up in drag is nothing particularly new . . . And it obviously worked and offended people, which was always the big thing, something new to offend them with. I think what we did in this era was take all these things that were unspoken in previous incarnations of rock 'n' roll and intellectualize them . . . rock 'n' roll mostly is a very butch thing, and it appeals to one hard side of the masculine character. But I don't think the Rolling Stones are only a rock band. They can be other things. They can be very feminine.

KEITH RICHARDS: Oh, you should have seen Mick really . . . I'll put it like this; there was a period when Mick was extremely camp. When Mick went through his camp period, in 1964, Brian and I immediately went enormously butch and sort of laughin' at him. That terrible thing . . . that switching-around confusion of roles that still goes on.

One final observation about the Stones and sexuality. It comes from one of the best essays about the group, written by Michael Lydon for his 1971 book *Rock Folk*. Lydon traveled with the group on their infamous 1969 tour of America and recorded the following exchange. I think it best illustrates the intersection of fame, sex, mythology, and perception as reality that this chapter is *really* all about:

CATHY: Two years ago my girlfriend Mary and I were married and living in Ojai. It was okay, but boring, and all we ever thought about was Mick Jagger. We loved him a lot more than our husbands. So one day we decided: we'll split, get divorces, and move down to the Strip. It was great, you know, hanging around the clubs. We got to know a lot of groups but never forgot Mick. So imagine how we felt in the Whisky one night when this guy said he was Sam Cutler and asked if we'd like to be with the Stones when they were in LA, and drive 'em around and stuff.

It was Sam who picked me up, and I felt loyal to him, but when we were up at Mick's house the first night—well, I'm only human. We were all sitting around, and Mick said he was going to bed. I was really disappointed. But he came down again and started pouring perfume on me, and sort of whispered, "Will you come up with me, then."

I almost died, but I managed to say, "Only if my friend Mary can come too." We had been together through two years, and had to make a pact not to leave the other out. He said okay.

It was funny, man, I could hardly get it on. He makes all the sexy noises in bed, like he does singing. I was laughing so hard, but know what was funniest? For two years I had been thinking with every guy, "He's great, but he's not Mick Jagger." And then with Mick, all I could think was, "He's great, but he's not Mick Jagger."

HAVE YOU SEEN YOUR MOTHER, BABY, STANDING IN THE SHADOW?

An early sign of the Stones' androgyny

CHAPTER 12

WAITING ON A FRIEND

WHEN BRIAN JONES took out an ad in *Jazz News* in May of 1962 looking for like-minded musicians, the first respondent was Ian Stewart. Stewart was working for a chemical company at the time.

IAN STEWART: [My] desk at ICI was the headquarters of the Stones organization. My number was advertised in *Jazz News* and I handled the Stones' bookings at work.

KEITH RICHARDS: He used to play boogie-woogie piano in jazz clubs, apart from his regular job. He blew my head off too, when he started to play. I never heard a white piano player play like that before.

Ian was a full-fledged member of the band for the first year or so, before Andrew Loog Oldham decided he should take more of a backseat role, saying that six members was one too many for a rock group and that Stewart, who was a burly guy, didn't fit the image he was trying to create for the Rolling Stones.

IAN STEWART: Nobody ever said, "You're out." But all of a sudden I was out. It happened one night when I went down to play a gig and there were five guys in band uniforms and none for me.

MICK JAGGER: It was obvious that Ian Stewart didn't fit the picture. He was still playing piano when we wanted him to; he didn't play on everything, anyway, because we were playing electrical instruments and he was playing an unamplified upright

Ian "Stu" Stewart

piano in a noisy club. You couldn't hear it. I'm not dissing him as though he wasn't part of the whole thing, but there were a lot of numbers which he didn't play on. It was plain that Ian didn't want to be a pop singer.

Stewart stuck around in his vital role as the "sixth Stone," becoming the band's road manager and continuing to play keyboards.

KEITH RICHARDS: [Stu] might have realized that in the way it was going to have to be marketed, he would be out of sync, but that he could still be a vital part. I'd probably have said, "Well, fuck you," but he said, "OK, I'll just drive you around." That takes a big heart, but Stu had one of the largest hearts around.

CHUCK LEAVELL: In the early days when they were playing Milwaukee or something, they'd be staying twenty miles away from the city in some hotel. "Why in the world are we out here?" Of course it was because there was a golf course Stu wanted to play nearby.

KEITH RICHARDS: We'd be playing in some town where there's all these chicks, and they want to get laid and we want to lay them. But Stu would have booked us into some hotel about ten miles out of town. You'd wake up in the morning and there's the links. We're bored to death looking for some action and Stu's playing Gleneagles.

But it was also clear that he was like family. Keyboardist Chuck Leavell was Stewart's protégé.

CHUCK LEAVELL: Everyone would get dressed up in their rock 'n' roll regalia before the show—me included—but Stu would come out in his golf polo shirt and jeans. He'd bring his camera and half a sandwich. He'd put the camera and the sandwich on the piano. Sometimes he would just stop playing and take pictures.

Stu was a universally beloved figure.

CHUCK LEAVELL: Stu and I really got on famously; I felt like his little brother. Stu was very particular. He didn't like playing on slow songs—ballads. He didn't like playing on things that had minor chord changes to them. He only liked playing the boogie-woogie and the rock 'n' roll stuff. So if it was a rock 'n' roll tune that he wanted to play piano on, that's what he did, and I played organ. If it was a ballad like "Angie" or if was something like "Miss You" that had minor changes in it or modal changes, then I took over the keyboard part . . .

BILL GERMAN: Ian saw what the Stones went through in terms of fame— they couldn't just go to the park—so he loved being anonymous. It's just the way it played out. In Stu's opinion, not being an official member of the band worked out for the best. He got to lead a normal life, while still being creative and still touring the world and still playing piano the best he could. He led a very happy life and he was a very humble guy. He was so glad not to be a rock star—fall into all the trappings of the drugs, and the booze, and the groupies, all that sort of stuff. He seemed to love it that way . . . He told me that the people he hung out with were not famous rock stars, for the most part . . . He knew every rock star, but basically the guys he hung out with on a day-to-day basis were pig farmers and local guys from his town.

Bill got the opportunity to meet Stewart in the early '80s when he was writing the Stones' fanzine *Beggars Banquet*.

BILL GERMAN: He famously used to call the Stones "His showers of shit." And they would take it from him because they had such a respect for him. That's what intimidated me: If he calls the Stones "showers of shit," what is he going to think of me? . . . It turns out that he completely puts me at ease. He was the nicest guy in the world. He was teaching me a little bit about boogie-woogie jazz.

Ian Stewart died in 1985 of a heart attack, but he remains inextricably connected to the band.

CHUCK LEAVELL: I think about Stu all the time. I know we all do. I miss that guy. He was so funny and such a great human being—a good person and enjoyable to be with.

MICK JAGGER: Stu was the one guy we tried to please. We wanted his approval when we were writing or rehearsing a song.

KEITH RICHARDS: Ian Stewart was the first to get us into the studio to make some demos. As far as I'm concerned, the Rolling Stones are his band.

Appropriately, the reception after the funeral was held at a golf course.

CHUCK LEAVELL: I can remember Keith saying, "I can hear Stu now saying that this is the only way that they'd let me in this club."*

*For what it's worth Keith tells this joke the other way, that the funeral lunch was the only way Stu could get Keith to go to a golf club.

CHAPTER 13

LET'S SPEND SOME TIME TOGETHER

TELEVISION IMPRESARIO ED Sullivan learned early on that a "new-fashioned" rock 'n' roll sensation could pump up the ratings of his "old-fashioned" Sunday night variety show on CBS. It happened with Elvis. It happened with the Beatles. And as we've noted, it happened six times, from 1964 to 1969, with the Rolling Stones.

BILL WYMAN: Well, I think Ed Sullivan can be summed up really easily. Do you remember when the Supremes came on his show and it came time for him to make the announcement? He said, "Ahnd naow, ladies and gen'lmen, for your enjoyment, the . . . the . . . the . . ." and the curtains open and he says, "the *Girls*." He had one line to say every ten minutes, but he couldn't handle it. Every time we were on the show he had to do four re-takes of whatever he was saying. "Heeeeeere's the Rolling Stones with their new record . . . er . . . uh . . ." He must have been all right at one time. Otherwise he never would have gotten the show, right?

As you might imagine, there was also headline-making controversy attached to some of these appearances. For every fresh-scrubbed, squeaky-clean performance by the Dave Clark Five, Herman's Hermits, or Gerry and the Pacemakers, there were an equal number of eyebrow-raising moments involving a few of the biggest names in music. In his third appearance on the Sullivan show, in January of 1957, Elvis was shown from the waist up only because of the uproar caused by his first two hip-swiveling performances in 1956. Bob Dylan walked off the show in 1963 when he was prohibited from singing "Talkin' John Birch Paranoid Blues." (He never did appear on the broadcast in its remaining eight years on the air.) Another famous incident occurred in 1967 when the show booked the Doors for an appearance on September 17.

RAY MANZAREK: "Light My Fire" went to number one and a day later we got a call from Ed Sullivan saying, "You're on the show in two weeks." So we get to New York, get in the rehearsal situation, and right at the end of "Light My Fire," some guy comes up to us, Ed Sullivan's son-in-law, actually [Bob Precht], and says, "Very good boys, very good. There's only one problem. You're going to have to change the word 'higher' . . . You can't say 'high' on nationwide TV." We said, "Hey, that doesn't have anything to do with drugs, or anything like that. That's not a drug song, it's a love song. We're so in love, our love couldn't get much higher." "I don't care what your rationale is boys. You can't say 'higher' on nationwide TV. You can say 'bite my wire' for all I care, but change it or you're not on!" We said, "Okay, okay, okay, okay, we'll change it. Yes sir, yes sir."

He left the room and we all looked at each other and said, "Let's not change it." It was only a five-second delay. It was virtually live. "They're not going to be able to edit it. Nobody's gonna even know. So it comes time to sing, man, and there we are: "Girl we couldn't get much HIGHER!" and we did it for all we were worth. After the show, this guy comes up to us and starts screaming, "You promised! You promised you wouldn't say 'higher.' Why did you do it?" And we said, "Hey, man, in the excitement of the moment—nationwide television—we just forgot. Our minds went blank. You know how musicians are, man. We're kind of dumb." And he said, "But you promised," and walked out of the room, and we never did another *Ed Sullivan Show* again.

Two famous eyerolls: Mick on Sullivan in 1967; Dean Martin from back in 1964

The Stones handled a very similar situation in a very different way. For their January 15, 1967, live appearance during which they were scheduled to perform and promote the new single "Let's Spend the Night Together" and "Ruby Tuesday," the group was famously asked by Sullivan himself to alter the lyric of the former to "Let's spend some time together." In this instance, the group complied with Sullivan's wishes, albeit with Jagger contemptuously rolling his eyes skyward at every opportunity during the song's entire three minutes and twenty-nine seconds.

BILL WYMAN: If it was England we probably wouldn't have bothered to go through with it. But the Sullivan show was quite important at the time, reached sixty million people or so, and it was our only shot since you had to agree not to do another big show one month before or after being on it.

Or, to put it another way, Mick Jagger didn't attend the London School of Economics for nothing!

CHAPTER 14

RUBY TUESDAY

THE STONES HIT the ground running at the beginning of 1967 with a two-fisted, two-sided, almost "too" controversial forty-five-rpm single called "Let's Spend the Night Together," backed with "Ruby Tuesday." The former was yet another hard-rocking, lewd, rude, and crude invitation by the Stones to cast off the pretenses and conventions of World War II era parents, and acknowledge that young people all over the world were engaging in all kinds of sexual relationships without the benefit of marriage. Well, once again, the Stones were a little bit ahead of their time, but a little bit behind the archconservatism of Big American Media.

As a result, the Stones ran into a thick brick wall of censorship when they tried to peddle the song on *The Ed Sullivan Show* (see chapter 13). And they also ran headlong into the same problem with the self-appointed guardians of culture and mores on the nation's airwaves. (Just a note to point out here that while all of this was going on, a young Howard Stern, who had just turned thirteen years of age, was attending Roosevelt Junior High School on Long Island!)

"Let's Spend the Night Together" was summarily banned on most of American radio, except for the new, more adventurous rock radio stations that had begun popping up on the FM dial in 1966—specifically WOR-FM in New York. But the law of supply and demand came into play, and the Stones were *definitely* in demand. Solution to the dilemma? "Let's see what's on the other side of 'Let's Spend the Night Together.'"

As it turned out, the flip side—"Ruby Tuesday"—was yet another soon-to-be legendary Rolling Stones ballad in the vein of "As Tears Go By" and "Lady Jane." No string quartet, but a very engaging recorder solo contributed by Brian Jones AND a very real-life love connection for Keith Richards. The song (mostly written by Keith and Brian, with not much input from Mick) was about a woman described by Andrew Loog Oldham as Keith's very first serious girlfriend, an English model named Linda Keith. Their relationship was coming to an end.

KEITH RICHARDS: It was probably written about Linda Keith not being there (*laughs*). I don't know, she had pissed off somewhere. It was very mournful, very, VERY Ruby Tuesday and it was a Tuesday.

That's one of those things—some chick you've broken up with. And all you've got left is the piano and the guitar and a pair of panties. And it's goodbye you know. And so it just comes out of that. And after that you just build on it. It's one of those songs that are easiest to write because you're really right there, and you really sort of mean it. And for a songwriter, hey, break his heart and he'll come up with a good song.

Good song? How about a GREAT song? And it not only captured the imagination of listeners all over the world, but also became the Stones' fourth number one single in America. (Without comparable airplay, "Let's Spend the Night Together" stalled at number fifty-five on the US charts.)

CHAPTER 15

2000 LIGHT YEARS FROM HOME

THE PUSH-PULL relationship between the Beatles and the Rolling Stones continued unabated for the balance of the '60s.

KEITH RICHARDS: Everybody was talking about the Beatles versus the Stones and all that crap, and yet between us, it would be, "You come out first and we'll wait two weeks." We would try never to clash; there was plenty of room for both of us. There was a time when "Paperback Writer" came out, and one of ours—"Paint It Black" or something like that—came out before or after; we had stitched it up with them. There would be surreptitious phone calls. It was, "OK, ours is ready, yours ain't" . . . "All right, you go first."

PAUL MCCARTNEY: We'd be hanging out with the Stones, working on their sessions, it was a very friendly scene. There must have been a bit of competition because that's only natural, but it was always friendly. We used to say, "Have you got one coming out?" and if they had, we'd say, "Well, hold it for a couple of weeks, because we've got one." It made sense, really, to avoid each other's releases. John and I sang on the Stones' song "We Love You"—Mick had been stuck for an idea and he asked us to come along. So we went down to Olympic Studios and made it up . . .

When we asked Brian Jones to one of our sessions, to our surprise he brought along a sax. He turned up in a big Afghan coat at Abbey Road. He played sax on a crazy record, "You Know My Name (Look Up the Number)." It's a funny sax solo—it isn't amazingly well played but it happened to be exactly what we wanted: a ropey, shaky sax. Brian was very good like that.

However, for every nice thing you can find a Beatle saying about a Stone, or a Stone saying about a Beatle, there is an equal and opposite devastating slag. Sometimes it got downright nasty. At his rage-venting-primal-scream best in 1971, John Lennon offered the following to *Rolling Stone* magazine:

JOHN LENNON: I think it's a lot of hype. I like "Honky Tonk Women," but I think Mick's a joke, with all that fag dancing, I always did. I enjoy it; I'll probably go and see his films and all, like everybody else, but really, I think it's a joke . . . I never do see him. I was always very respectful about Mick and the Stones, but he said a lot of sort of tarty things about the Beatles, which I am hurt by, because you know, I can knock the Beatles, but don't let Mick Jagger knock them. I would like to just list what we did and what the Stones did two months after on every fuckin' album. Every fuckin' thing we did, Mick does exactly the same—he imitates us. And I would like one of you fuckin' underground people to point it out; you know *Satanic Majesties* is [*Sargeant*] *Pepper*; "We Love You," it's the most fuckin' bullshit, that's "All You Need Is Love."

I resent the implication that the Stones are like revolutionaries and that the Beatles weren't. If the Stones were or are, the Beatles really were, too. But they are not in the same class, musicwise or powerwise, never were. I never said anything. I always admired them because I like their funky music and I like their style. I like rock 'n' roll and the direction they took after they got over trying to imitate us . . .

He's obviously so upset by how big the Beatles are compared with him; he never got over it. Now he's in his old age, and he is beginning to knock us, you know, and he keeps knocking. I resent it, because even his second fuckin' record, we wrote it for him. Mick said, "Peace made money." We didn't make any money from Peace.

A quarter of a century later, and fifteen years after John's death, Mick was still grappling with some of those brickbats hurled in 1971. He told *Rolling Stone*:

MICK JAGGER: [John Lennon] said something in your magazine. It wasn't to do with appearance, more with music. When asked about the Rolling Stones, he said, "I like the butch stuff, and I don't like the faggy stuff." But you don't want to be butch the whole time. It would drive you mad, wouldn't it?

Admittedly, Mick has tempered his thoughts about the Beatles since John's demise in 1980, but there are many recorded instances where he would casually drop a comment such as this in 1977:

MICK JAGGER: We were not the Beatles . . . the Beatles were a pop band . . . and, though we liked them . . . you know . . . I mean . . . Keith and Brian sort of liked them, but I didn't really. I mean they were sweet and all that, but we were a blues band. We played blues and we played in clubs and we didn't play ballrooms and we just played in clubs and we played blues . . . we didn't play that kind of music, pop music. We didn't play like . . . what was it? "Please Please Me" . . . we didn't play adolescent love songs at all . . . we were doing "I Just Want to Make Love to You."

So maybe the real questions here are: How do you define a love/hate relationship? Or can you have a sibling rivalry with someone who isn't actually your brother or your sister? We could ask Don and Phil Everly about this. Or Paul Simon and Art Garfunkel. Or Ray and Dave Davies. Wouldn't all of those be interesting conversations to listen in on? You could literally fill volumes about the dynamics and nuances of the personal and professional relationships between John Lennon and Paul McCartney, or Mick Jagger and Keith Richards. Here are Mick's thoughts about this very question:

MICK JAGGER: You don't have to have a partner for everything you do. But having partners sometimes helps you and sometimes hinders you. You have good times and bad times with them. It's just the nature of it . . . People also like partnerships because they can identify with the drama of two people in partnership. They can feed off a partnership, and that keeps people entertained. Besides, if you have a successful partnership, it's self-sustaining.

This is certainly true of Mick and Keith. Unfortunately, we'll never know how things might have turned out for John and Paul had they each been given an equal number of years on the planet.

Sometimes the rivalry between the bands was light-hearted and playful. For example, the Beatles putting "Welcome the Rolling Stones" on the cover of *Sgt. Pepper*, or the Stones putting the four tiny, semi-camouflaged faces of the Fab Four on the cover of *Satanic Majesties*.

It is difficult, though, *not* to acknowledge the plausibility of John Lennon's "imitators" accusation. After all, didn't "Paint It Black" owe something to "Baby's in Black"? Couldn't "You Can't Always Get What You Want" be seen and heard as a close, seven-minute-plus companion of "Hey Jude"? Aren't there parallels to be drawn between the two made-for-TV specials *Magical Mystery Tour* and *The Rolling Stones Rock and Roll Circus*? And, certainly, wasn't *Their Satanic Majesties Request* just a blatant, knee-jerk response to *Sgt. Pepper's Lonely Hearts Club Band*? Well, not necessarily.

KEITH RICHARDS: I don't know. I never listened any more to the Beatles than to anyone else in those days when we were working. It's probably more down to the fact that we were going through the same things. Maybe we were doing it a little bit after them. Anyway, we were following them through so many scenes. We're only just mirrors ourselves of that whole thing. It took us much longer to get a record out for us; our stuff was always coming out later anyway.

MICK JAGGER: I can't remember anything that happened in 1967 I'm afraid . . . I'm sure there's lots of other people who can't remember either . . . everyone was wanting to do something else at that point. Everyone was fed up with just playing straight-ahead rock 'n' roll, so they just . . . we just went in and just looked around . . . It was a very weird time for us because we were in and out of jail and were on kind of drug charges and we didn't know what we were doing and . . . It was very peculiar and so we played very peculiar music that year . . . I think we were just taking too much acid. We were just getting carried away, just thinking anything you did was fun and everyone should listen to it. The whole thing [*Satanic Majesties*], we were on acid. We were on acid doing the cover picture. I always remember doing that. It was like being at school, you know, sticking on the bits of colored paper and things. It was really silly. But we enjoyed it (*laughs*). Also, we did it to piss Andrew off, because he was such a pain in the neck. Because he didn't understand it. The more we wanted to unload him, we decided to go on this path to alienate him.

Mission accomplished! Oldham walked out in the middle of the recording sessions at Olympic Studios never to return.

There's no denying that the album had its moments ("She's a Rainbow," "2000 Light Years from Home"), but it seldom appears on any lists of favorite, best, or most successful projects by the Rolling Stones. And *Pepper* eclipsed it by . . . well, about two thousand light years. It is a curio. A timepiece. A graphic reflection of the excesses of the period in which it was recorded.

BILLY ALTMAN: The *Satanic Majesties* album had been their first misstep really in their entire career. They'd always been kind of following the Beatles, but kind of doing things their own way. The Beatles would do something and then the Stones would do something in a similar vein, but also different and controversial that set them apart.

GLYN JOHNS: Recording *Satanic* was really boring. It really didn't come off. I've never listened to it since its release.

Once the purple haze began to lift, it actually accelerated and paved the way for a soon-to-be new Stones era: a break with Andrew Oldham; a new producer; the sad departure and death of Brian Jones; and the eventual winding down of the Beatles as a day-to-day functioning reality. In a very real sense, the Stones were poised to finally step out of the shadow of the Fab Four, and make a run for Greatest Rock 'n' Roll Band in the World status. That journey began in earnest in 1968.

This photo from 1965 at RCA Studios in Hollywood presaged the Stones' psychedelic stage

ROLLING STONES IN DRUGS SWOOP

Evening News

CHAPTER 16

MOTHER'S LITTLE HELPER

You can't write about the Rolling Stones without writing about a place called Redlands. Redlands was Keith Richards's home and the site of one of the most notorious drug busts in all of rock 'n' roll history. Among the guests at Keith's that day were Mick Jagger and Marianne Faithfull, as well as George and Pattie Harrison, and an art dealer named Robert Fraser. There was also a soon-to-leave-England-never-to-return informant named David Schneiderman, aka the Acid King, who it was learned years later had tipped off the police that there were drugs on the premises. Brian Jones was supposed to be there, but was in a fight with his girlfriend, Anita Pallenberg, and stayed in London. George and Pattie left early, and weren't there when police arrived at five thirty P.M., search warrant in hand.

Keith and his friends had spent a long day outdoors before the trouble began.

KEITH RICHARDS: We were just gliding off from a twelve-hour trip. You know how that freaks people out when they walk in on you. The vibes were so funny for them. I told one of the women with them they'd brought to search the ladies, "Would you mind stepping off that Moroccan cushion? Because you're ruining the tapestries." We were playing it like that. They tried to get us to turn the record player off but we said, "No. We won't turn it off but we'll turn it down."

MARIANNE FAITHFULL: My clothes were all covered with sand, dirt, twigs in my hair, the normal sort of wear and tear of being on a trip outside. It was such an intense trip that I was quite relieved when we started to come down. That's when I went and took my bath. I was the only one who hadn't brought a change of clothes and I dealt with it by wearing this beautiful fur rug. It was very large, six by nine feet or something. It would have covered a small room. I remember having this absurd idea of telling everyone to be still. "If we don't make any noise, if we're all really quiet, they'll go away."

The cops did not go away; they kept knocking and eventually got inside, where they discovered Faithfull dressed scantily, and oddly. When it came out later, the story of the woman wearing only a rug titillated the English press, and became a focal point of the coverage. (There is a rock 'n' roll urban legend about Marianne, Mick, and a Mars bar, but it's been disproved in enough places to dispense with it parenthetically.)

At some point, with the cops searching the premises, somebody put on Bob Dylan's "Rainy Day Women #12 & 35," with its refrain, "Everybody must get stoned."

The police found cannabis and amphetamines, and if they'd searched harder they'd have found cocaine and LSD as well. Still, they had enough evidence to eventually sentence Mick and Keith to prison for three and twelve months, respectively. Jagger spent a night in Brixton prison; Richards a night in Wormwood Scrubs. An editorial written by William Rees-Mogg of the *Times of London*, headlined WHO BREAKS A BUTTERFLY ON A WHEEL?, railed against the severity of Jagger's sentence and helped turn the tide of public opinion in favor of the band.

There's a great story from engineer George Chkiantz about the period when Jagger and Richards were out of jail and waiting for their appeal. Nobody at that day's recording session wanted to talk about the trial or the fact that this episode could possibly destroy the band. The silence, and simultaneously the tension, was finally broken by a late-arriving Charlie Watts. "So how are the two jailbirds?" he said.

At last, in July, the guilty verdict was overturned and Mick and Keith were free from the hassles of the law . . . for the moment, at least.

Brian Jones wasn't as fortunate. He was first busted for possession in May of '67, and was fined and given probation. But when he was busted a second time, in May of '68, he had to plead guilty to avoid jail time. This meant that he'd be unlikely to gain a visa the next time the band wanted to tour the United States, a fact that would soon become significant.

CHAPTER 17

JIGSAW PUZZLE

AT THE START of 1968, the Stones were a group in turmoil, coming off what was mostly a lost year. The rift between Brian and the rest of the band was deepening. Brian had been abusive to his girlfriend of two years, Anita Pallenberg, and she ended up leaving him for Keith. Did Keith feel guilty about this?

KEITH RICHARDS: Brian, in many ways, was a right cunt. He was a bastard. Up to a point, you could put up with it. In the last year or so, when Brian was almost totally incapacitated all of the time, he became a joke to the band. It was the only way we could deal with it without getting mad at him. So then it became that very cruel, piss-taking thing behind his back all the time . . .

Things only got worse after Jones's second bust for marijuana possession in May. Now, not only was Brian in danger of no-showing gigs in the UK, but his legal problems might prevent him from joining the band if and when they decided to return to America.

KEITH RICHARDS: There was no immediate necessity to go through the drama of replacing Brian because no gigs were lined up. We first had to recognize the fact that we needed to make a really good album. After *Satanic Majesties* we wanted to make a STONES album.

And that's where Jimmy Miller came in.

GLYN JOHNS: Jagger came to me after *Satanic Majesties* and said, "We're going to get a new producer, an American." I thought, "Oh my God, that's all I need. I don't think my ego can stand having some bloody Yankee coming in here and start telling me what sort of sound to get with the Rolling Stones." So I said, "I know somebody! I know there's one in England already and he's fantastic," and he'd just done the Traffic album: Jimmy Miller. And it was a remarkably good record he made, the first record he made with Traffic. I said, "He's a really nice guy." I'd met him, he'd been in the next studio room and I said, "I'm sure he'd be fantastic." Anything but some strange lunatic drug addict from Los Angeles. So . . . Jagger actually took the bait and off he went, met Jimmy Miller and gave him the job. And the first thing Jimmy Miller did (*laughs*) was fire ME. 'Cause he'd been using Eddie Kramer as an engineer. And so, naturally, quite obviously, he wanted to use his own engineer, the guy he knew.

Miller was exactly what they needed at that time. His roots-based approach allowed the Stones to do what they did best.

ANDY JOHNS: Jimmy Miller made the Stones into the band they should have always been, and tried to be in the beginning.

BILLY ALTMAN: He was a tremendous producer. Mick especially was very impressed with the last Spencer Davis album and that first Traffic album that he had done. He was able to get them a very big sound that they had never really managed to have prior to that. I don't know how much of that was attributable to Andy Oldham nominally being their producer up until then, but I think on a sonic basis, Miller really got to the heart of what they sounded like as a band, really honing in on Keith's guitar and Charlie Watts's drumming.

EDDIE KRAMER: I think they'd had enough at that point. Thank God they found Jimmy Miller. Certainly Mick and Keith and the boys had heard what we'd done with Traffic. And it was amazing. When you put *Dear Mr. Fantasy* up against *Satanic Majesties* it completely blows that away. So the Stones probably think, "Who is this guy Jimmy Miller?"

If not for him, I don't think the Stones would be in the place they are today. Because what he did is that he went to the heart and soul of where they came from. And he was so adept at milking the inner psyche of the band. And he was so clever at production. And he's the guy I've always modeled myself after in terms of how to get a session going, how to make the artists really get excited about what they're playing. Even to the point where Charlie couldn't play the drum part the way he was hearing it, he would go and sit in on the drums.

ANDY JOHNS: Jimmy was an extremely talented man. His main gift I think was his ability to get grooves. Which for a band like the Stones is very important. Look at the difference between *Beggars Banquet* and *Satanic Majesties*. He put them right back on the rail. So he was quite influential then and came up with all sorts of lovely ideas for them. In fact that's him playing the cowbell at the beginning of "Honky Tonk Women." He sets it up.

ROBERT GREENFIELD: Jimmy Miller was a lovely guy. He had this great disposition. And if you want to talk about his greatness as a producer, look at his Traffic albums. What Jimmy brought to the Stones was groove. Jimmy gave them a soul groove, a rhythm groove that they never had before.

The Stones in the studio with producer Jimmy Miller (far left)

JIMMY MILLER: Musically they were just coming out of their psychedelic period, which hadn't been too successful for them, and I think that was lucky for me, because I didn't insist that they change direction but they were ready to do so, as was evident from the new songs that they played me. What they had written was rock 'n' roll, yet I subsequently received a lot of credit for getting them back on course, so I benefited a lot from being in the right place at the right time. There again, I think it's fair to say that being American also helped, because—as was the case with many successful British bands during that era—they had been raised on American records. As things turned out, it was not always easy—they could take a long time over certain things—but it was always a pleasure, especially when they'd eventually hit those magic moments as they inevitably seemed to do. The first of those just happened to be on the very first track that I produced for them, "Jumpin' Jack Flash."

KEITH TALKS "JUMPIN' JACK FLASH"

"Jumpin' Jack Flash" was released as a single in 1968 and remains one of the Stones' most identifiable songs. It's also significant in that it essentially kicks off the next period in the band's existence, Rolling Stones "Mach Two," as Keith has called it. In *Life*, Keith tells the story of how the tune got its name:

KEITH RICHARDS: Mick and I had been up all night, it was raining outside and there was the sound of these heavy stomping rubber boots near the window, belonging to my gardener, Jack Dyer, a real country man from Sussex. It woke Mick up. He said, "What's that?" I said, "Oh, that's Jack. That's jumping Jack." I started to work around the phrase on the guitar, which was in open tuning, singing the phrase "Jumping Jack." Mick said, "Flash," and suddenly we had this phrase with a great rhythm and ring to it. So we got to work on it and wrote it.

Keith gives himself some of the credit for the reinvention of the Stones' sound as well.

KEITH RICHARDS: "Jumpin' Jack Flash" and "Street Fighting Man" came about because I had become fascinated by the possibilities of playing an acoustic guitar through a cassette recorder, using it as a pick-up, really, so that I could still get the crispness of an acoustic—which you can never get off an electric guitar—but overloading this tiny little machine so the effect was that it sounded both acoustic and electric. Technology was starting to increase in sophistication, but I just wanted to reduce it back to basics. I bought one of the first cassette machines—a must for a budding songwriter—and then day in, day out recorded on it. Then I began to get interested in the actual sound of the machine, how close you could put the microphone to the guitar and what effect you could get out of it . . . When we were in the studio I would bring in that little Philips cassette recorder, get a wooden extension speaker, plug that into the back of the recorder, shove a microphone in front of the speaker in the middle of the studio and record it. We would all sit back and watch this little microphone record the cassette machine in the middle of the studio at Olympic, which was the size of Sadler's Wells. Then we'd go back, listen to it, play over it, mash it up, and there was the track.

EDDIE KRAMER: We used Jimmy Miller's Wollensak—a cassette machine with a microphone in it. We put it on the floor of the studio and we recorded Keith's guitar, and I believe Charlie was just using a brush or a stick on the snare for the backbeat. After we cut the track on the cassette machine, we played it back on a

**Jumpin' Jack Flash
Rolling Stones**

little speaker, then rerecorded that on one track of a four-track machine. That was the guide track, then everybody overdubbed to that. When you hear the beginning of the song, you can hear the amount of wow— on a cassette machine when you play the straight chord you hear "bo-wow-wow-wow" because the movement of the tape against the pinch wheel was never very steady. It wasn't a professional machine . . . You hear the movement of the pitch, which is the reason that it has this funky sound which everyone dug at that time.

The resulting album would go on to be one of the Stones' collective favorites. Its back-to-basics approach was natural for them.

BILL WYMAN: It's probably because we listened to and played so much early blues material. Musically, it was very simple, so you had to put a lot of feeling into it to make it work. Whenever we rehearse and learn new numbers, every other thing we play is a jam on an old Elmore James or Muddy Waters or Chuck Berry thing. I know a lot of people say, "What are you playing that old stuff for?" But we're not doing it for sentimental reasons, we're doing it to retain the feeling of those blues and R&B things.

You can't have everybody flying off everywhere and showing off your chops. Besides, our chops aren't always that good! I think the great thing about the Stones is the simplicity of it—that slightly ragged rhythm that sounds like it might fall apart by the next bar but never does. We always have scrappy endings; we play with kind of a pulse that fluctuates between being slightly behind and slightly in front of the beat but it swings like that. And it works for us. I hate bands that play on eighths or sixteenths, there's no feel there, nothing seems to be coming from inside them.

On the contrary, the bluesy feel of *Beggars Banquet* still resonates. One album track that stands out is "No Expectations."

BILLY ALTMAN: "No Expectations" to me is one of the great Stones songs in their entire body of work. And it really stands out to me because it's one of the last things of substance that Brian Jones was able to contribute to the band, his slide playing on there. It's Robert Johnson, it's Delta blues, it's everything about their connection to the American blues. For me, that remains one of the high points of the album.

MICK JAGGER: That's Brian playing [slide guitar]. We were sitting around in a circle on the floor, singing and playing, recording with open mics. That was the last time I remember Brian really being totally involved in something that was really worth doing. He was there with everyone else. It's funny how you remember— but that was the last moment I remember him doing that, because he had just lost interest in everything.

BILLY ALTMAN: Even though Brian was already out the door, there's more of him on there than he's usually given credit for. His spots are few, but they are significant. In addition to his work on "No Expectations," his sitar on "Street Fighting Man" and his harmonica on "Prodigal Son" give him a real presence.

With Brian fading toward the background, other musicians stepped up as well.

BILLY ALTMAN: Nicky Hopkins added a tremendous amount to *Beggars Banquet*. I'm not sure how much of this was Jimmy Miller, but it seems like someone realized that they need some other voice instrumentally besides Keith's guitar, and Nicky Hopkins is the secret weapon of *Beggars Banquet* and then again on *Let It Bleed*. He is really one of the great unsung heroes of British rock during that period. And the combination of Nicky Hopkins and Ian Stewart during that period works wonderfully and adds dimension because Stewart is such a good boogie-woogie blues pianist.

ANDY JOHNS: Nicky is on everything. He was the best and the greatest. God bless Nicky Hopkins. He added so much to that band. Sometimes you wouldn't really notice it. But if you take the piano out then the house of cards collapses a bit. He was always coming up with gorgeous little melodies. Earlier, "She's a Rainbow." That's Nicky. Of course he was doing a lot of things like that. Plus he was extremely rhythmic. People don't remember him for being rhythmic. But he was.

   When people think of Nicky Hopkins they think of his right hand. But he would make the groove happen sometimes. If you took him out, it's "Oh, what happened here?" Which is normal. If they are listening to him they are gonna play around him. Or with him. And if you take one of those elements out: "What happened here?" It's music. See. That's how it works.

The album's focal point became one of the Stones' most famous songs, "Sympathy for the Devil."

CHARLIE WATTS: "Sympathy for the Devil" was tried six different ways. I don't mean at once. It was all night doing it one way, then another full night trying it another way, and we just could not get it right. It would never fit a regular rhythm. I first heard Mick play that one on the steps of my house on an acoustic guitar. The first time I heard it, it was really light and had a kind of Brazilian sound. Then when

COUNTRY HONK

Beggars Banquet also featured another new, rootsy element for the Stones: country music.

KEITH RICHARDS: It is the other side of rock 'n' roll. Rock 'n' roll, basically, is blues, and then put in a little bit of white hillbilly melody. It's that lovely coming together of one culture hitting another which is what music's always about. What I've always loved about rock 'n' roll is that it's a beautiful synthesis of white music and black music. It's a beautiful cauldron to mix things up in.

Keith's budding friendship with Gram Parsons was the inspiration.

KEITH RICHARDS: I first met Gram in 1968, when the Byrds were appearing in London . . . I knew the Byrds from *Mr. Tambourine Man* on . . . But when I saw them with Gram, I could see this was a radical turn. I went backstage, and we hooked up. Then the Byrds came through London again, on their way to South Africa. I was like, "Man, we don't go there." The sanctions and the embargo were on. So he quit the Byrds, right there and then. Of course, he's got nowhere to stay, so he moved in with me.

Others, notably Chris Hillman of the Byrds, have doubted that apartheid had anything to do with Parsons's decision to leave the band. Hillman went so far as to suggest that Parsons was a Rolling Stones groupie. A friend of Parsons and employee of the Stones from that time refutes this idea:

PHIL KAUFMAN: Nothing could be further from the truth. Gram was one of the only guys in the world who hung out with famous people like the Stones and who carried his own weight. If anything, Keith was the "groupie" of Gram. Gram was teaching the Rolling Stones country music. Quite often we'd just sit around the house—Gram, Mick, Keith, and I. They had been to Ace Records and bought every country album they could find: George Jones, Merle Haggard, Dave Dudley, Ernest Tubb—you name it. Gram would say, "Here is an example of this," and he'd tell me which record he wanted and I'd play the record. They'd listen to it, tap their toes to it, listen to the chords, and then Gram had me play George Jones, . . . That was what Gram was doing. I recorded Gram and Keith singing together, but sadly those tapes are long gone.

Here's Mick's take on the Stones first foray into country:

MICK JAGGER: As far as country music was concerned, we used to play country songs, but we'd never record them—or we recorded them but never released them. Keith and I had been playing Johnny Cash records and listening to the Everly Brothers—who were SO country—since we were kids. I used to love country music even before I met Keith. I loved George Jones and really fast, shit-kicking country music, though I didn't really like the maudlin songs too much . . . The country songs, like "Factory Girl" or "Dear Doctor," on *Beggars Banquet* were really pastiche. There's a sense of humor in country music anyway, a way of looking at life in a humorous kind of way—and I think we were just acknowledging that element of the music.

BILLY ALTMAN: There is a lot of humor in the country songs on *Beggars Banquet*. At the time, I'm not sure how much of it any of us got. Back then, with everything that was going on with the tensions of 1968, they just seemed kind of weird. But listening now, "Dear Doctor" and "Factory Girl" are a lot of fun. And I think that's one of the nice things about the album. They provide a balance against things like "Sympathy for the Devil" and "Street Fighting Man."

we got in the studio we poured things on it, and it was something different. I could never get a rhythm for it, except one, which is like a samba on the snare drum. It was always a bit like a dance band until we got Rocky Dijon in, playing the congas. By messing about with that, we got the thing done.

One critic correctly identified a source of inspiration for "Sympathy for the Devil —the Stones' own blues roots.

MICK FARREN: One of the major devices used by the Stones (and a lot of blues singers—Howlin' Wolf, Robert Johnson, Lightnin' Hopkins) to accentuate the shock of their music is consistent use of first-person involvement in their lyrics. Jagger doesn't sing about the Devil, he sings about *being* the Devil.

KEITH RICHARDS: "Sympathy" is quite an uplifting song. It's just a matter of looking [the Devil] in the face. He's there all the time. I've had very close contact with Lucifer—I've met him several times. Evil people tend to bury it and hope it sorts itself out and doesn't rear its ugly head. "Sympathy for the Devil" is just as appropriate now, with 9/11. There it is again, big time. When that song was written, it was a time of turmoil. It was the first sort of international chaos since World War II. And confusion is not the ally of peace and love. You want to think the world is perfect. Everybody gets sucked into that. And as America has found out to its dismay, you can't hide. You might as well accept the fact that evil is there and deal with it any way you can. "Sympathy for the Devil" is a song that says, "Don't forget him." If you confront him, then he's out of a job.

UNDERCOVER OF THE NIGHT

The original cover for *Beggars Banquet*

Both Decca in the UK and London Records in the US rejected the planned album cover for *Beggars Banquet*.

CHARLIE WATTS: The toilet one. The graffiti one around the toilet, which they used in an ad later. That was the first one and they refused to put it out.

MICK JAGGER: We really have tried to keep the album within the bounds of good taste. I mean we haven't shown the whole lavatory. That would have been rude. We've only shown the top half! Two people at the record company have told us that the sleeve is "terribly offensive." Apart from them we have been unable to find anyone else who it offends. I asked one person to pick out something that offended him and he quite seriously picked out "Bob Dylan." Apparently "Bob Dylan's Dream" on the wall offends him . . . We've gone as far as we can in terms of concessions over the release of this sleeve. I even suggested that they put it in a brown paper bag with "Unfit for Children" and the title of the album on the outside. But no, they wouldn't have it. They stuck to their guns . . . It was simply an idea that had not been done before and we chose to put the writing on a lavatory wall because that's where you see most writings on walls. There's really nothing obscene there except in people's own minds . . . We'll get this album distributed somehow even if I have to go down the end of Greek Street and Carlisle Street at two o'clock on Saturday morning and sell them myself.

In the end, Mick's guerrilla marketing strategy wasn't necessary. After several months of delay, the record was released with an album that looked like a wedding invite, complete with the letters RSVP.

CHAPTER 18

ROCK AND ROLL CIRCUS

FILMED IN DECEMBER of 1968, *Rock and Roll Circus* became one of the great, lost Rolling Stones projects. It was the brainchild of Mick Jagger and a TV producer named Michael Lindsay-Hogg, who worked with the Stones on *Ready Steady Go!*

MICHAEL LINDSAY-HOGG: I turned up at *Ready Steady Go!* around four in the afternoon and there were some bands rehearsing for the show. On the stage were these guys. I had never heard of the Rolling Stones before. There was this amazing kid, Mick Jagger, doing dance steps, and slides and movements and stuff which of course he perfected over the years . . . I thought, "Jesus Christ. Something is going to happen to these people, because this guy's amazing."

Lindsay-Hogg ended up filming the Stones on *Ready Set Go!* several times, including iconic versions of "Satisfaction" and "Paint It Black."

MICHAEL LINDSAY-HOGG: I thought it would be great if after every chorus he'd put his hands up and take out the lights. The lights would go down verse by verse until you end up with a spotlight on him at the end. I said, "Think of it as you're Lucifer and you're taking out all of the light in the world." I think the very best single song I ever did on *Ready Steady Go!* was that "Paint It Black." It does start in full light and certainly by the end, it's just Mick in this little bit of light and darkness. And then, what happens, we put up the credits over the darkness; the music is still playing; and when we come back there are all these shots of Mick. And I'm doing the thing with the zoom extender and faces shuddering, and it's very quick cut. And it's very mesmeric. As we were shooting it, someone kicked loose the junction of his vocal mic. So you couldn't actually hear him singing. All you could hear was him saying "ahhhahhhah." So there were no more lyrics, just sound and these strange, rapidly cut camera shots.

Michael Lindsay-Hogg was a real pioneer in music video, working with both the Beatles and the Stones.

MICHAEL LINDSAY-HOGG: Then in '68 Mick called me up and said, "We're thinking of doing some promos. Come and talk to me. We got this song called 'Jumpin' Jack Flash.'" During the break our makeup person started playing around with some makeup and they started to paint their faces. I said, "Let's paint everyone's faces."

As their partnership with him continued to have success, the Stones brought a new idea to Lindsay-Hogg: a television special that blended various rock acts with actual circus performers. The final lineup included John Lennon, Yoko Ono, the Who, Eric Clapton, Mitch Mitchell, Marianne Faithfull, Taj Mahal, Jethro Tull, and lastly, members of a small touring English circus group, Sir Robert Fossett's Circus. The last (musical) slot came down to either Tull or Led Zeppelin.

MICHAEL LINDSAY-HOGG: Mick and I had seen Jethro Tull on a very late-night BBC show and we were very taken with Ian Anderson, their front man. I think partly what Mick felt was that Jethro Tull would be an interesting addition to the show and fun to watch, but was not in any way threatening to the Rolling Stones or the Who. Maybe Led Zeppelin would have brought more testosterone to the mix than the room could stand.

The original choice to host *Rock and Roll Circus* was Brigitte Bardot. Lindsay-Hogg hand-delivered a note from Mick to the actress asking her.

MICHAEL LINDSAY-HOGG: I felt like an emissary, prince to a princess. She wanted to do it because she was as famous in Paris and France as Mick was in London; and she could see herself in the outfit. It's just that she had a TV deal and they wouldn't let her.

Here are a couple of eyewitness testimonies from the music trades of the time (from Keith Altham and Chris Welch), along with a more modern perspective (from Gary Pig Gold).

KEITH ALTHAM: Michael Lindsay-Hogg, who directed some of the more memorable *Ready Steady Go!* sagas, produced this epic with a little help from his illustrious friends John Lennon, Yoko Ono, Marianne Faithfull, Eric Clapton, Mitch

Mitchell, Jethro Tull, classical pianist Julius Katchen, the Who, and "perpetual" violinist Ivry Gitlis.

GARY PIG GOLD: Director Michael Lindsay-Hogg, who'd already captured the best of the small-screen Stones on various UK pop shows of the moment, masterfully translated Mick Jagger's vision of "taking out the normal and making a slightly surreal circus" onto celluloid. The primary reason for this may be that Lindsay-Hogg, who had pioneered his amphetamine-paced quick-jump style on the landmark *Ready Steady Go!* television series (expertly shooting the Stones' "Paint It Black" in '66 for example), stretched his skills to supreme effect throughout the *Rock and Roll Circus*, cleverly cutting his shots to the beat of the songs themselves, and in the Who's landmark "A Quick One While He's Away" herein especially, turning an already red-hot performance into a downright incendiary one.

And the quality of the overall show?

GARY PIG GOLD: This particular carnival absolutely provides a nice bright, loud, swinging sixty minutes full of music and merriment, with fire-eaters and trapeze artists unapologetically sandwiched between Taj Mahal and Yoko Ono as only *The Ed Sullivan Show* had dared to before.

CHRIS WELCH: It was a group fan's dream, when the giants of pop held a three-hour jam session, while rehearsing for the Rolling Stones' *Rock and Roll Circus* last week.

Eric Clapton and John Lennon on guitars, Mitch Mitchell on drums, and Mick Jagger adding a few vocals formed a supergroup that would rock most propagators of rhythm into a cocked hat.

"This is so like the Stones used to sound," said a road manager as the strains of "Sweet Little Sixteen" boomed through the corridors of Intertel Studios, Wembley. "I don't think they want anybody in with them," said Jagger as he dashed about getting the show together and trying to find Keith Richards who hadn't showed up and was supposed to be on bass.

Then, of course, there were the actual circus performers.

CHRIS WELCH: In the main studio gentle chaos ensued with a tiger dozing fitfully in its cage, the odd dwarf or two wandering about in top hats and huge bow ties, and the stars of stage, screen, and gasworks looking dreadfully bored, with the exception of Keith Moon, as always enjoying himself heartily.

Keith was attempting to play his drums encased inside a glittering clown's suit, complete with pointed hat and white makeup. He looked pretty terrifying, but it didn't stop him kicking up a storm of percussion as the Who thundered into "mini-opera," their contribution to the *Circus*.

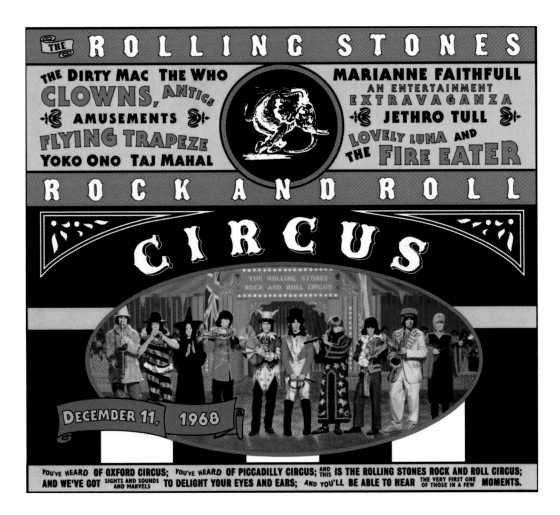

THE ROLLING STONES

THE DIRTY MAC THE WHO   MARIANNE FAITHFULL
CLOWNS, ANTICS   AN ENTERTAINMENT
                         EXTRAVAGANZA
AMUSEMENTS   JETHRO TULL
FLYING TRAPEZE   LOVELY LUNA AND
YOKO ONO TAJ MAHAL   THE FIRE EATER

ROCK AND ROLL
CIRCUS

DECEMBER 11, 1968

YOU'VE HEARD OF OXFORD CIRCUS; YOU'VE HEARD OF PICCADILLY CIRCUS; AND THIS IS THE ROLLING STONES ROCK AND ROLL CIRCUS; AND WE'VE GOT SIGHTS AND SOUNDS AND MARVELS TO DELIGHT YOUR EYES AND EARS; AND YOU'LL BE ABLE TO HEAR THE VERY FIRST ONE OF THOSE IN A FEW MOMENTS.

And what about the Stones' performance?

CHRIS WELCH: Around about two A.M. the Stones were on stage and warming up with "Route 66." They got through "Jumpin' Jack Flash" and "No Expectations" to prove they still have the most exciting group sound in the world and the most interesting visual vocalist in Jagger. "Sympathy for the Devil" was Mick at his provocative best. He whipped off his shirt to reveal a Devil's head tattooed on his chest.

Both contemporary observers were always optimistic about the final product.

KEITH ALTHAM: The Rolling Stones put in some overtime last Wednesday when they spent seventeen hours working on their telethon production of the *Rock and Roll Circus* which is likely to become a pop classic when it is shown.

CHRIS WELCH: If the superstars aren't knifed, scorched, slap-sticked, or eaten by mistake, the *Rock and Roll Circus* looks like a winner.

But a funny thing happened on the way to the television: the Stones decided to put the whole thing away. The rumor was always that they backed off because they thought the Who were better than they were.

MICHAEL LINDSAY-HOGG: It's not that they thought the Who were better than the Stones. The Stones had a very accurate view of who they were: the Greatest Rock 'n' Roll Band in the World. But they thought on that particular day the Who had gone on stage at four in the afternoon; they were fresh; they also had been touring; they'd been on the road; their act was really together. The Stones hadn't been on the road. They didn't think the Who were better as much as they thought the Stones weren't as good as they could be.

BILL WYMAN: We weren't really satisfied with our performance on that. Mick, in particular, wasn't happy. We thought about reshooting our sequence, but it would have involved redoing the whole three- or four-day spectacle to preserve continuity, or else you would have seen the differences in lighting or whatever.

There was also another major reason that *Rock and Roll Circus* stayed buried: legal hassles.

BILL WYMAN: And then we broke with [manager] Allen Klein, and to have done anything about *Rock and Roll Circus* at that point would have involved enormous legal hassles and negotiations about ownership. So in the end it was just shelved. Permanently.

What happened to the film?

MICHAEL LINDSAY-HOGG: Before the Stones went to France [see chapter 28], they had a very large, commodious office in London. To save money, they moved into very small offices. So the cutting room was closed down and all of the cans of film were moved to this very small office, where there really wasn't room for them. They were in the bathroom and on top of the toilet seat.

There was talk of just chucking this stuff out because nobody was ever going to want it. That day, when there was this kind of low-level discussion, Ian Stewart was in the office. And he thought, "Maybe someone will want this stuff someday." His van was outside and he put all the cans of film in his van and he drove it out to his house in the country.

There it was, and there it remained, until 1985, when Ian Stewart passed away.

MICHAEL LINDSAY-HOGG: Then Ian died young and Cynthia, his widow, was looking around the property to see what was where and what was what, and she went into the barn and up against the wall with a rake leaning against it were these cans with tape on the side of the cans peeling off saying, "The olling stones ock and oll ircus." It had been there for like fifteen years.

And how did it finally see the light of day?

MICHAEL LINDSAY-HOGG: The information of it being found got to Allen Klein because Allen, because of an agreement when he split from the Stones, was given the right to the pre-1970 Stones material. Also, he had the rights to the footage. And he's the one—we took the cut to New York. He found some stuff that had been lost. [The Who's] stuff had been used in the documentary *The Kids Are Alright*. That's where their *Circus* performance was. We got it all back. We put it together . . . and there was *Rolling Stones Rock and Roll Circus*, which was not shown until the New York Film Festival in 1996. I was thrilled to see it on the big screen. The reviews were good. We knew we had something special. Brian had died; Keith Moon had died. It had a poignancy to it as well as vibrancy.

GARY PIG GOLD: This archival hour provides perhaps the best existing audiovisual documentation of a time truly in turmoil; of a musical and even social changing of the guard between, well, "All You Need Is Love" and Altamont.

CHAPTER 19

LET IT BLEED

BY LATE 1969, the Stones rediscovered and reasserted their in-studio recording chops with the widely acclaimed and very well-received *Beggars Banquet* album. But what the *Rock and Roll Circus* undeniably proved was that the group's live-performance skills were very, very rusty. For reasons of money, pride, and self-respect, 1969 was the year that something had to be done about it, but there were many obstacles in the way. First and foremost among them was the continuing disinterest, disintegration, and, eventually, the death of Brian Jones. Jones's personal struggles were a factor during the recording of *Beggars Banquet*, and it became clear that it was going to be an even bigger factor during the *Let It Bleed* sessions. Mick expressed his frustration and dissatisfaction to Roy Carr:

MICK JAGGER: We weren't playing, that was the thing, but we were recording a lot of good material on our own . . . the four of us Keith, Bill, Charlie, and myself. Brian played on some of *Beggars Banquet* . . . not all of it. Let's say he was helpful. I don't know exactly how many tracks he played on but that was his last album. We did *Let It Bleed* without him. But Brian wasn't around towards the end. What we didn't like was that we wanted to play again on stage and Brian wasn't in any condition to play. He couldn't play. He was far too fucked-up in his mind to play.

In June 1968, Mick, Keith, and Charlie informed Brian Jones that the band was going to move on without him.

MICHAEL LINDSAY-HOGG: It is sad and I think he felt life had gone the wrong way for him because originally it had been his band and they took it over. But he was drinking and drugging and it wasn't doing him any good. I think what happened partly, he couldn't play well anymore. He'd been to north Africa a few months before to record an album with a Joujouka tribe. He'd broken his wrist. So he couldn't play; he couldn't finger the way he was used to doing . . . And that depressed him and then he drank and that depressed him. His emotional constitution wasn't strong anyway.

Charlie's overview on "The Life of Brian" is even more personal:

CHARLIE WATTS: For a long time he was the most popular person in the band, fan letters and all that, for what it's worth. It was Brian, Brian, Brian. Then it became Brian and Mick. Then it became Mick and Brian. Then it became Mick, and Keith and Brian. And Brian slowly faded off and his ability to play on many, many instruments, which was his best thing, to be able to pick up any instrument that was lying around in a studio and perform on it, not as an expert but to use it in a recording, like a harp. All those early albums was Brian using marimbas and sitar and anything. He would just pick it up and play it and it made a track different, did something to another song. He just got worse . . . I think the whole band as a whole got better performing on their instruments and Brian didn't get better, he stayed where he was. And eventually he wasn't where he should have been and it did create a lot of conflicts.

They were conflicts that *had* to be addressed. The great American guitar virtuoso Ry Cooder was brought in to work on the *Let It Bleed* sessions, and later described Brian as a phased-out, sad character who spent most of his time in the corner of the studio sleeping or crying! Others insist that the Stones had given Brian every benefit of the doubt for a very long time, but that their patience had worn thin. They ALL wanted to get back out on the road, yet realized that Brian's deteriorating mental and physical condition would certainly make that impossible just as it had in 1968. And even if he were able to rally, he might not get the proper paperwork to reenter the United States because of his drug arrests. It all came to a head on June 9, 1969, when Mick, Keith, and Charlie paid an anticlimactic visit to Brian's home to work out the details of his departure from the Rolling Stones. A press release went out the next day with this quote from Brian: "I no longer see eye to eye with the others over the discs we are cutting. The Stones' music is not to my taste any more . . . I have a desire to play my own brand of music rather than that of others. We had a friendly meeting . . . I love those fellows."

British blues icon John Mayall offered us this sad memory:

JOHN MAYALL: The week before [Brian's death], Alexis Korner and I both had been to Brian's house and talked to him about putting a band together of his own that never came to pass unfortunately . . . He was definitely a casualty. By the time we met with him near the end of his life, the damage had already been done. The coordination between his right hand and his left hand was definitely off. His rhythm was all over the place. It was one of the side effects of the drugs, all very sad. The drugs and all that were going around really took their toll. It's a tragedy that was all too familiar at that time with Jimi Hendrix, Janis Joplin, Jim Morrison. It was that time where the drugs really took over.

Eddie Kramer recalls Jones dropping by the studio when he was working with Jimi Hendrix on *Are You Experienced*.

EDDIE KRAMER: He adored Jimi. Brian used to come over to Jimi's sessions. You could hear him on the tape. I have a multitrack of when we're cutting "All Along the Watchtower." You can actually hear him as he stumbles into the control room and he stumbles out to the studio. He's trying to play the piano and Jimi says, "No, no, no." Jimi would wink at me. "See if you can get him out of here." Because he was out of his mind . . . He would come into the control room and collapse in a heap . . .

We've heard all our lives that a rolling stone gathers no moss, so it shouldn't come as any surprise that a solution to the "Jones problem" was already in the works well before the June 9 confrontation. The mental decision to ease Brian out of the group was probably made in May. Eric Clapton was always a possible candidate, but at the time he was completely wrapped up in his newly formed "supergroup" Blind Faith with Steve Winwood, Ginger Baker, and Ric Grech.

Young Ron Wood was another possibility after he was let go by the Jeff Beck Group, but he wasn't available for long, opting to join the Small Faces soon after. Ron had a passing acquaintance with the Stones and recalled a visit with them in 1968:

RON WOOD: I went to Olympic Studios in London when they were doing *Beggars Banquet* and I saw little odds and ends going down and I was very impressed then. And I met Brian then. Nicky Hopkins introduced me to Brian and I used to think he was a very nice character, very outlandish; he was wearing all these brilliant colored clothes and floppy hats, feather boas, and I used to think, "Christ this guy gets away with murder." He was a great character.

Would Wood have joined the Rolling Stones? We'll never know. Here's why:

RON WOOD: I must put in another bit here . . . Before the Small Faces started with Rod and myself in the lineup, Ronnie Lane very nicely said no to the Stones before they got Mick Taylor, because apparently they'd asked me then but I knew nothing about it. Ronnie Lane said, "No, Ronnie won't do it. He's gonna stay with us."

That was thanks to Ian Stewart, occasional member of the Stones, and he's like the old sixth Stone going back many years. He said, "Why don't you get this guy Ronnie Wood. Let's give him a try." So he rang up Laney [who] said no on my behalf. I don't blame him. I had a fantastic time with the Faces. And chronologically everything took its own form and shape.

Brian Jones in happier times

Okay. No Clapton and no Ron Wood. Where would the Stones find their replacement for Brian Jones? John Mayall told us:

JOHN MAYALL: Mick Jagger called me up. He reckoned if there was a guitar player around, I'd know who to recommend. I recommended Mick Taylor. This was before the tragic death of Brian Jones. Mick was talking to the other Mick and they got something primed for the future . . . Mick actually sat in with us one night when Eric [Clapton] didn't show up. That was the first time I got the opportunity to hear him and it was pretty special that he had a handle on all the tunes we were playing at that time. He was obviously someone who was on the horizon, so to speak, and fortunately I was able to get a hold of him after Peter Green and Mick Fleetwood left. He joined the band and of course he's still playing. He's part of the Bluesbreakers history. He always seems to crop up over the years. It's always a pleasure to play with him. Mick's one of the all-time greats.

ALAN CLAYSON: He had a very supportive family. His uncle took him to see Bill Haley and the Comets in 1958. They bought him his first guitar, then an electric guitar. At this time, you have to understand that a boy saying he wanted to be a rock and roller was the equivalent of a girl saying she wanted to be a stripper.

Mick Jagger made the initial offer (one hundred fifty pounds per week). Mick Taylor accepted. And Keith Richards made the necessary adjustment from Brian to the new Mick.

KEITH RICHARDS: I'd been working with Brian for a long time. At the same time, Brian had gone off the guitar for a long period of time. He wasn't interested in it. In sessions throughout most of the '60s, I just overdubbed the guitar. Brian was more interested in playing other instruments that were around, like the marimbas on "Under My Thumb" or harp on something else. He was one of those guys who could just pick up an instrument and by the time we'd worked out the song, he'd have worked out how to play this instrument enough to make the record.

So I had to adjust in a way even in the latter part of Brian being in the band to doing virtually all the guitar work on record. With Mick Taylor, this was somebody who was a definite lead-guitar player. It was very easy right from the beginning. Number one because he's such a master guitar player with what he does. It's very easy for me to stick to my role of writing songs and playing chord. As long as I accepted my role of laying down the rhythm, then Mick and I would work very well together.

Taylor's first task as a Stone was to overdub the guitar part on the hot new single "Honky Tonk Women." Then there was the matter of how the new member would be presented to the world. The answer to that one actually came on June 8 when Mick Jagger attended a free Pink Floyd concert in Hyde Park where he met another soon-to-be very important person in the Stones' universe. His name was Sam Cutler and he was the production supervisor, stage manager, and MC of the event, and he suggested to Mick backstage that the Stones do a Hyde Park free concert as well. Mick was taken with the idea of launching the new single and the new guitarist in such a low-risk, high-profile manner. The date chosen was Saturday, July 5, 1969. The rest of June was spent recording, rehearsing, and preparing for the big day. But no one was quite prepared for the news headline that was flashed around the world on July 3: BRIAN JONES OF THE STONES FOUND DEAD.

Brian's famous teardrop guitar

Many books have been written exclusively about this tragedy. This isn't one of them. We will offer a few first person accounts to illustrate the scope of the mystery, and then move on. Sam Cutler's reflection is a concise recap of the events:

SAM CUTLER: On July 2, three days before the Hyde Park concert, Brian Jones died in mysterious circumstances, apparently having drowned in his swimming pool. The police made a complete shambles of the investigation and the coroner eventually ruled that Brian had died through "death by misadventure" . . . Many older people in England were not at all sympathetic to Brian and basically thought that as a drug-taking rock star, he had got what he deserved . . .

All that I know is that the day after Brian's death a certain person took a truck to Cotchford Farm and removed everything of value; none of Brian's belongings have been seen since that day. Valuable guitars, clothing, furniture—the lot was simply stolen. While this was going on, every scrap of paper that made reference to financial matters was burned on a bonfire in the garden. This happened in a place where someone had died in suspicious circumstances less than twenty-four hours earlier. The police didn't even bother to secure the crime scene.

The person who removed the articles was a close friend of Frank Thorogood, the builder whom many suspect of murdering Brian because he was there at the scene. Thorogood is supposed to have made a deathbed confession to Brian's murder, but this was in front of only one witness, and those who know both the witness and the history of his relationship to the Stones remain unconvinced. What is beyond dispute is that several people who were present when Brian died were subsequently threatened and forced to leave the country so that they had no input into the enquiries made by the police or the coroner . . .

The coroner was unable to establish who was present on the night Brian died . . . The whole case for his cause of death seemed to rest on an asthma inhaler conveniently found beside the pool; the coroner found that "on the balance of probabilities" Brian had died from an asthma attack while swimming. No one who knew Brian, or knew the people who were around him at the time of his death, believed the verdict for a minute. I am firmly convinced that he was murdered.

Here's what Keith says in *Life*:

KEITH RICHARDS: I'm always wary of deathbed confessions . . . Whether he did or not, I don't know. Brian had bad asthma and he was taking quaaludes and Tuinals, which are not the best things to dive under water on . . . He had a high tolerance for drugs, I'll give him that. But weigh that against the coroner's report, which showed that he was suffering from pleurisy, an enlarged heart, and a diseased liver. Still, I can imagine the scenario of Brian being so obnoxious to Thorogood and the building crew . . . that they were just pissing around with him . . . At the very most, I'd put it down to manslaughter.

Interviewed in tandem in 1977, Charlie Watts and Bill Wyman offered this heartfelt assessment when asked if they were shocked at the news of Brian's demise:

CHARLIE WATTS: It was to me. I was more shocked for him to die than anybody since.

BILL WYMAN: The thing is—looking back on it—I think he was a very weak, I mean, ill person. He had been very ill before that.

CHARLIE WATTS: He couldn't handle that fame. He used to have a lot of things like asthma and all kinds of allergy things. He was a nervous type of sensitive person. An article in the newspaper would really freak him out if it was bad; whereas everybody else would tear it out and throw it away and laugh, when they used to say we smelled and never took baths and had fleas and filthy clothes. It was really stupid. But he really took it to heart and he used to write letters back.

BILL WYMAN: He took himself and his image very seriously, which I never saw at the time.

CHARLIE WATTS: He found it very difficult to change from the '63 thing that was happening, to suddenly he was world known. He couldn't really handle it. Maybe we did it to him.

On another occasion, Charlie clarified what he meant by these chilling words:

CHARLIE WATTS: We took away the one thing that he had—the band.

EDDIE KRAMER: The drug problems only exacerbated the health problems he had. He had a mischievous side to him—a genius musician. He would try any goddamned instrument you could think of just to get a different sound. He added these tone colors that no one else thought of.

Of course, Brian's death put the Hyde Park concert in jeopardy. Bill Wyman gave me his up close and personal view:

BILL WYMAN: We came very close to canceling the whole thing. Brian had left the band about a month before, and he'd come around to tell us that he was getting a band together with Alexis Korner. He was really excited about his new project, and he was kind of hanging out with us a bit. Then we got the news while we were recording in London and, of course, we all thought we should cancel the Hyde Park thing. Then we realized that Brian would have probably wanted us to go on—it had been announced for weeks in the papers, and they were estimating there'd be half a million people there. So we went ahead, basically to keep our minds off what happened, I suppose. We had a photo of Brian on the stage and . . . it was exactly like he was there. There was a special atmosphere, and Mick said that poem and they released ten thousand butterflies. It was the most peaceful concert—there was no trouble, no problems. And afterwards gangs and gangs of kids went around and cleaned up, and we promised everyone who came back with a sack of litter a free album. And by the next morning, apart from a few broken branches, you wouldn't have known anything about it, it was so well done.

SAM CUTLER: There were five hundred thousand people. No one was injured. No one got sick. I think two people had to go to the Red Cross to have tea and a biscuit.

Documentary filmmaker Leslie Woodhead was brought on board to shoot the concert.

LESLIE WOODHEAD: My next encounter with the Stones was in 1969, when Mick Jagger got in touch to ask if Granada wanted to film their upcoming free concert in Hyde Park. At that time I was part of a group of documentary makers making films on everything from the capture of Che Guevara to the London production of *Hair*— and Jagger's notorious drug bust. With a fellow producer, I met the Stones in their London office with manager Allen Klein, and we agreed to shoot the concert with six film cameras—a logistical challenge back then. On the day, surrounded by half a million fans, I was shooting the concert on stage alongside Marianne Faithfull with one crew, while a colleague shot backstage with the Stones, and four other teams were located at various locations round the stage. We filmed as Mick read a Shelley poem for Brian Jones, a closing act of '60s innocence, just before Woodstock—and Altamont.

The poem that Bill and Leslie referenced was "Adonais" by Percy Bysshe Shelley and the excerpt included the following lines:

> *Peace, peace! he is not dead, he doth not sleep*
> *He hath awakened from the dream of life*
> *'Tis we, who lost in stormy visions, keep*
> *With phantoms an unprofitable strife,*
> *And in mad trance, strike with our spirit's knife*
> *Invulnerable nothings.—We decay*
> *Like corpses in a charnel; fear and grief*
> *Convulse us and consume us day by day,*
> *And cold hopes swarm like worms within our living clay.*

Our eyewitness at the event would go on to have a long career as the music critic for the *Boston Globe*—Steve Morse.

STEVE MORSE: It was a magical show. Mick's elegy, where he released thousands of butterflies in the air, was a magical cathartic moment, with the Stones set up in front of mock palm trees to give it kind of a tropical air, and they were right down by the lagoon in Hyde Park. And then they just started ripping. It was Mick Taylor's first show with the Stones.

There was instant rapport between Mick Taylor and Keith on guitar. Some of the British reviewers from the time didn't think that highly of the show. They didn't think that Taylor and Keith played that well together. They thought that "Honky Tonk Women" had kind of a herky-jerky rhythm that didn't cut it, but I don't know what concert they were seeing. I've seen two hundred fifty concerts a year for the past thirty years and from my vantage point of thirty feet away, it was just overpowering. And with the added emotion of being a tribute to Brian Jones—who knows what happened in that swimming pool—but the Stones came out of it just kicking on all cylinders. It was just a phenomenal concert experience.

You gotta give Keith and Mick Taylor credit, when they got together it was just a blues duel, that down and dirty, real blues sound. In the trenches. The synergy is what made it. Mick Taylor arrived at the right place at the right time. And to think that they played the Hyde Park concert within the same week as when Brian Jones died is almost inconceivable, really. That they were able to get it together and perform that well, with that level of emotion cutting through that Hyde Park field. I'd never seen anything like it, and I've never seen anything like it since.

And the Stones had an unusual security force for the event.

SAM CUTLER: Tom Keylock, the Stones "security man" and apparently a former member of the parachute regiment, briefed a bunch of motorcycle riders with hand-embroidered "Hells Angels" signs on their backs on how to deal with "screamers," girls who might try to get to Mick on stage.

STEVE MORSE: The day was further highlighted by security from the Hells Angels. The Angels in Britain did an exemplary job. Jagger was complimenting them throughout the day and it was a peaceful day, beautiful sunny day.

LESLIE WOODHEAD: I vividly recall the Angels doing sterling work in Hyde Park. The film I made [*The Stones in the Park*] has lots of cheery Angels sporting cheery swastikas. The benign London Angels undoubtedly did seduce the Stones into believing that the San Francisco brothers would be similar pussy cats. Big mistake.

SAM CUTLER: Most of the bikers were no more Hells Angels than any other young rock 'n' roller in England. They were a joke. In fact there was no officially sanctioned Hells Angel chapter in England in 1969, just a bunch of risible wannabes who were barely old enough to shave.

The Rolling Stones (and some butterflies) at Hyde Park, July 5, 1969

How about the performance itself?

STEVE MORSE: They did fifteen songs, "No Expectations," "Stray Cat Blues," "Midnight Rambler," "Satisfaction," "Street Fighting Man," and they finished with "Sympathy for the Devil." I was just completely blown away by "Sympathy for the Devil." Before the show they had put in the paper asking fans to bring tin cans to use as percussion. Today, that would never be allowed at a concert, no way. It would be considered a real safety violation. It was like Britain's Woodstock that summer. And to hear them all with the tin cans, banging them on percussion during "Sympathy for the Devil," the sound was just deafening, the stereophonic percussion running all around Hyde Park. At the end, they got into a boat and started going back over the lagoon, to get away that way. And Jagger had said to the crowd that they were going to see Chuck Berry that night, and suggested that the crowd go too. Chuck was at Royal Albert Hall that night with the Who. I didn't get to that one. I was just thankful I made it to Hyde Park. It was a show and a summer I will never forget.

Before we move on to the next story, I would just like to weigh in personally with a final thought about Brian Jones. This is a book about the fifty-year odyssey of the Rolling Stones. But the truth is that there were at least four distinct and separate eras in those fifty years: the original Stones from 1962 to 1969; the Mick Taylor Stones from 1969 to 1975; the Ron Wood Stones from 1975 to 1992; and the Bill Wyman–less Stones from 1992 to the present. But for those first seven years, when the band burst onto the scene, there is no question about it: No Jones, No Stones.

And that's how we like to remember him.

CHAPTER 20

GIMME SHELTER

"GIMME SHELTER" is regarded as a socio-political anthem, but Keith Richards's tale of writing it is at once highly personal and also quite literal. It was penned during a storm while Anita was off with Mick filming *Performance*. Keith knew they were having an affair. And depending on whose account you read, he was either devastated or quite blasé about it. We'll go with Keith on this one. From *Life*:

KEITH RICHARDS: I didn't find out for ages about Mick and Anita, but I smelled it . . . I never expected anything from Anita. I mean, hey, I'd stolen her from Brian.

Keith is then quick to point out that he'd had an affair with Marianne as well. He goes on to explain the song:

KEITH RICHARDS: Of course, it becomes much more metaphorical with all the other contexts and everything, but at the time, I wasn't thinking about, oh my God, there's my old lady shooting a movie in a bath with Mick Jagger. My thought was storms on other people's minds, not mine . . . Only later did I realize, this will have more meaning than I thought at the time.

Bringing in a female foil for Mick on "Gimme Shelter" was Jack Nitzsche's brilliant idea. Merry Clayton, a former backup singer for Ray Charles, got the gig.

MERRY CLAYTON: Jack called me at home from the studio in the Los Angeles area one night where I lived with my husband, Curtis Amy. Jack called our home and

Curtis told him I was just about ready to go to sleep. See, I was pregnant, but Jack insisted that he had to talk to me about this Stones' session immediately as I was about to go to sleep. Curtis then woke me up. Jack was on the line. "Merry, I really need you to do this part. There is no other singer who can do this. Please." I always loved Jack; like Lou Adler, he always took a chance on me. And I worked with Jack on the *Performance* soundtrack he did and I had worked with Jack earlier on a record he did with Neil Young in 1968 or '69. OK . . . I was really tired that night, but I got up, put on my coat, got in the car with Curtis and we drove up La Cienega from LA to Hollywood later that evening where the studio was located.

They played me the song and asked if I could put a little somethin' on it . . . I said, stop the song and tell me what all this stuff meant before I went any further. "It's just a shout or shot away" was something in the lyrics. I said, "I'm gonna put my vocal on it and I'm gonna leave. 'Cause this is a real high part and I will be wettin' myself if I sing any higher!" 'Cause my stomach was a little bit heavy . . .

So, we went in and did it. Matter of fact, I did it three times. I didn't do an overdub. Mick's vocal was already on it when I heard it and I recall he did a bit of touching up after I left. But they got what they wanted. "It was so nice meeting you guys." "Oh Merry you sound incredible. We just love you. We're gonna work with you" . . . I was walkin' out the door as they were talkin'. "OK, love you guys, too! See you some other time." And I got in the car with my husband who took me right home and I went right upstairs to bed. And that was the "Gimme Shelter" session.

The song has a legion of admirers, including a certain well-known film director. After the release of *Shine a Light*, Martin Scorsese was asked to compare the subject matter of the Stones with another of his familiar subject matters—gangsters.

MARTIN SCORSESE: It reminds me of when I went to see *Threepenny Opera* back in 1959, 1960, at the Theater de Lys, and how the music affected me and what that was saying, and what that play said, and the lyrics. The lyrics were so important to me. I grew up in an area that was, in a sense, like *The Threepenny Opera*, and I think at times, the music, the Rolling Stones' music, had a similar effect on me. It dealt with aspects of a life that was growing up around me, that I was experiencing and trying to make sense of. And so it was tougher, it had an edge, it was beautiful, honest, brutal at times, and powerful. And it's always stayed with me and become a well of inspiration to this day. Mick said to me in Berlin, "I want you to know that *Shine a Light* is your only film that 'Gimme Shelter' is not played in." And when I use "Gimme Shelter" in a film, it's just as apropos today; and when I use it in a film I don't remember that I did it before. Someone might say, you did it before, and I say, that's alright, let's put it in. It's something that has been very important to me over the years.

CHAPTER 21

HONKY TONK WOMEN

THE ROLLING STONES hadn't had a number one hit in the States since "Ruby Tuesday/ Let's Spend the Night Together" in March of 1967. They wouldn't have another one, "Brown Sugar/Bitch," until May of 1971. But in 1969, a year of chaos and crisis for the world and the band, they unleashed a brilliant, instant Stones classic—"Honky Tonk Women/You Can't Always Get What You Want"—that ascended to the top of the charts on August 23 (my twenty-fourth birthday by the way, and less than a month after I had joined WNEW-FM).

Brian Jones left the band on June 9, and was found dead in his swimming pool less than a month later on July 3. His final work with the group was two tracks on the *Let It Bleed* album: percussion on "Midnight Rambler" and autoharp on "You Got the Silver." Mick Taylor joined up at that point and his first session with them was for the single version of their fifth number one American single, "Honky Tonk Women."

The record came out on July 4 in England, the day after Brian's death, and on July 11 in the States, the day after his funeral. About four hundred promotional copies were given away to fans who helped to clean up after the Hyde Park concert on the fifth. (See chapter 19.)

Big hit singles are either from albums of new material, or released independently, then quickly collected on packages of greatest hits. Before it even finished its run on the singles charts, "Honky Tonk Women" turned up in September of 1969 on a compilation called *Through the Past, Darkly (Big Hits Vol. 2)*; the successor to *Big Hits (High Tide and Green Grass)*. In another blaze of originality, artistic flair, and marketing genius, the cardboard cover for the collection was not the typical twelve-and-a-quarter-by-twelve-and-a-quarter-inch jacket. Instead, it was cut out octagonally, like a stop sign, featuring the five group members as if they were pressing and distorting their faces right against the sealed plastic wrapper that enveloped the recording. Instant collectible, anyone?

An earlier version of "Honky Tonk Women," when it was still a rollicking barroom drinking song called "Country Honk," featuring Sam Cutler honking an actual car horn, ended up as side one, cut three on the *Let It Bleed* album released in December. Also on that album was the full-length version of "You Can't Always Get What You Want," clocking in at seven minutes, twenty-eight seconds. A four-minute, forty-nine-second edited version ended up as the B side of "Honky Tonk Women," minus the chorus and some horn parts.

It's as interesting a story as the A side. One of my favorite rock 'n' roll performers of all time is the legendary Al Kooper. Aside from his ample credits as a musician, writer, arranger, teacher, and producer, he has also authored one of the best and most entertaining books about the rock 'n' roll life, *Backstage Passes and Backstabbing Bastards*, a must-read for anyone interested in the roller-coaster ride of the music biz. Al has never been accorded the acclaim commensurate with his talents—he belongs in the Rock and Roll Hall of Fame.

Al also earned an asterisk for his unexpected contribution to the sessions for "You Can't Always Get What You Want." Many regard the song as yet another attempt on the part of the Rolling Stones to equal or surpass an accomplishment by their bosom buddies/arch-rivals the Beatles—namely "Hey Jude." It's a reasonable assumption, isn't it? One last Hail Mary pass as the Fab Four were beginning to implode, and the Rolling Stones were about to take the title Greatest Rock 'n' Roll Band in the World!

The Stones were in Olympic Studios in London putting *Let It Bleed* together. Al Kooper, burned out from all his recording responsibilities in the States, booked a trip to England to unplug, decompress, and do nothing but relax. The Rolling Stones had other ideas. Hearing about Al's proximity from the rock 'n' roll grapevine, Mick and Keith found him, wore him down, and got him to agree to play organ and piano at the session, very much in his comfort zone, of course. The recording went extremely well, and, when it was finished, Al had a brainstorm. I'll let him pick up the story:

THE ROLLING STONES

Honky Tonk Women
You can't always get what you want

AL KOOPER: I told Jagger that if he ever wanted to put horns on it to call me 'cause I had a great part for it. Almost nine months after that session, an eight-track master of the song arrived at my office one day at CBS. There was a note which said, "Dear Al, you once mentioned you could put some great horn parts on this. Well, go ahead and do it and send us the tape back. Love, Mick."

What a memory that Jagger had. I wrote out a horn chart, leaving a spot in the intro where I could play a French horn solo. The intro itself took me three hours to get 'cause I'm not the world's greatest French horn player, and I wanted to sound like I was . . . It was a bad night in the studio for me, and the part didn't come out nearly as good as I thought it might. I crossed my fingers and sent Jagger back his tape. A year later it came out, and they had ditched all the horn parts except my little French horn intro. It sounded fantastic on the radio. You could hear the piano and the organ, and they actually gave me credit on the single. Nice guys . . . over the years, the Stones have always been honorable, great people to hang out with, and the best people to play after-hours music with.

Here's another asterisk for you, Al. * You're the best!

CHAPTER 22

YOU CAN'T ALWAYS GET WHAT YOU WANT

FROM JULY TO August of 1969, the attention of the rock 'n' roll world shifted from a concert in Hyde Park, London, by the Rolling Stones that was supposed to be free to one in Upstate New York that *wasn't* supposed to be free, but turned out that way nonetheless. The Woodstock Music and Art Fair created a sea change in the economics of rock 'n' roll that would have reverberations right up to this day, and even though the Rolling Stones were not a part of it, they would play a huge role in the ways and means by which the music industry would generate capital from that day forward.

Woodstock became iconic without the participation of the holy trinity of '60s rock: the Beatles were in the death rattle phase of their existence knocking off one last masterpiece—*Abbey Road*. Bob Dylan sat home petulantly sixty miles away from the festival, opting instead to perform at the Isle of Wight in September; and the Stones were consumed by a litany of personal and professional obligations and responsibilities. Stones engineer Eddie Kramer ended up doing the sound at Woodstock.

EDDIE KRAMER: I think the Stones would have done enormously well at Woodstock. The competition would have been so fierce. Having Jimi Hendrix, the Who, and the Stones. It doesn't get much better than that.

During the research phase of my previous book—*Back to the Garden: The Story of Woodstock*—the question about why the Stones weren't there came up quite often. The most consistently offered answers were that they were too expensive to sign up and would bust the already fragile budget of the event. And that the group's dark, demon-riddled simulacrum at the time would have clashed too drastically with the peace, love, and music brand that the event was cultivating.

I think with the wisdom of hindsight, we can see that an appearance by the Rolling Stones would only have enhanced and magnified even further the cachet of Woodstock. More than anything else, pragmatic considerations made that fantasy booking impossible. Certainly Brian Jones's death was still at the top of the list. And when they weren't mourning their lost friend or otherwise attending to his passing, finishing up *Let It Bleed* and preparing for a fall tour of America were the band's main priorities. On top of all that, Mick Jagger was learning his lines for *Ned Kelly*, the motion picture he was about to shoot in Australia; and Keith and Anita were having a son, Marlon, who was born on August 10. It was, simply, a lot. It didn't preclude, however, the band's thoughts of a big event of their own during the upcoming tour of the US . . .

The Stones regrouped at the end of October in Los Angeles. First up on the agenda was finishing up

The poster for the Rolling Stones 1969 tour of North America

the work on *Let It Bleed* that had begun over a year before. Next up was an unexpected journalistic stink bomb hurled at the group by a very respected and influential columnist in San Francisco. It makes me laugh to consider what Ralph J. Gleason, who died in 1975, would think about the totally outrageous ticket prices charged for an "A" list rock concert in the twenty-first century. Gleason, who was also a co-founder of *Rolling Stone* magazine, wrote the following after details were announced about the Stones tour in 1969: "Can the Rolling Stones actually need all that money? If they really dig the black musicians as much as every note they play and every syllable they utter indicates, is it possible to take out a show with, say, Ike and Tina and some of the older men like Howlin' Wolf and let them share in the loot? How much can the Stones take back to Merrie England after taxes, anyway? How much must the British manager and the American manager and the agency rake off the top?"

When the issue was raised at a press conference promoting the tour at the Beverly Wilshire Hotel, Mick was clearly stung by it, and responded thusly:

MICK JAGGER: We were offered a lot of money to play some very good dates— money in front in Europe, before we left, really a lot of bread. We didn't accept because we thought they'd be too expensive on the basis of the money we'd get. We didn't say that unless we walk out of America with X dollars, we ain't gonna come. We're really not into that sort of economic scene. Either you're gonna sing and all that crap, or you're gonna be a fuckin' economist. I really don't know whether this is more expensive than recent tours by local bands. I don't know how much people can afford. I've no idea. Is that a lot? You'll have to tell me.

He also left the door open for some kind of "free" event on the West Coast to calm the storm—more on that in chapter 24.

Opening night was set for November 7 at Colorado State University. Based on his triumphant handling of the Hyde Park concert, Sam Cutler was brought on board as the tour manager, which led to a fateful and long-lasting decision by Cutler:

SAM CUTLER: The Rolling Stones had pretty much been away from the music scene for three years. At the height of their fame, their concerts would last for perhaps twenty minutes before the stage was swamped by screaming teenagers and the show would have to be abandoned. Production value seemed to be of little concern. The forthcoming American tour, the Stones soon realized, was going to be different; they were going to have to deliver the goods. In America, people actually listened to music.

It was quite a challenge. How would the Stones reinvent themselves as a live act?

SAM CUTLER: We were rehearsing in LA. Mick Taylor was still learning all the parts and the rehearsals weren't going very well. I asked a couple of beautiful California blonde sisters who were standing there what they thought of it. They just gushed, "Oh, they're the greatest rock and roll band in the world." Well, I didn't think so.

   We eventually left to do our first show in Colorado and we were on the plane and Mick said, "Oh, we have nobody to introduce the band." He said, "Sam can do it." I didn't think any more about it until I went on stage, then it just popped into my mind, "The Greatest Rock 'n' Roll Band in the World, the Rolling Stones." Mick was furious. It wasn't a very good gig. He said, "Don't say that about us." Well either you fucking are or you aren't. What's it going to be? And that was the end of it. They had that kind of frailty about them. They never knew if they were going to make it. But that's what makes them a great band and they produce wonderful music. The moniker has stuck ever since.

The tour was under way. Next stop, Los Angeles for two shows on November 8, then up to Oakland for another two shows on November 9. It was here that the group would encounter another formidable figure in rock 'n' roll with whom they would have an on-again, off-again relationship for the next twenty-two years—rock impresario Bill Graham.

SAM CUTLER: Bill Graham was like a lot of people around the Rolling Stones; it went to their heads. Bill Graham was arrogant to the extreme, a pain in the butt. People were getting really fed up with him. Some girl was trying to get on stage and Bill Graham was pushing her back into the audience and she kept on coming and Bill Graham then started slapping her. Charlie Watts and I were standing backstage and Charlie saw that and said, "Get that guy out of there." I said, "It's the promoter." Charlie didn't give a fuck who it was. "You can't be doing that. Get him out of there."

So I went and told him, "Get off the stage, man." He said, "Do you know who I am? I'm Bill Graham. This is my stage." At which point I said, "It's the Rolling Stones' stage. Fuck off." At that point there was a fight. We got separated by security guys. He said that the second show wouldn't go on unless I was out of the building. He didn't care how much it would cost, he would cancel the other show. Which was all bullshit. Finally, Mick agreed to see Bill. Bill came in the dressing room while I was standing there. Mick was standing there putting his makeup on. Bill said to me that if I wasn't out of the building, there wouldn't be a second show. Mick was very good about it. He said, "First off, Sam works for me, not for you. I decide what happens with Sam. Number two, who are you?" He said, "I'm Bill Graham. I'm the promoter." Mick said, "Didn't I speak to you on the telephone from London? Oh yes, you were rude to me. You shouted at me. I hate people who are rude on the telephone. Now listen Bill, we'll be on in five minutes." He just turned back around and continued putting his makeup on and that was the end of that.

Bill Graham's version of the same story is very different:

BILL GRAHAM: The problems started right away during the first show. The Stones went on forty-five minutes late. Jagger told the crowd it was because no one had picked them up at the airport but the truth was that Tina Turner had killed the audience to such a degree that the Stones did not want to play right after her.

When they started doing "Satisfaction" during the first show, all the kids who had been dancing in the aisles rushed the stage. I was under the piano when it happened. I got to my feet and I went to the front edge of the stage to keep the kids from coming up or getting hurt in the crush. Sam Cutler tried to have me removed by a tall black security guard.

"We'd like to know who you are," Cutler said.

"Get your fucking hands off me!" I screamed at him. "I'd like to know who you think you are. This is my stage."

I went crazy on him. We grabbed one another and started wrestling right on stage as the Stones played "Satisfaction." But they broke it up and nothing really came of it. Between shows, I went back into the dressing room to talk to the Stones. I tried to make them understand. "Look," I said. "We've got two shows tonight. Please be ready on time for the second one."

WE NEVER REALLY GOT IT ON UNTIL DETROIT

Once again on the '69 tour, the Stones shared the stage with black artists they idolized such as B.B. King and Chuck Berry, and supported up-and-coming black artists like Tina Turner. The Stones saw firsthand the racial divide that was happening in America. Shows in Alabama created concern among the band.

SAM CUTLER: There were a lot more black artists on the stage than there were black guys in the audience. That's for sure. It was shocking and we hated it. The Stones championed black music the whole of their lives. To have to go to the University of Alabama and go through that was shocking.

The Stones loved playing in Detroit. I think they loved it because it was a black audience. They could play what was essentially black music to black people. Anyone that was anyone in Detroit showed up wearing their bling, looking like a million dollars. Brown sugar wall to wall. Mick loved it; everybody loved it. It was a cracker of a show. Things built up throughout the tour until we did Madison Square Garden which in some respects was the height of it all.

Here's Keith Richards's delicious postscript to the Oakland saga:

KEITH RICHARDS: I remember a poster of Bill Graham up in the dressing room. I want to look at Bill Graham in *my* dressing room? With his finger up, giving me the "fuck you" sign. You know, fuck *you*. We threw food at it. We trashed the dressing room. At the time, the deal was, "Fine. We won't work for him again." And I really didn't see Bill for a long time after that.

Rock writer and musician Michael Lydon was one of the handful of journalists who covered the tour from Fort Collins to Altamont. His coverage was originally commissioned by editors at the *New York Times*; but at one hundred pages long, Lydon's article was ultimately rejected. It first appeared in *Ramparts* magazine, and was eventually collected in his 1971 seminal rock music anthology *Rock Folk*. In a follow-up piece about *Gimme Shelter*, the documentary made about the tour, Lydon offered the following reflection: "As one who was there, I most want *Gimme Shelter*'s new viewers to know how deeply the disturbing drama of this film sprang from the disturbing drama of the times. Nostalgic journalism has made the sixties an innocent time of love, peace, and flowers, but living through the decade didn't feel like that to me. Becoming a hippie was fun but at the same time a scary, soul-wrenching process. Altamont was one of many dark and dangerous bummers I, and seemingly everyone else, stumbled into as we reached for new ideals and possibilities."

Rock critics Dave Marsh and Robert Christgau respectively labeled the '69 tour, "one of the benchmarks of an era," and, "history's first mythic rock and roll tour." Christgau added: "The most sexually exciting man in rock had always been the most androgynous, deliberately counterposing his almost girlish stage demeanor to Keith's droogy leer. In fact, all the Stones had posed in drag on a forty-five jacket back in 1966. So even when Mick performed "Midnight Rambler," that psychotic little showpiece, it could be said that he was merely exposing the petty rape fantasies of his male audience for what they were. Yet no matter what music historians will say, that wasn't the way his male fans—not to mention his female fans—could be expected to take it. Maybe this was obtuseness, but it was also common sense. After all, the spate of antiwoman songs that appeared between 1965 and 1967 can be passed off as a devastating catalog of sexist stances, but Keith's explanation ought to be kept in mind: 'It was a spin-off from our environment . . . hotels, and too many dumb chicks.'

"The 1969 tour was a triumphant exploration of the complexities of the Stones' stance. All that irony and enigma was magnified into a complete drama of good and evil, aspiration and frustration—a joyous, bitter celebration of what could only be designated The Truth. With an omega emblazoned on his black shirt and an Uncle Sam top hat, Jagger took each of us as far as he or she wanted to go. Contradictions within contradictions—Uncle Mick could always show you one more. The triumphant sexist of 'Under My Thumb' became the desolate supplicant of 'Love in Vain.' The nasty triumph of 'Midnight Rambler' turned into the candid need of 'Gimme Shelter.' As for Altamont, it was simply the final contradiction in a long series."

The Stones play Madison Square Garden on Thanksgiving weekend, 1969

CHAPTER 23

SYMPATHY FOR THE DEVIL

It STANDS ALONE in rock 'n' roll history: Altamont. It shouldn't even have been at Altamont.

SAM CUTLER: [Ralph J.] Gleason and [Bill] Graham bear a lot of the responsibility for the fact that the Stones' free show was supposed to be in the center of San Francisco in Golden Gate Park. The problem was Gleason and Bill Graham basically stopped that from happening. There was no place for the concert to go. It just slowly spiraled out of control. It got moved to Sears Point. They got greedy and wanted a huge slice of the film. At the last minute, the site at Altamont came up, which I never saw before the actual show. We should have called it off. Needless to say, when the concert turned to shit, the Stones unfairly got the blame, and I have been living with my share of that opprobrium for forty years.

Bill Wyman's hindsight is more sanguine:

BILL WYMAN: Don't do free concerts in America (*laughs*). Don't say thank you . . . just jump on the plane and wave. We'd had such a good tour that we felt we'd make a gesture to the American people and just do a concert for all the people that couldn't make the concerts and wanted to, and could hitchhike there, and didn't have to pay money and all that. It was a shame that it became the focal point of the entire tour because if you ever talk about the '69 tour, all anybody remembers of it is not the great shows we had for seven or eight weeks, it's the Altamont program. And even that's out of all proportion, because there were an estimated four hundred thousand people there—some people say more—and the trouble was all in the front. I would say 80 percent of the audience didn't know anything about the trouble because they couldn't see it, they weren't aware of it, except that we kept starting and stopping playing. But it was focused around forty people in a crowd of four hundred thousand, so that was really out of proportion, too. It was just very unfortunate.

We interviewed one of the four hundred thousand people who showed up that day expecting a very different kind of experience:

AKI KANAMORI: I was an undergraduate at Caltech entering my senior year. My mother and brother and I had heard about Woodstock. We thought this would be the West Coast version of it. So we all drove out there that morning. We got there too early or something because we had to wait for quite some time. The first band I remember playing was Santana. There were large intervals of time when nothing was happening. I also remember the Flying Burrito Brothers. Of course, the Stones came up much later. That was the problem. There were these long intervals when people would go away and come back, and you didn't know what was going on. We asked around; nobody seemed to know that much. And finally, my mother and brother got tired; it was getting cold. We started thinking, "Maybe they're not playing at all." There was a lot of tension in the air. Then it seemed like something was going on and they were finally setting up. It was starting to get dark. The sun was going down. It was a very bright reddish sunset. Then it got very dark.

One of the strong indicators that Altamont wasn't going to be a day in the park (even though it was *supposed* to be a day in the park!) was the treatment accorded to Marty Balin of Jefferson Airplane earlier in the proceedings. I asked Marty about it:

MARTY BALIN: We came back from a tour and I had just gotten home and they said, "We're flying off to Altamont to do a gig with the Stones," and it was that afternoon. So I remember getting a helicopter with the Stones, getting there and going on stage. And we started the first number . . . and I had my eyes closed and I was singing the first number. And I looked up and there were these Hells Angels with pool cues beating up this naked guy who was obviously on acid and he wanted to get out of the crowd, you know, like people did in those days. And they were like beating this guy, and thousands of people just stepped back and let it happen. Then I just figured the guy needed some help, so I dove over. I figured no one was listening to us sing anyway. It looked like a good fight, so I just jumped in and started punching with them and helped him out. They sort of stopped. Then I got back up and started to sing again. Then pretty soon the guy got to the back of the stage and they were beating him up behind me. I looked behind me and they were fighting again so . . . God, I was mad, you know, I just got mad. I went back and started jumping in with them again. I started kicking and punching. They had this leader guy with a wolf head helmet on his head, so I went after him. I had a few drinks and I was doing pretty good. Suddenly they got me from behind and that was the last thing I remembered.

But when I woke up, I had boot marks all over me—tattoos and everything. But you know it was real sad because there were all these people, and they just stepped back and let them kill this guy in front of them, and I thought, "That wasn't the '60s." It wasn't right.

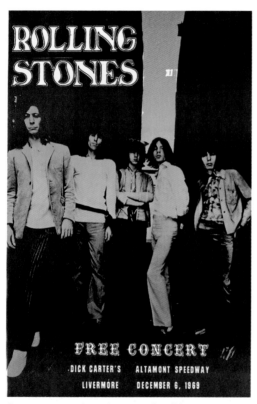

A rare promotional poster for Altamont

For anyone not familiar with the basic facts of Altamont, the *New York Times* printed this basic summation on April 13, 2000, by Gerald Marzorati: "The Hells Angels had been hired to provide security at the free, outdoor Altamont festival, which drew 300,000 people and was to feature not only the Stones but also the Grateful Dead (whose manager had recommended the Angels' services), Santana, the Jefferson Airplane and Crosby, Stills, Nash and Young. The Angels, many of them new recruits to the club with something to prove, spent much of the afternoon clearing the area in front of the stage with the help of weighted pool cues. Then, a few songs into the Stones' closing set, several of the Angels developed a particular interest in an 18-year-old black man 10 or 15 yards from the stage. Meredith Hunter was attacked by one of the Angels, and when he pulled a gun and ran, was chased down, stabbed and beaten to death by a pack of them. None of the Stones could see this, but they knew something was happening—it was there in the confusion of their playing, and in the fear they conveyed to one another in those quick glances with which longtime band mates say all that needs to be said."

Filmmaker Albert Maysles offered this synopsis of the "security" issue:

ALBERT MAYSLES: I got to understand the problem was that the guy who would normally be in control of the Hells Angels somehow or other wasn't there. And instead they got this other guy who was totally inexperienced and things fell apart.

SAM CUTLER: Who brings a gun to a rock 'n' roll show? None of the Hells Angels had guns. Here's this black guy, who's a speed dealer and had all kinds of convictions against him, and a member of a black Oakland gang that as part of their membership had to be armed. I had to go up and tell Mick. I saw the whole thing. I was about twenty meters from it. I had to go tell Mick, "Listen, there's somebody in the audience with a gun." I said, "Mick you got to get off stage now." Mick went, "No, we got to finish." He had balls of brass. He was so courageous. I take my hat off to him. He saw it through to the end . . .

Here's Hells Angel Sonny Barger's version:

SONNY BARGER: They say that was the end of the Age of Aquarius, but actually to us it's just another day in the life of a Hells Angel. A guy pulled a gun on us, he got killed and that's the bottom line. We got movies of him shooting at us; we got movies of him getting killed and nobody went to jail for it. There was a trial, everybody was acquitted.

PLEASE ALLOW ME TO INTRODUCE MYSELF...

To understand the absolute anarchy that was the Altamont concert, look no further than the case of a stout swindler named John Jaymes.

Already a career criminal by the time he joined the tour in '69—passing checks, forgery, and grand larceny—Jaymes got on board the Stones' touring party by promising to procure free ground transportation for the Stones and their entire entourage. Then, he deftly went to Chrysler claiming to represent the Stones, and offered them advertising in exchange for free rental cars and limos. Once he successfully delivered the cars, no one questioned his credentials.

When the free concert was moved from Sears Point to Altamont, Jaymes sped ahead to the racetrack to sign the contract for the site in the name of his alleged company, Young American Enterprises. He even assumed liability for any security issues associated with the show. Predictably, the security Jaymes had promised for the show was seriously lacking, leaving the Stones to find quick replacements.

No one was exactly sure who Jaymes was. The *New York Times* called Jaymes "promoter of the Stones' nationwide tour." To many in the Stones' entourage, the whispered rumor was that the shadowy Jaymes represented mob interests in New York City. Stones' tour manager Sam Cutler had a different idea. He intimated that James was working with the FBI. Speculation aside, one thing was for sure, James was another necessary, insane facet of the Stones tour. Furthermore, he was just hitting his prime as a hustler.

After Altamont, Jaymes went on to greater grift. Under his new name, John Ellsworth, he fronted a phony charity called the International Children's Appeal.

The scheme got the endorsement of no less than the United Nations and First Lady Rosalynn Carter, who unwittingly helped Jaymes poach more than a million dollars from Senator Edward Kennedy, NFL legend Rosey Grier, and Hollywood bombshell Jane Russell among many others. Little did they know all of their kind contributions went to fund an international drugs and weapons laundering scheme.

How could Jaymes assume so much power unquestioned? How did he get on the tour to begin with? How did the so-called head of security come out of Altamont unscathed after the fallout from so many security lapses? Only the madhouse that was the Altamont concert could give shelter to a three-hundred-pound gorilla of a con man like John Jaymes.

As Barger notes, the whole thing was captured on camera by documentary filmmakers Albert and David Maysles. David died following a stroke in 1987 at the age of fifty-four. Albert is eighty-five years old at this writing and offered us the following crystal clear recollections of the events at Altamont and his documentary *Gimme Shelter*:

ALBERT MAYSLES: I got a call from Haskell Wexler one day, who was an old friend of ours, and he said he'd just been talking with the Stones and they were about to begin their tour and they were going to be at the Plaza Hotel the next day and we might want to look them up. So we went to the Plaza, knocked on their door. We didn't really know their music but we went to their concert the next day, which was in Baltimore, and we said, "These guys are good." We wanted to make something that was not just a concert film.

We spent a lot of the next two years filming them and ended up making two movies, *Gimme Shelter* and *Get Yer Ya-Ya's Out!*, though that was more of the Madison Square Garden concert. We didn't establish any ground rules, it was just, "We'll tag along." We didn't start filming it any way other than as a process of discovery.

Were they influenced by any of the other existing rock 'n' roll movies?

ALBERT MAYSLES: We didn't draw upon any of the rock 'n' roll movies that had come before; we were just focused on what was happening in those moments. We had developed a filmmaking philosophy which was totally observational. We never asked questions, no interviews, no host, just what's happening.

SAM CUTLER: Albert Maysles had the wonderful facility of making a film and you weren't really ever aware that it was a film you were in. They never got in the way. They never appeared in anything. They never asked for anything to be staged. They just filmed what was going on. It's an amazing film.

ALBERT MAYSLES: We were lucky in so many ways. Pennebaker's film on Dylan is a very good film but I think he was unlucky in that, due to no fault of Pennebaker's, Dylan is not that easy to film, very distant. Not so with the Stones, we were right in close with them all the time.

Scenes from Hell: The Stones at Altamont

Could Altamont have turned out differently?

ALBERT MAYSLES: The events at Altamont really turned out to be a characterization of that era. It's interesting to speculate what would have happened if drugs had been legalized, as they should have been then and now. I think there would have been a proper security force and none of that ruckus from the Hells Angels.

Both the Stones and the Maysles brothers were excoriated afterward in the press.

ALBERT MAYSLES: The press got it wrong when they called it a murder. To this day, we don't know what the motive may have been. It really should be called a killing. The *New York Times* piece by Vincent Canby was titled "Making Murder Pay." Did you read Pauline Kael's review of *Gimme Shelter*? It was totally, totally wrong. The basic premise of her article was that we staged everything. We didn't stage anything. I still get so angry when I see the journalists from that time who accused the Stones of being responsible for the tragedy, because of the titles of the songs and so forth. It's terrible. It's unfortunate and unfair.

People have described *Gimme Shelter* as portending the demise of the '60s. When you look at it, and you know how things turned out even worse in the next two years, you look at it like a prediction of the future. And the people who said that when we filmed the Beatles in '64 and then the Stones in '69, that the films are sort of like the bookends of the '60s.

That's one way to look at it. Here are a couple of others: Calendar purists will tell you that the '60s ended on December 31, 1969, at midnight. Some historians will tell you that what we think of culturally and politically as the '60s began on November 22, 1963, with the assassination of President John Fitzgerald Kennedy, and ended on August 9, 1974, with the official resignation of Richard Milhous Nixon as president of the United States. And finally, any true fan of '60s rock 'n' roll will tell you that the '60s ended on the evening of December 6, 1969, at a decrepit motor-sports racetrack in northern California named Altamont.

CHAPTER 24

BROWN SUGAR

However the '60s may have ended, one thing was clear: the Rolling Stones were beginning the 1970s with a clean slate. All the new elements were in place: Jimmy Miller was a producing whiz; Mick Taylor was an acclaimed new guitar hero; the Decca deal was almost over and done with; a new label was in the works. The Stones needed a debut single to launch it, at least as successfully as the Beatles launched their Apple label with "Hey Jude" in 1968. So what was it gonna be?

Back in 1969 when Mick was in Australia filming *Ned Kelly*, he injured his hand on the set, and while recuperating, conjured up a riff to which he gave the working title "Black Pussy." (Guess what that was going to be about?!?) The basic tracks were recorded at the Muscle Shoals sessions in early December, after the tour-closing final concert in Florida and the Altamont show. The reason the track stayed on the shelf for more than a year was because of the legal and contractual issues the group was dealing with both with their old record label and their then-manager Allen Klein. (Both "Brown Sugar" and "Wild Horses" were recorded at Muscle Shoals and, in the end, the two songs appeared not only on the first Rolling Stones Records release, *Sticky Fingers*, but also on the *Hot Rocks* compilation album on ABKCO. Since they were recorded while the group was still under contract to Decca, the two songs are co-owned by the Stones and Allen Klein.)

On some level, songs intended to be hit singles have to have the widest possible reach. It is somewhat bizarre then, yet totally in character, that the Stones' first mass-appeal success of the new decade is also one of the group's most controversial efforts. How many taboo subjects could the boys cram into one three-minute, forty-eight-second recording? Let's see—miscegenation, rape, cunnilingus, slavery, racism, sexism, and for good measure, a veiled reference to heroin—all set against another one of the Stones' top-ten riffs of all time!

The only concession to potential outrage and censorship was the changing of the title from "Black Pussy" to "Brown Sugar." It brings to mind a quote about the way rock 'n' roll works:

KEITH RICHARDS: Music isn't something to think about, at least initially. Eventually it's got to cover the spectrum, but especially with rock 'n' roll, first it has to hit you somewhere else. It could be the groin; it could be the heart; it could be the guts; it could be the toes. It'll get to the brain eventually. The last thing I'm worried about is the brain. You do enough thinking about everything else.

"Brown Sugar" hit the bull's-eye. Following its release on April 16, 1971, it zoomed up the charts, landing at number one on May 29—the sixth Stones single to do so.

The promotional shoot for *Sticky Fingers*

CHAPTER 25

LIKE A ROLLING STONE

IN 1970, THE Stones were dealing with massive issues financially. The problem was twofold. They were soon to discover that their deal with former manager Allen Klein kept them from owning their publishing rights. They also owed an awful lot of money in taxes.

MICK JAGGER: I just didn't think about [taxes]. And no manager I ever had thought about it, even though they said they were going to make sure my taxes were paid. So, after working for seven years, I discovered nothing had been paid and I owed a fortune.

This would become a larger issue the next year. But for now, the more pressing matter was that after the *Beggars Banquet* cover fiasco, the Stones had reached the end of their rope in dealing with their record companies, Decca in the UK and London Records in the States. From an American perspective, it had never made much sense that the Stones were on London Records.

CRAIG BRAUN: London Records were a very proper record label, they did things like Mantovani. Their most outlandish recording artist was Engelbert Humperdinck. They couldn't relate to this bad boy image that the Stones had.

BILL WYMAN: Henry Mancini, Boots Randolph. The only reason for that is that in England we were assigned to Decca and their parent company in America was London Records. And all the best records in the '50s that came over to England from America were London Records on forty-fives, Buddy Holly and the Crickets, the Coasters, etc. All those things were on London in England and they were distributed through Decca. So London Records, in England, was quite big as an outside record company, an outside-England record company. It was the biggest rock 'n' roll record company. But when we came to America we realized that it wasn't quite the right record company to be with. I used to go to their vault to look for records to nick and there was nothing. When we went to Chess, you could find fifty of the greats.

CHARLIE WATTS: With London Records there were always problems with everything you did, album covers, publicity photos.

BILL WYMAN: With Decca we had one every month. And the horrible thing was Decca never really worked on selling our records.

CHARLIE WATTS: They didn't really care.

BILL WYMAN: They just let them go out and sell. They put barriers in our way whatever we tried to do. They were against us.

The time had come for a new solution: the birth of Rolling Stones Records, which would be distributed by Ahmet Ertegun and Atlantic Records. Before striking a deal with Atlantic, the Stones reached out to an old acquaintance. Designer Craig Braun is a lifelong friend of Marshall Chess. He picks up the story:

CRAIG BRAUN: Chess was the roots of English rock 'n' roll. That's how the connection was made. Marshall was very involved in the label and he felt that when the time came, his father would pass the baton to him. He knew the whole business by the time he was in his mid to late twenties. The Chess brothers then got involved in owning a radio station and they sold the label. I guess it wasn't unbeknownst to Marshall but he was certainly not happy about that sale. Even though he ended up being the president of Chess Records, he was now dealing with a very unsophisticated, industrial, duplicating company called GRT. There was a major showdown and Marshall got out of his contract, and that left the door open for other opportunities.

MARSHALL CHESS: Then, completely unexpectedly, my father died of a heart attack. He was fifty-two. If he'd possessed a crystal ball, he'd never have sold Chess Records. He wasn't to know how historically important and how valuable that music would become. No one knew.

Everything unraveled at that point. Not only did I lose my dad but I also lost a fortune. I'd been promised a lot of money from the sale of Chess to start my own label. But my father died without signing his will and I never got the money. The problem with the will meant that 70 percent of the proceeds from the sale of Chess went in tax. The people who bought Chess had no idea how to run it. They made me president of the label after quite a struggle on my part. But it was never going to work out. These people didn't know the first thing about music. The first indication of the nightmare to come was that they called me in to discuss forecasts. They expected me to predict the kind of profits the shareholders could expect in the next year. It had never worked like that. To us, it was simply a question of making the next hit record. So they sent me to management school in New York for a week. I hated it. During all my time at Chess it never felt like a job. It was a joy. Suddenly it was a different ball game. For the first time in my life I felt I was at work rather than doing what I enjoyed. It was drudgery. That was a tough time for me. There was a lot of psychological turmoil. I really didn't know what I was going to do next.

Then there was some divine intervention—or something like that.

CRAIG BRAUN: About 1969 I was with my girlfriend and Marshall was with his wife and we took a week's holiday in the wintertime in Jamaica, and one of the things we did when we were there—I don't know why—was to look for witch doctors. We wound up making a long and arduous trip up the side of a mountain there. He was in a state of flux at that point, not really working, looking for guidance. He was given this regimen by this very shaman-like, wise witch doctor where he'd light two yellow candles one day and one blue candle the following day and two red candles the day after that. He told me, "As soon as I get back to Chicago, I'm going to do it." And he did it for about a week, and then he called me and said, "After I started doing this candle trip, I got a call from Mick Jagger and he wants me to run their label." We were incredulous! And a few months after that we got together to work on *Sticky Fingers*, their first release.

MARSHALL CHESS: He invited me round to his house in Cheyne Walk, Chelsea. It was a slightly bizarre meeting. I sat on the sofa and outlined my idea of running the Stones' new label and Mick was dancing around the room to Clifton Chenier's "Black Snake Blues." Straight after that I walked up the road to meet Keith Richards. He was sitting at this big psychedelic yellow piano, jamming with Gram Parsons. First thing Keith does is remark how badly dressed I am. In the Chess days we were always sharply dressed because the artists respected that. I always wore a suit and tie, a ring on the little finger. Now I looked like Al Pacino in the *Serpico* movie—scruffy jeans, T-shirt, long hair. Anyway we shook hands on a deal and I was now the founding president of Rolling Stones Records.

TONGUE LOGO

The Rolling Stones' tongue logo is the best-known and probably the most identifiable logo in rock 'n' roll history. Ever wonder how it came about?

MARSHALL CHESS: The Stones were in Amsterdam. I landed at Rotterdam airport. I was driving along to meet the band and saw a Shell petrol station with the classic yellow logo. It was so beautifully simplistic. I mention this later when I'm sitting around with the Stones, saying that we should come up with a design that is totally recognizable without having the band's name on it.

MICK JAGGER: It's a funny history, really, because lots of people think it was designed by Andy Warhol, which isn't true. Andy would have loved to have designed it and we'd never be able to use it, probably. I was looking for a logo when we started Rolling Stones [Records] in 1970. I had this calendar on my wall, it was an Indian calendar which you'll see in Indian grocery stores and things; and it's the goddess Kali, which is the very serious goddess of carnage and so forth. And she has apart from her body, this tongue that sticks out— like that. So I took that tongue and I go into this designer called John Pasche, and he "modernized" it somewhat. And that's how it started.

The Warhol confusion arose because the *Sticky Fingers* cover was shot by Andy Warhol and the inner sleeve of that record was the first appearance of the tongue. But it was Pasche who was responsible for the design.

JOHN PASCHE: At this time, I was in my final year of a graduate design course at the Royal College of Art in London. I was suggested as the most suitable student to take on the job.

MARSHALL CHESS: As label manager it was my job to audition a variety of artists who came up with an extraordinary variety of tongues. As soon as we saw John Pasche's now famous design, there was no doubt that was the one and we bought it outright.

JOHN PASCHE: The design concept for the tongue was to represent the band's antiauthoritarian attitude, Mick's mouth, and the obvious sexual connotations. I was paid fifty pounds for the design which took me about a week to complete. In 1972, I was paid an additional two hundred pounds in recognition of the logo's success.

CRAIG BRAUN: Marshall gave me this little logo of this rubber stamp that John Pasche was working on, who was a kid in London in some kind of graphic arts studio.

Braun didn't know about Mick's Indian calendar but he suggested another possible inspiration for Pasche's illustration.

CRAIG BRAUN: My contention is that John Pasche lifted this logo from an illustrator's book, a guy named Alan Aldridge from a book called *Beatles Illustrated*. It's on page 110. It's not the same, but it's very similar. It's particularly applicable to the Stones and that's why it resonated with such power. But it's not a new concept; it's been around for thousands of years.

Other than branding the albums themselves, was there a larger vision for what to do with the logo?

MICK JAGGER: I always took a bit of a strong slight to a lot of rock 'n' roll merchandising, just basically 'cause it was the same thing over and over . . . "That's very nice—black T-shirts with tongues on them. We have no real objections to them. It's just that perhaps we should do something as well as that."

CRAIG BRAUN: We did a lot of different marketing things. I redrafted the logo that John Pasche had done. I refined the original because it was very rough and I needed to blow it up. It was a perfect logo.

And what did that entail?

CRAIG BRAUN: I basically outlined the highlights, the lips and the tongue, and made it reproducible in any way from silk screening to rubber stamping to letter press, offset, embroidery. I wanted to create a line of not only promotional items to help launch the label and the first record but also to create a line of merchandising items. It was the advent of licensed merchandising: T-shirts, canvas shoulder bags, pendants, key rings, etc. I called them Licks, based on the tongue and lips logo.

CHAPTER 26

STICKY FINGERS

CHARLIE WATTS describes the first of the *Sticky Fingers* sessions, which are captured as part of *Gimme Shelter*:

CHARLIE WATTS: During the tour of the States we went to Alabama and played at the Muscle Shoals studio. That was a fantastic week. We cut some great tracks, which appeared on *Sticky Fingers*—"You Gotta Move," "Brown Sugar," and "Wild Horses"— and we did them without Jimmy Miller, which was equally amazing. It worked very well: it's one of Keith's things to go in and record while you're in the middle of a tour and your playing is in good shape. The Muscle Shoals studio was very special, though—a great studio to work in, a very hip studio, where the drums were on a riser high up in the air; plus you wanted to be there because of all the guys who had worked in the same studio.

Other sessions for *Sticky Fingers* took place in the UK.

ANDY JOHNS: We set up at Mick's house, Stargroves, and they were using these really cool amps. It was ideally suited because it was a big mansion. I put Mick Taylor in the fireplace and stuck a mic up the chimney—it was kind of a baronial hall—I put Charlie in the bay window and it worked. I remember when we were doing "Bitch" and Keith is yet to show up . . . I go out to the hall and there's Keith leaning up against the wall eating a bowl of cornflakes. With "Moonlight Mile" you can tell by the vibe on the track that it was about five o'clock in the morning. Everyone was either drunk or tired or stoned or whatever. It was a five o'clock in the morning track. You can hear that coming through . . .

As with *Beggars Banquet* and *Let It Bleed*, the Stones were looking for new sonic elements to add to their portfolio.

CHARLIE WATTS: *Sticky Fingers* was the first time we added horns—that was the influence of people like Otis Redding and James Brown, and also Delaney and Bonnie, who Bobby Keys and Jim Price played with. It was to add an extra dimension, a different color, not to make the band sound any different.

BOBBY KEYS: I was staying with Mick for a brief period of time, and they were working on *Sticky Fingers*. I think Otis Redding and the Memphis sound was big on everybody's minds at the time and the Stones wanted to do something that had horns on it. Jim Price and I were available; we did a couple tracks, then they said, "Let's do a couple more." One thing led to another and forty-some years later here I am.

Keith acknowledges being "out of it" during a lot of that period.

ROBERT GREENFIELD: Keith had been relatively impossible during the recording of *Sticky Fingers*. The reason he's not on "Moonlight Mile": he never showed up. He would come ten, twelve hours late.

MICK JAGGER: We made [tracks] with just Mick Taylor, which are very good and everyone loves, where Keith wasn't there for whatever reasons . . . People don't know that Keith wasn't there making it. All the stuff like "Moonlight Mile," "Sway." These tracks are a bit obscure, but they are liked by people that like the Rolling Stones. It's me and [Mick Taylor] playing off each other—another feeling completely, because he's following my vocal lines and then extemporizing on them during the solos.

Marshall Chess was now a member of the Stones inner circle. How was his transition into that group?

MARSHALL CHESS: It happened straightaway. They accepted me immediately because of my connection with Chess Records. For a time I lived with Keith at Cheyne Walk. I had the servant's quarters at the top of the house. Keith wasn't your typical housemate. He would stay up for three days, then sleep for three days. He always did have a unique physiology. I'd always been a morning person. At Chess, it was a case of start working at nine A.M., finish at seven P.M. It was a very structured life. Working with the Stones played havoc with my body clock. Meetings would start at eleven P.M., one A.M., whenever. Working with the Stones becomes your life. It's not like a job at all. The only way to survive it was to live it.

What was his main contribution to the band in the studio?

MARSHALL CHESS: Attitude. Of course, the Stones already had plenty of that, but I definitely added to it. It was a case of "Fuck everybody, fuck the label, fuck the cost, because we're going to make the greatest music and nothing is gonna get in the way of that." In the seven years with the Stones, I spent more time in the studio than anybody with the exception of Mick and Keith. I've always loved recording studios. For me it's like entering a church or a temple. I love the mood of those places. I love sitting behind that mixing-desk, watching events unfold. I find it completely fascinating.

Also I'd learned so much from watching my dad and uncle work with the Chess musicians. They knew exactly how to push their artists so they got the best out of them. There were times when my father would take over on the drums during Muddy Waters sessions to get the exact sound he wanted. The thing with the Stones was that they were surrounded by people who were completely enamored of them. So everything was great all the time. But I used to push them and push them some more. Doing *Sticky Fingers*, Mick would be laying down the vocal on "Moonlight Mile" and I'd be screaming, "Come on you motherfucker, another one." Because I thought it could be improved.

The critics, evidently, appreciated the extra effort.

BARNEY HOSKYNS: *Sticky Fingers* has always been taken for granted. Fans and critics alike have drooled for decades over *Let It Bleed* and *Exile on Main St.*, but *Fingers* is surely the Rolling Stones' greatest single long-player. It captures the group at the absolute top of their game—imperiously sexy, decadently jet-setting, above all passionate. (If Mick Jagger has never moved you, listen again to the line "You know I can't let you/Slide thru my hands," on "Wild Horses.") All this and a brilliantly homoerotic Andy Warhol sleeve—complete with real zip.

Fingers is tighter and more focused than the basement-tapes jam-session sprawl of *Exile*. It finds Jagger and Richards mastering every American roots genre they touch, from swaggering rock 'n' soul ("Brown Sugar," riding on one of Keith's rawest riffs) through Gram Parsons–infused country soul ("Wild Horses") and delta blues ("You Gotta Move") to churchy Muscle Shoals soul ("I Got the Blues," with its peerless Billy Preston organ solo).

"Bitch" is as thumpingly funky as it is politically incorrect. "Sway" may be the band's greatest hard rock outing, as well as a potent illustration of Mick Taylor's fluid lead guitar . . . "Dead Flowers" is gnarly country rock born of the Stones' frequent stints in turn-of-the-decade LA. Only the sub-Santana extemporization of "Can't You Hear Me Knocking" can be said to let the record down.

The Marianne Faithfull co-write "Sister Morphine"—with the late Jack Nitzsche on piano and his protégé Ry Cooder on cold-turkey slide guitar—is the ultimate late '60s junkie lamentation. Closing the record, "Moonlight Mile" is one of the band's true peaks—a cocaine-comedown ballad boasting a magisterial Paul Buckmaster string section and a thing of wasted, desolate beauty.

A few more points before we move on from *Sticky Fingers*. The first is about Barney's criticism of the jam at the end of "Can't You Hear Me Knocking." Many Stones fans love that part of the song.

BILLY ALTMAN: The jam at the end of "Can't You Hear Me Knocking" gives a lot of space for Mick Taylor to make a real impact.

KEITH RICHARDS: We didn't even know they were still taping. We thought we'd finished. We were just rambling and they kept the tape rolling. I figured we'd just fade it off. It was only when we heard the playback that we realized, "Oh, they kept it going." Basically we realized we had two bits of music. There's the song and there's the jam.

MICK TAYLOR: That song had such a fantastic groove going, they just left the tape running for my solo at the end. Generally, I tried to bring my own distinctive sound and style to *Sticky Fingers* and I like to think I added some extra spice. I don't want to say "sophistication"—I think that sounds pretentious. Charlie said I brought "finesse." That's a better word. I'll go with what Charlie said.

The other issue to follow up on is about "Sister Morphine" and Marianne Faithfull.

MARIANNE FAITHFULL: I wrote this song with a guy I used to know called Mick Jagger. I made the mistake of telling my mother I was doing drugs. She immediately had me committed to a hospital. I had one phone call. I called Mick Jagger and he came and got me out. He showed very good form.

We asked her to expand further on her relationship with Mick and Keith for this book but she politely declined.

MARIANNE FAITHFULL: I don't talk about the Stones anymore. Proud as I am, of having been in that generation and having been around the Rolling Stones at such a wonderful moment, and being so grateful for "As Tears Go By," and also writing "Sister Morphine" and just being around them because they're great, I really can't go on like that, it's finished. It kind of diminishes me so forget it.

Given this quote from Mick about her contribution to "Sister Morphine," we can't really blame her for not wanting to talk about the Stones.

MICK JAGGER: [Marianne Faithfull] wrote a couple of lines; she always says she wrote everything, though. She's always complaining she doesn't get enough money from it. Now she says she should have got it all.

A key witness seems to support Marianne's view.

KEITH RICHARDS: Marianne had a lot to do with "Sister Morphine." I know Mick's writing, and he was living with Marianne at the time, and I know from the style of it that there were a few Marianne lines in there.

To this day, *Sticky Fingers* remains one of the best things the Stones have ever done.

BILLY ALTMAN: I think on *Sticky Fingers* and then again on *Exile on Main St.*, the Stones moved back closer to their blues roots than they'd been in a while. And I attribute a lot of that to Mick Taylor. But Keith Richards also deserves a lot of credit for understanding what a great blues player Taylor was and moving out of the way for him on "All Down the Line" and "Stop Breaking Down." Keith let Mick Taylor really take over there and that required a lot of security in his ego. And at the same time, Keith was still really honing that choppy ringing guitar that's a part of so many great Stones songs. Keith really got in that middle space with his guitar playing.

ANDY JOHNS: Mick Taylor in the studio in France or Sunset Sound was just a shining light, as a person somewhat taciturn. When he plays his guitar, and we'd do a hundred takes on something, he would come up with something slightly different every time. Faultless. He'd put a bottle on his little finger and then he'd do chords with the rest of his hand. So he could do both at once. Usually it's a separate deal but that was part of his style. His sense of melody was unbelievable. Every time I knew it was Mick Taylor, I'd be sitting at the edge of my seat. He was wonderful.

And what about the band as a whole?

BILLY ALTMAN: I think when they made *Sticky Fingers* they were really focused, in terms of the song and their playing. It's such a wonderful multifaceted album. I think the fact that this was their first release for Atlantic on Rolling Stones Records made them really want to deliver a terrific album. I get a very professional sense of purpose from them on *Sticky Fingers*. And from there on, that's what they've been.

CRAIG BRAUN: It was a very special album. I remember sitting around a table in Los Angeles with various record executives listening to a test pressing and just knowing it was going to be a hit. When the record finished, people stood up and cheered.

The next question was: what should the new album cover look like?

MICK JAGGER: It's always good to have something that's a bit groundbreaking, and that causes a bit of a stir, as well.

Andy Warhol was at the forefront of album designs that did just that.

CRAIG BRAUN: I met Andy Warhol in '65 when he was venturing into all kinds of things. That was my beginnings in the music business. And in those days the art world and all the photographers and design studios and people in the fashion world started to meld together. Hip crossed many lines. Andy had a place called the Factory down in Union Square, which was basically a loft. The Velvet Underground and Nico had recorded an album and they wanted to put a piece of art he'd designed, a banana, on the front cover of the album. This was antithetical to the way music was merchandised. Usually it was the band's name on the front. But he wanted this banana. And he wanted it to become a peelable banana, and then he wanted to print underneath, and he wanted the banana under the peel to be pink, essentially a phallus. I had to find a custom stock that would be pre-coated in the yellow of that banana that was on the original art and also a removable adhesive that could be peeled back and reapplied. It was a project that was given to me.

What happened with the *Sticky Fingers* jacket?

CRAIG BRAUN: When this opportunity came to pass with Marshall and the Stones, Andy had already met Jagger a number of times and they had talked about doing an album cover. Andy had suggested the idea of maybe one day using a real zipper on an album cover. That was his idea. And Mick never forgot that.

But they didn't want to just settle on that first concept, so Braun was tasked with coming up with other ideas as well.

CRAIG BRAUN: I went to work on it and I used a number of different concepts using the zipper and the blue jeans. We did about three or four zipper ideas and maybe six other album cover concepts. One of them was a black cover, preprinted with images of the Stones' faces in a black, encapsulated, crystal ink that was heat sensitive. So if you'd put your hand on top of this black cover, all of a sudden the images of the Stones' faces would come out of it in this eerie, bluish-green color.

One of Craig's ideas really crossed the line.

CRAIG BRAUN: Another idea was to take a photo from the perspective of the bottom of a swimming pool; looking up and through the water you'd see the Stones' faces standing around the pool. The idea was to come up with something shocking, to push the envelope. But that was too sick even for the Stones.

The band objected, of course. Brian Jones's death was not something worth having a sense of humor about. But there were other ideas as well, including a crushed velvet cover with

Mick's face on it, and another design that featured a decapitated Mick! In the end, the correct choice was made:

CRAIG BRAUN: The zipper thing was at the top of their charts. Marshall called me and told me they liked everything but they still want the zipper. So I put together a comp and they approved it. The cost was such, twice of a normal package, so I'm sure that the Stones had to absorb some of the cost from their royalties. They considered it worth the investment in their future.

One mystery that still persists to this day is whose waist is pictured on the *Sticky Fingers* cover. Warhol superstar Joe D'Allesandro believes it's him:

JOE D'ALLESANDRO: It was just out of a collection of junk photos that Andy pulled from. He didn't pull it out for the design or anything, it was just the first one he got that he felt was the right shape to fit what he wanted to use for the fly. It had nothing to do with anything else. There was no photograph session set up where they were taking shots of crotch areas.

Craig Braun disagrees.

CRAIG BRAUN: Marshall is convinced that the model was Joe D'Allesandro. I'm pretty sure it wasn't. There were very good-looking twin guys from down south, Jed and Jay Johnson. I think it was Jed Johnson who was on the outside cover. There was also the mention of a model there, Corey Tippin, who was a hanger-on, hairdresser, stylist, model, that he might be the guy. Glenn O'Brien, who was the first editor of *Interview*, claims it was him. Frankly, I don't know who it was but we wanted the impression to be, at the point of sale, that it was Mick's dick.

Indeed, that became the rumor. Mick himself acknowledges that it isn't him, though. And while Mick doesn't have *the* answer, he does have a cheeky answer:

MICK JAGGER: It's one of Andy's . . . "protégés" is the polite word we used to use.

The cover is widely recognized as one of the best ever made. But it was almost a total disaster.

CRAIG BRAUN: I thought there might be problems with the zipper. Vinyl is so easily scratched or dented. We instructed the pressing plant to use corrugated cardboard between each album to nest the zipper, and stagger the albums top and bottom when they were packed. I didn't take into account the weight that would be cumulative in the back of these big semis. They were stacking boxes very high. And as the truck started moving, that weight started to settle down. But I got a call from

Atlantic almost right away that they were getting returns because there was the same dented track—"Sister Morphine"—on a lot of the albums because of the zippers. I was devastated. The corrugated inserts didn't work. And I got a big lecture about how I should have dissuaded the Stones and Marshall from doing this. They wanted me to pay for it. I went home and tried to think of a way to salvage this thing for everybody. Somehow in the middle of the night, I must have been divinely inspired. The idea came to me that if the fabric was glued with a very strong glue that they would adhere enough in the factory that they could have people pull the zippers down. And if they pulled the zippers down, then that zipper pull would be on the center disc label of the LP. Who gives a shit if that's dented? They hired these little old ladies whose sole job at the plant was to pull down the zipper. Lo and behold it worked, man.

CHAPTER 27

WANG DANG DOODLE

THE LONDON HOWLIN' WOLF SESSIONS is a fascinating recording, pairing blues legends Howlin' Wolf and Hubert Sumlin with the generation of English rock 'n' rollers who discovered and helped to make their music a worldwide phenomenon, including Bill Wyman, Charlie Watts, and Ian Stewart.

HUBERT SUMLIN: I was glad that they helped us record the *London Sessions*. We recorded numbers we'd already recorded in the States but we did them all over again.

Initially, producer Norman Dayron reached out to Eric Clapton to see if he'd be interested in playing with Wolf. He most certainly was.

HUBERT SUMLIN: The record company wanted Eric Clapton but they didn't want me. But Eric Clapton called the record company and said, "If Hubert isn't on the *London Sessions*, then neither am I." I didn't even have a passport, but the next day I had a visa.

NORMAN DAYRON: Hubert isn't right about that. He was one of the first people I wanted to bring. I thought for Clapton to play his best on lead, he'd need his idol, Hubert, holding down the rhythm.

Initially, the band was supposed to feature another guitarist as well.

HUBERT SUMLIN: Keith Richards was supposed to have been with us too. But

Eric Clapton beat him out some kind of way. Keith still talks about this today. He told me, "I was supposed to be on there."

NORMAN DAYRON: He's right about that. I was going to put together new arrangements nothing like the originals, I wanted as many piano players and guitar players as possible because I had a master plan of doing overdubs, but I still wanted to get as much as I could in London. Eric invited Keith to join him to play both lead and rhythm but he didn't show up.

Later on, several musicians including Steve Winwood would add overdubs to the initial tracks. Also joining in on the first day of sessions were an array of Chess all-stars, including eighteen-year-old harmonica prodigy Jeffrey Carp (who drowned shortly after), as well as Klaus Voormann and Ringo Starr. The latter two didn't last long.

Howlin' Wolf and Mick at the recording of the *London Sessions*

KLAUS VOORMANN: Howlin' was singing, he took the mic off the mic stand, and was walking around in the studio. He came right up to me, looked at me right in my eyes while he was singing and I was playing. I thought that was great and very inspiring, like he was talking to you: "Come on, boy, do your thing!" Then he went over to Ringo, but Ringo—as he often does when he loves playing—had his eyes closed, so he didn't notice that Howlin' was right in front of his face. When Ringo opened his eyes, he got a real shock and nearly fell off his chair with fright.

Ringo left and took Voormann with him, though Ringo still appears incognito in the liner notes, credited as "Richie."

The sessions weren't without other challenges.

ERIC CLAPTON: There's that thing of him teaching me how to play "Little Red Rooster" and when that was happening it was awful. I wanted to just die. He kept grabbing my hand and shoving my wrist up and down the neck of the guitar. And he was angry. He was very angry.

Wyman recalls a kinder, gentler Wolf.

BILL WYMAN: It was very nice, actually. Except Wolf wasn't feeling too well at the time. I remember on some of the tracks there was someone standing behind him whispering the lyrics into his ear because he was getting blanks which he couldn't remember. But it was a good session—he showed us how to play "Little Red Rooster." We cut the tune and he says, "No, it shouldn't go like that." We were playing it kind of backwards—the way white kids would play it, but the way we felt it. He started to show us the right way to do it, but the Chess people ended up using the old "backwards" take anyway.

NORMAN DAYRON: That was me whispering the words to him. I don't think Wolf was angry at that point, but I do remember him being upset about something earlier on. It was my idea to have Clapton ask Wolf about the changes on "Little Red Rooster." I didn't think we'd use it for the record but I needed to break the ice.

Hubert confirmed Bill's view of Wolf's health, and remembers another celebrity visitor.

HUBERT SUMLIN: Wolf had doctors tending him night and day. He was so sick that on a couple of nights we didn't even record; we just sat in the studio and got high. Mick Jagger and Bill Wyman came in, and we partied all night long, man. The cleaning lady came in the next morning and everyone was laying there on the floor. Mick Jagger had his head up inside the bass drum (*laughs*). It was wild. We had a ball.

NORMAN DAYRON: Mick was there, but that's the only part of that that's accurate. I had to get Wolf to take his pills but once he did, he was fine, he outworked all the other musicians. Mick played percussion on about five songs. He had perfect rhythm. I was not a producer who sat in the control room, I was out with the musicians conducting. I don't think Mick liked that at all. He thought I was a prima donna. I remember him saying after one take, "Well, I do hope that her majesty the queen is satisfied with that take," but Wolf stuck up for me.

The record stands as an amazing document and a great record that's a lot of fun to listen to: it's hard not to enjoy the coupling of "new" and old bluesy sounds. At the time, however, there was a bit of a backlash.

NORMAN DAYRON: The snobs and the blues-nerds who wrote for the magazines at the time generally resisted liking the album. These were people of a similar ilk to the ones who booed Dylan when he went electric at Newport.

But soon Dayron received the ultimate approbation.

NORMAN DAYRON: When I sent a copy of the record to B.B. King, he called me up and said, "That's a good record, son. You ought to be proud of it."

ABOUT THEM SHOES

One of the lasting achievements of the Rolling Stones is the consistency of their desire to pay back the blues heroes who inspired them. This isn't just lip service or good PR. This is a real sense of urgency to honor and remember all of the giants whose shoulders they stood on during their fabulous trajectory to a level of fame and fortune that their own idols never attained. It began as far back as the group's insistence that Howlin' Wolf appear with them on the American television program *Shindig* (see chapter 6). It continues to this very day, ironically, with yet another connection to that same blues idol. In 2004, Wolf's guitar player, Hubert Sumlin, recorded a solo album with a little help from his friends. Eric Clapton, Levon Helm, David Johansen, and Keith Richards all appear on various tracks on *About Them Shoes*.

In *Life*, Keith Richards wrote about his admiration for the record, noting that he especially liked the title. In a 2004 interview, I asked Hubert what those words meant to him:

HUBERT SUMLIN: Everybody walked in these shoes, everybody in this blues line. I named the album *About Them Shoes* for everybody who walked in them shoes. I'm a blues guy. The people who make music, I don't care if it's blues or rock or country and western, if they got soul, they say, "We been in these shoes, too." This is what it's all about. I got a little bit of all of it. If you feel it, somebody's gonna feel it too.

When Hubert died of heart failure in New Jersey on Sunday, December 4, 2010, at the age of eighty, Mick and Keith once again stepped up to the plate for one of their idols. They insisted on picking up the costs of the funeral.

KEITH RICHARDS: He was an uncle and a teacher, and all the guitar players must feel the same as myself.

MICK JAGGER: Hubert was an incisive yet delicate blues player. He had a really distinctive and original tone and was a wonderful foil for Howlin' Wolf's growling vocal style. On a song like "Goin' Down Slow" he could produce heartrending emotion, and on a piece like "Wang Dang Doodle" an almost playful femininity. He was an inspiration to us all.

It is that kind of consistency, empathy, and respect that will be remembered long after the Rolling Stones themselves cease to exist.

CHAPTER 28

TUMBLING DICE

ROBERT GREENFIELD: The Stones are way beyond peace, love, and flowers; they're way ahead of the culture in America.

DON WAS: I think you can use the Stones as markers. The peace, love, hippie, acid thing, that was long gone. There was definitely the sense that the '60s didn't work and you had to blow up the system or flee from it.

The Stones chose to flee. Their new business manager, Prince Rupert Loewenstein, determined that they'd be able to save a tremendous amount of money if they left the country for twenty-one months.

MICK JAGGER: We'd sold a lot of records but we weren't getting paid for it because we had such a low royalty. We found out that we had a management company guy [Allen Klein] who claimed that he owned everything that we were doing. So we had to get rid of him and try to get out of this ridiculous, byzantine mess that you'd created for yourself.

BILL WYMAN: Tax, under the labor government, Wilson, was 93 percent. If you had a million quid, which we didn't, you'd end up with seventy grand. It was impossible to earn enough money to pay back the inland revenue and stay in our own country.

The next step was to find a place to record.

ROBERT GREENFIELD MEETS THE STONES

Robert Greenfield has done some of the best writing on the Stones, touring with them in 1971 and again in 1972. In fact, his landmark 1971 interview with Keith for *Rolling Stone* is quoted throughout this book. Here's the story of how he came to cover—and be accepted by—the band.

Bob Greenfield in the *Rolling Stone* magazine offices in London

ROBERT GREENFIELD: I was the associate editor of the London bureau of *Rolling Stone* magazine, and the Stones were about to do their English farewell tour before they moved to France. The first day I just showed up at King's Cross Station. The band came walking down the platform, got into this train heading for Newcastle, and no one had told anyone who I was. We were just sitting in compartments. It was the band, the Stones, the supporting musicians, the tour personnel . . . and no one knew who I was. I wasn't going to introduce myself to anybody. We got to the hotel and somebody handed me a key. And I went upstairs and I was twenty-five years old, straight out of Brooklyn, and it was the first time in my life I had stayed in my own hotel room . . .

They do the show that night and I'm standing right behind the piano—Nicky Hopkins and Ian Stewart are taking turns. Chip Monck, who was the stage manager, introduces them. I'm standing next to Chip, right behind the piano. Maybe there are one thousand people there and they're doing most of *Sticky Fingers*. That's dandy, except *Sticky Fingers* hadn't come out yet. I'd never seen them play. I'm standing on stage with them watching them play. What I left out: the only person who's not on the train is of course Keith Richards. Because Keith, at this point in time, unbeknownst to me, is pretty smacked-out. He's traveling separately with Anita and Marlon, and Gram Parsons. They're a separate entity. They get to every gig late. Nothing happens until Keith gets there.

They finish the gig and we go back to this hotel we're staying in . . . The gig is over by eleven thirty, twelve o'clock. You can't get any food. There's no restaurants open. England shuts . . . So, they have a big dinner catered in a ballroom in the hotel. I'm sitting between Charlie Watts and Jim Price, who's a trumpet player. Neither one of them knows who I am . . . Charlie, who is one of the great jazz fanatics of all time. Charlie is trying to remember, "Harry James. 'We Meet and the Angels Sing.' Who's playing the trumpet solo on that?"

I'm eating and I say "Ziggy Elman" and I go back to eating. Charlie looks at me and says, "Yeah. Ziggy. Nice." After that, Charlie figures I'm probably one of the crew . . . I don't know if they ever get my name. They travel by bus; they travel by train. There are no limos. There are no cars. They walk up the street to all these town halls. And I'm on the road with the Rolling Stones.

I'm hanging out with Marshall Chess, who knows who I am, and I get off with Marshall right away because Marshall is just wild. He's taking over the Stones; he's at the peak of his power; he's hysterically funny. All we do is laugh together. As happens the first time you go out with the Stones, I'm getting crazier.

The key to the whole thing with them is I never take notes where they can see me. I never write anything down. I listen and then I go to the bathroom and I sit in the bathroom and I take copious notes—I think I still have the notebook—and I write down everything they are saying.

They work a terrible place in Brighton called the Big Apple; it's freezing cold and we're waiting to get in the dressing room. Down the hallway, as only he can, comes Keith. He sweeps. He's not walking. It's a royal procession. Anita with the tiger-skin coat, with Marlon and Gram Parsons. "What's going on?" Keith right away goes off on a riff: "My baby. My baby's freezing."

The next thing I know, Keith is taking the door off the hinges with a buck knife. I pull something out of my pocket—could have been a comb—and he and I who have never spoken, we take the door off the hinges. He throws it in the fucking hallway: "Right! Now we're in. If nobody saw us do it, nobody is going to rat us out." So I qualified with Keith.

I still hadn't qualified with Mick. On the last night of the tour, he waited to get me. He said to me in the dressing room, "You haven't taken a single note on this tour. You've been as fucked-up as anyone. You have no idea what's going on, have you?" I said, "Mick, I don't know. I had a good time." Then when the article came out, he saw that I remembered everything. I passed the Mick test after the tour was over.

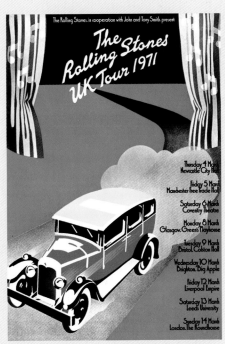

Poster from the Goodbye Great Britain tour

KEITH RICHARDS: We looked around for studios but there were no good rooms and the equipment was shabby. Nobody felt comfortable anywhere we looked.

JIMMY MILLER: We tried various cinemas and public halls, we just never found a suitable site and in the end we chose convenience, I suppose, over sound, and went for the basement of Keith's house.

Nellcôte was built by an English admiral, Admiral Byrd, and was a Nazi stronghold during World War II.

ROBERT GREENFIELD: The house was literally surrounded by a jungle. You could not see the house from the road. You had to turn in and drive up. That's how overgrown it was. It was really dense. It was lush. You could get lost on the grounds. It wasn't a huge estate. Everybody sat on the back steps. Then you went down from the back steps and there was a flat area. Then there was a private staircase.

There was a set of very old moss-covered stone steps leading down to the private beach. Off the beach, Keith kept the speedboat moored. The back patio overlooked the Bay of Villefranche, which is a deepwater port. The US Navy would have ships of war in there. Anita was obsessed with looking at them through her binoculars. Onassis's ship would be there. All the richest men in the world would bring their private yachts into that harbor. The villa was literally on the edge of the western world. You walk down from the villa to the water. It overlooked the ocean.

It had been beautiful inside. But Keith had the ability to make any space look like a trashed hotel room in three days. So there were cardboard cutouts of Mick Jagger standing in the living room . . . The music was non-stop and it was fabulous . . . For some reason, one night I seemed to be the last one up . . . *Mud Slide Slim and the Blue Horizon* had just come out, James Taylor. Something that would never be played in that house. And I loved James Taylor and I put it on. I was listening to this . . . and here comes Keith. He gives me this look like, "You fuck, you're listening to James Taylor" . . . It's midnight and he's working his way through the living room before heading upstairs and he stops and he looks at the rug. And there's some kind of pill, like a large capsule. He looks at it a second, picks it up and throws it in his mouth and goes upstairs.

I was there during the good time it was a party. Keith was happy; they were having a good time. The weather was beautiful. And it seemed like paradise. Then it became hell.

In May, Mick married his finacée, Bianca, who was pregnant during the recording of *Exile on Main St.* He was frequently visiting her in Paris.

JIMMY MILLER: I think that was Keith's album. Mick was always jumping off to Paris 'cause Bianca was pregnant and having labor pains. I remember many mornings after great nights of recording, I'd come over to Keith's for lunch. And within a few

THE MIGHTY MOBILE

Recording at Nellcôte wouldn't have been possible without the Mighty Mobile Unit.

KEITH RICHARDS: The Mighty Mobile, as we called it, was a truck with eight-track recording machines that Stu had helped to put together. We didn't realize when we put it together how rare it was. Soon we were renting it out to the BBC and ITV because they only had one apiece. It was another one of those beautiful, fortuitous things that happened to the Stones.

The Mobile Unit was first used to record the Hyde Park concert and then used again at Stargroves.

ANDREW MOSKER: Ian Stewart felt that given the lifestyle of the Rolling Stones, this idea of having a mobile recording studio at their disposal was a good one. So that they could remove themselves from the confines of having to go into a stand-alone recording studio that was booked at a certain time at a certain day. The mobile was able to catch some of that improvised, unplanned, spontaneous music making that came out of *Sticky Fingers* and *Exile on Main St.* The space became part of the sound. The mobile became an enabler for the Rolling Stones and their creative process.

ANDY JOHNS: Dick Swettenham put the truck together. It was his very cool stuff with four speakers in Lockwood cabinets. It could sound very nice in there but it could also be very difficult. The confined space. The camera never worked. The talk back never worked. So you couldn't see or talk to people. You had to keep runnin' out of the truck. "Stop!" Jimmy and I went to France with that truck.

minutes of seeing him I could tell something was wrong. He'd say, "Mick's pissed off to Paris again." I sensed resentment in his voice because he felt we were starting to get something, and when Mick returned the magic might be gone.

Keith himself isn't so sure.

KEITH RICHARDS: I don't really get that. Mick was incredibly involved. Look how many songs there are. And he wrote the bulk of the lyrics. He was very involved. I don't think I was putting in more than anybody else. Charlie was amazing. Everybody was in great form.

The journalist in residence certainly noticed the tensions between Mick and Keith.

ROBERT GREENFIELD: They weren't coming up with any new songs. The thing that drove Mick crazy was that Keith would sit around all day long playing country-western songs with Gram Parsons. Gram was teaching Keith the lexicon of country. Gram was a scholar of that music. Then when Mick needed to write with Keith, he was nowhere to be found. When Mick needed to record with Keith, he had to go put Marlon to sleep, then he'd shoot up and fall out. By no means should Mick be construed as the villain here. He was just trying to get this album made. He couldn't make it without Keith.

Mick would put up with a lot from Keith. I never saw him get angry, but you could tell how frustrating it was for him. Then he starts going to Paris to be with Bianca because he couldn't take it for too long.

JIMMY MILLER: The basement of Keith's house was in fact a series of rooms. And in the end, the separation was so poor that we'd have to have the piano in one room, an acoustic guitar in the kitchen, because it had tile and it had a nice ring. There was another room for the horns. And then there was another main studio, where the drums were, and Keith's amp. And Bill would stand in there but his amp would be out the hall. And every time I would want to communicate, I'd have to run around to all the rooms and give the message.

Andy Johns describes the bizarre scene at Nellcôte:

Mick marries Bianca Pérez Morena de Macias on May 12, 1971

ANDY JOHNS: I come out the trucks, through these big front doors and down the steps, and I look down the floor: blue marble, it was. The heating vents were in the shape of swastikas—solid gold swastikas. I said, "Keith. What's this swastika shit?" "Oh, I didn't tell you? During the last war, this was the headquarters for the Gestapo in the south of France." They were torturing people to death in this basement. Upstairs, they were having sumptuous dinners. Which was kind of what was going on with us.

"Happy" is one of the record's signature tracks, featuring a rare-at-the-time Keith lead vocal.

KEITH RICHARDS: It was mainly because we had the track, we liked it, but we hadn't worked on the lyrics or the vocal at all until we were in there doing vocal overdubs. And it came around to the point where Mick said, "Even if I spend three days on it, I don't think I'm going to do it as well as you're doing it trying to teach it to me." It's one of those, "I think you're wrong, but if you want me to I'll go ahead and do it anyway." And either if he wants to do it again later he can, or it stays as it is. If I manage to pull a good vocal off then it'll stay there.

I [like singing lead] . . . but it's very rare that I can do it as well as Mick can do it, that's why he does it so well. It just occasionally happens that we come across a song that either I've written or I've gotten the hang of it so quickly for some reason or other or Mick can't get round to it or he just prefers the way I do it. And I might disagree but he'll say no, you're doing it better than I'd do it and that's the way it happens.

Marshall Chess was there in France. He had a lot of responsibilities during that time, including helping with the album, setting up a world tour, and making a film.

MARSHALL CHESS: Then I was summoned to Holland Park in London for a meeting with Prince Rupert Loewenstein, who looked after the Stones' finances. I'm sitting there with him and Keith Richards. After polite preliminaries Rupert got down to business and asked me what the hell I was thinking about, spending two hundred thousand pounds and building a kitchen. All of a sudden Keith, who is obviously inebriated on something or other, starts flapping his arms around and says, "Whatever Marshall says, we're gonna go with." And he's spilling this tea all over Rupert's forty-thousand-pound carpet. The Stones always stood up for me when necessary. They were very loyal in that way.

What does he remember most about his time at Keith's house?

MARSHALL CHESS: The meals. Soon after we arrived it dawned on everyone that there was fifteen people to feed every day and we needed a chef. In this fabulous mansion there was this great long baronial table that was half inside the house and

The Rolling Stones
new single
"HAPPY"
KS-19104

half outside but covered, looking out on the bay. To make this work, I had to restore a kitchen in the cellar and all the food was sent up in one of those dumbwaiters. Then I had to hire a chef. Every afternoon at five o'clock we all gathered around this long table for our first meal of the day. Most of us had just got out of bed. I'd pass around bowls of joints as we waited for the food to arrive. It was like something from a King Arthur movie, quite a thing for a boy from Chicago.

ANDY JOHNS: This French chef would put out these lavish spreads for lunch and you'd walk out to a big table of artichokes, stuffed tomatoes, sautéed asparagus, salads, and lobsters. Wonderful stuff. Big luncheon on the terrace overlooking the Mediterranean and these big yachts.

ROBERT GREENFIELD: There's sixteen people at lunch every day on the patio; we're drinking blanc de blancs . . . Lunch is three hours. Joints are being smoked. Then we're in the speedboat on the bay. I'm trying to water-ski. Keith is laughing because I can't water-ski. We're walking on beaches. I teach Keith how to skim stones. He loves it. We skim stones for twenty minutes. "This is great, man."

KEITH RICHARDS: We had a couple of French chefs who blew it up. Fat Jacques, he certainly blew it up.

That's not a compliment; Keith was being literal. Jacques once left the gas on too long before lighting the stove and caused a big explosion. A possible explanation:

KEITH RICHARDS: He was a junkie, too. He used to go to Marseille. You'd say, "Where's Jacques?" "It's Thursday." "Oh, right, he's gone to score."

Kidding aside, drugs became a real problem at Nellcôte.

ANITA PALLENBERG: I walked into the living room and this guy pulled out a bag of smack. The whole thing kind of disintegrated and we got heavily into drugs, like breakfast, lunch, and dinner. At the end especially, I thought I was cursed.

ANDY JOHNS: One night I go into my room to change my shirt, and Keith's there and he's got a needle and a spoon. I said, "What are you doing Keith?" "I thought I'd jack myself up a bit. Do you want to try this?" It's Keith Richards so I say, "Yeah, OK." He says, "This needle's a bit bent. Why don't we go back to my place?" We go into the Nazi basement. Afterwards he went, "Now you're a man." I thought that was a strange thing to say. I went upstairs and I can't even see my feet. And Stu came in, and he looked at me and said, "You've been hanging out with Keith, haven't you?" He said, "Andrew, what time is it?" I looked at my watch. I could see the watch, but I couldn't see what time it was. I said, "I think it's twelve thirty." "It's eight thirty! I know what's been going on and I'm going to tell your brother." I went, "Stu, don't do it. OK?" He said, "I'm going to have to have a chat with little fairy boy Keith."

Reportedly, Miller and Mick Taylor developed heroin habits as well.

ROBERT GREENFIELD: Jimmy was also using heroin by the time they got to Nellcôte. The thing that I think really blew Jimmy out was the combination of using smack and that they were playing endlessly without getting anywhere, and he just kind of lost it. What the Stones always did—Keith and Mick—brought in a genius, sucked everything the genius knew out, and got rid of the genius.

The French authorities became aware of what was going on at Nellcôte and launched a probe. Since there's no habeas corpus in France, Keith and Anita could have been imprisoned for months while they were being investigated.

KEITH RICHARDS: Prince Rupert Loewenstein came into play. Later he would set up a global network of lawyers, of top-ranking legal gunslingers, to protect us. For now, he managed to acquire the services of a lawyer named Jean Michard-Pellissier. You couldn't have reached higher. He had been a lawyer for de Gaulle and was a friend of the prefect of the region. Nice one, Rupert.

And what happened at the hearing?

KEITH RICHARDS: Instead of the prospect of jail, a real possibility, Anita and I got one of several skin-of-teeth legal agreements that I've received in my time. It was decreed that we should leave French territory until I was "allowed back," but I had to keep renting Nellcôte, as some kind of bond, at twenty-four hundred dollars a week.

ANDY JOHNS: I remember talking to Keith in his basement in France. Just Keith and I, and I said, "Look, the next step is that we've got to go and finish the overdubs and mix. Why don't we go to Sunset?" And they worked there before. So, "Yeah, all right." And of course, I loved LA. Twenty-one-year-old English guy, and I had done a couple or three projects there. So I knew people and chicks eventually. "Yeah. Let's do that then."

THE STORY OF THE 1971 *ROLLING STONE* INTERVIEW

ROBERT GREENFIELD: I get to Keith's house, I'm standing there waiting, a little nervous. He sweeps down the stairs. "Oh man, Bob Greenfield!"

I wind up living with him for two weeks in Nellcôte. A day or two after I got there, we do the first interview and he's great. The second one, Keith and I drinking tequila from the bottle, something that no one was doing back then. The interview degenerates to monosyllabic grunts that have no meaning whatsoever.

Keith's unbelievable to talk to. Any question I ask him, he answers. And he's smoking a spliff constantly throughout the interview. After I've got two sessions done with him, it goes to the next level, which is: I'm a guest; it's a party; but we're not sitting down to talk. He's dodging me. I was starting to lose my mind. I talk to Marshall Chess on the phone. I said, "This is bad, man. I can't get him to sit down and talk to me. I need to finish this." Marshall shows up . . . He brings some form of chaotic law and order to the house and we do two more sessions . . . On the last one, the only sound you hear is the sounds of the birds in the trees and the scratching of the matches against the box as Keith lights and smokes another spliff.

I spend a week transcribing the interview in Cannes. I drive back to the villa. I walk in and say, "Keith, I want you to read this." He's reading the original. It's ninety-eight pages long, and as he reads each page, he throws it on the floor. It must've taken forty-five minutes or an hour . . . He flips the last page on the floor and says, "Yeah man, I said it. Print it." It eventually ran on the cover in August. It was a big deal. No one had heard Keith talk before. He had never been the face of the band.

Upon release, the record received mixed reviews and some harsh notices even from within the Stones camp.

JIMMY MILLER: I was never happy with the sound of that album, especially after *Let It Bleed* and *Sticky Fingers*.

MICK JAGGER: *Exile* . . . is not one of my favorite albums, although I think the record does have a particular feeling. When I listen to *Exile* it has some of the worst mixes I've ever heard. I'd love to remix the record, not just because of the vocals, but because generally I think it sounds lousy. At the time, Jimmy Miller was not functioning properly.

MARSHALL CHESS: We certainly didn't think we were working on an album that would be hailed as a masterpiece all these years later. You never hear something that way. Also you never hear it like a member of the public hears it when he drops the needle on the vinyl or pops the CD into the deck. I'm hearing the album from the acoustic versions when they first play the songs, through the tracks and vocals being laid down, to the final mixes. When you're involved you see it more like a sculptor does, remembering how it evolved from a block of stone. You don't ever hear it fresh. Besides, there was no time to think about posterity. Everything about the making of *Exile* was so intense.

Keith on the other hand was more immediately proud of *Exile*.

KEITH RICHARDS: I always thought, somewhere in the back of my mind that what we were doing, it wasn't just for now. There might have been some sort of feeling since we had to move out of England while we were doing it, well, we better make this bloody work.

And work it did . . . a few final thoughts about *Exile*:

ANDY JOHNS: With *Exile*, its mostly blues-based stuff. "Stop Breaking Down" is probably my favorite track. I remember getting Mick to play harmonica on that. It did not seem like it was finished. My brother [Glyn] had recorded earlier. I said, "We've got to use this," because Mick Taylor plays some gorgeous lines and I'm very sure that it's Mick Jagger playing the rhythm guitar as well. That's why it's a little choppier.

ROBERT GREENFIELD: At the time, *Exile* confused people. There was so much music on it and it was so dense. It was made under the influence of heroin and mixed under the influence of cocaine. The album reflects what Keith wanted to be in the Stones' music: blues, funk, who gives a shit if it ain't perfect, it fucking sounds good to me. It took a long time for it to reach masterpiece status. It took a damn long time.

Interestingly, Greenfield himself has some reservations about *Exile* musically.

ROBERT GREENFIELD: For me the songs go on too long. The endings trail away. The thing about *Exile* is that it is a very dark stew.

And why is *Exile* so great?

ANDY JOHNS: It's an intangible. *Exile* just turned out to be a great collection of music. And I think it was good that it was a double album. Some people say it should have been a single album, but you get the feeling of what they were going through at the time, and the confusion and the angst and the joy and the drugs and they moved out of England. There were a lot of emotions.

ROBERT GREENFIELD: They were so estranged from everything. They were in control of this album because of Rolling Stones Records. *Sticky Fingers* had made so much money that they could tell Ahmet, "We're not ready." They could say no. That's why Marshall set it up the way that he did. Mick was never going to be under the thumb of someone like Allen Klein again. He was going to control what was going on with the Stones' product. Mick was so smart. He knew this would be a bombshell and it was. *Exile* is the closest they ever got to pure art. Everything on there is basically not commercial. There is no precedent for *Exile*. It's a leap; it's an inductive leap. And when a band makes an inductive leap, they leave people behind . . .

CHAPTER 29
LET IT LOOSE

THE ROLLING STONES' 1972 tour has been described as the first modern rock 'n' roll tour. Many feel it was the best that any band has sounded live, ever. It amounted to more than just a series of concerts.

ROBERT GREENFIELD: That tour was special. It was a social event. It was a cultural event. It was a business event. It's the kind of thing that rock 'n' roll can't do anymore. It has to do with timing, it has to do with setting; it was a perfect crossroads. This is what's called history.

One of the many interesting people who traveled with the Stones on the '72 tour was Swiss-born iconic photographer and observer of the American condition Robert Frank. Frank was making the never-to-be-officially-released documentary of excess on the tour called *Cocksucker Blues*.

ROBERT FRANK: I have never been on anything like this. I have been on trips with extraordinary people before but they were always directed outward . . . this totally excludes the outside world. To never get out, to never know what city you are in . . . I cannot get used to it.

Marshall Chess describes the Stones' partying during this period:

MARSHALL CHESS: Oh, it was right up there. To the max. It was at the very start of that whole sex, drugs, and rock 'n' roll lifestyle. I was the same age as the

Unused ticket from one of the most famous concerts of all time, Mick's Birthday Show

Stones and fell right in with all that. What was there not to like about any of it? I was in my twenties. My marriage had broken up so I had no responsibilities in that way. I wouldn't say I was a major womanizer but I definitely knew how to enjoy myself. Like any man I appreciate a pretty woman. On those Stones tours there was a lot of very hot women around the band and a lot of extra ones to go around.

The bigger issue for Marshall was drugs.

MARSHALL CHESS: Before I joined the Stones I'd smoked marijuana, that was it. Suddenly every drug on the planet was freely available. As soon as we started touring, I found myself with multiple addictions. By the end of the first big tour I was doing everything there was to do. I liked to be high all the time. When you're living that life you don't stop for a moment to think that there's gonna be a long, dark tunnel waiting for you somewhere down the line.

ROBERT GREENFIELD: The brilliance of Keith was you didn't know about the junk unless you were using junk. You didn't get in the room with him unless you were using junk. They had lived in public since they were eighteen, nineteen, twenty. They were very clever at presenting a public face, a second face, a third face. Then it was a secret life even further back than that. They had everything compartmentalized. You had to really pass tests to get to the inner circle.

Marshall was in that inner circle. When did things get out of hand for him personally?

MARSHALL CHESS: It was on tour that the real partying went on, after the shows. I did seven years of sex, drugs, and rock 'n' roll. I came out of it a better man than when I went in. I made it out. Jimmy Miller and Nicky Hopkins didn't make it out alive.

What was it like touring with the Stones in those days?

MARSHALL CHESS: Those tours were epics. I even got to play on stage with the band a few times. On the 1973 tour of Europe I played trumpet and conga drums on the last three numbers of the Stones' set, finishing up with "Street Fighting Man." I used to be a bugler in the Boy Scouts, then I played in my high school band. My dream was to become a musician but my family discouraged that. They thought it was a stupid life. They had a point. In those days being a musician was a hard road to travel. There were no rock stars. But I regret it to this day because I think I'd have been a great musician. I had it in me.

The Stones were using Stevie Wonder's horn section to fatten their sound and they insisted I join them on stage. Walking out to play in front of twenty thousand people, that was a thrill. I blew so hard my lips were bruised. My abiding memory is Mick showering me with rose petals at the end of the show and thirty thousand people focusing their energy on me. It was such an intense feeling.

PETER RUDGE: THE RINGMASTER

Before Peter Rudge got the job as road manager of the Stones, he was on the road with the Who.

PETER RUDGE: We were making a rock opera called *Tommy*. That attracted the attention of Mick and the Stones and Rupert Loewenstein, because they were coming off the back of Altamont. I got a call from somebody saying, "The Stones would like to meet with you." I went in and I met the Stones at the Beverly Hills Hotel at Rupert Loewenstein's bungalow. It was hysterical: Keith kept leaving the room. Mick was in and out of the room. Rupert was the only constant. We just talked. I sensed even then that Mick ran the show. Keith was the conscience of the group. There were a lot of discussions about the ticket prices. They were mindful of all the pitfalls of the '69 tour. About two or three months later I got a call that said, "Hey, the Stones would like you to come work with them on the '72 tour." I was a pretty young kid.

How was his experience on the '72 tour?

PETER RUDGE: That tour is unique in terms of what we accomplished. It was a fusion of rock 'n' roll and celebrity that transcended music and attracted a huge media curiosity at that time. It was Ahmet Ertegun and all his social circles. Mick reached out to people like Bob Ellis, who managed Billy Preston [and] happened to be married to Diana Ross. We had parties at Diana Ross's house in LA and [Motown founder] Barry Gordy was there.

It was a self-contained traveling tour. We controlled everything. I was the guide horse. It was kind of like playing the media themselves because there was such a fascination with the Stones: here comes the devil incarnate, lock your daughters up. We created the template for the modern tour from a structural, organizational, and a production point of view. And the gigs were phenomenal.

Is it true that the Stones had issues with disgruntled Hells Angels on the tour?

PETER RUDGE: There was the underlying issue of the Hells Angels. They wanted the Stones to pay their legal fees from Altamont. The Stones said, "It's your problem. You killed the kid. You're the ones who decided on taking that course of action." So we were constantly being harassed by Hells Angels. Once, I was walking down Madison Avenue, two bikers rode up the side of me when I was pushing my three-month-old kid down the road. I was wired up by the FBI, because the Angels were trying to shake us down for money. On that tour, you had Hells Angels trying to knock the back door down and Truman Capote sitting in the dressing room with Jackie Onassis's sister.

What were the Stones themselves like during the '72 tour?

PETER RUDGE: The Stones knew that the gig didn't finish when they walked off stage. They really understood that everything they did would either add or subtract from the Stones legend. So they were really good at working that. Mick and Keith had an incredible chemistry. Keith, the dark gypsy, with his rat retinue that hangs on, and Mick prancing around with Ahmet, prancing around with Nancy Reagan, prancing around with David Geffen. No one could pin him down.

Charlie was probably the only one that could speak to all five of them. Mick was coming along—the new boy, the baby. Dear old Bill would plod along being Bill, worried more about the football results back home than anything else. But it worked. If bands like each other, they don't last long. If bands don't like each other, they tend to last forever.

The official tour chronicler was Robert Greenfield.

ROBERT GREENFIELD: Now we hear that the Stones are going to go on tour in America. I want to write about the tour, but I'm not really the choice of *Rolling Stone* magazine. Then, they're informed by the Stones that I'm the only guy acceptable. I didn't pay for anything on the tour. Nor did *Rolling Stone* pay for anything. My expenses were covered by the Stones. I'm on the Stones' touring party . . .

Peter Rudge is running the tour. I fall in love with Peter because he's a character of major proportions. He's hysterically funny and he's so smart.

In effect, Greenfield was an honorary member of the group. And his memories of the time were as extraordinary as anyone's. Remember the Stones' trip to Alabama in 1969? Three years later, things weren't that different but were maybe just starting to change.

ROBERT GREENFIELD: We got to Mobile, Alabama—my distinct memory was that there were these little shacks all around the gig in which black people lived, where old black men were rocking back and forth on the porches. There were thousands of white kids to see the Stones. I don't think there was a single black person in the audience. Stevie Wonder opened every night. Every night, a bunch of us would go up and watch Stevie. I saw all these white kids and I have to believe that was the start of cultural change in America. That once you love black music, you're going to have some problems thinking black people aren't as good as you are.

Across the country, the audience was changing before their eyes.

ROBERT GREENFIELD: The other amazing thing was being in Minneapolis, where everybody was white and blond and seeing seventeen-year-old guys in full makeup and drag. Mick knows all about Bowie, that's why he looks that way on the tour. He's wearing this beaded onesie that's cut down to his navel. He's wearing eye makeup; he's got a full-time makeup man on the tour. He's well aware of the transgender, cross-sexual vibe that's going on in England. It's not going on in America, that we know about, yet here are these kids who have already tuned into T. Rex and it's already starting. The '60s have ended and the weirdness of the '70s is beginning.

Another notable stop on the tour was the Playboy Mansion.

ROBERT GREENFIELD: In Chicago, the Playboy Mansion scene was insane. It was hot and cold running bunnies and playmates. The bunnies were keeping score, I later learned, keeping track of how many Stones they had slept with. One of my great memories was going into Keith's bedroom there—he had been out that day buying guitars at pawnshops—and I swear to you a playmate I recognized came in while he was talking to me about the guitar, and Keith said something to her like, "That's alright darling. I'll fuck you later." She said, "OK," and she walked out.

The other great moment: there was a grand piano in the living room and Stevie sat down to play, and I was leaning on the piano. And he's singing this show tune I'd never heard before. It was stunning.

The tour was marked by a large number of outsiders backstage, including a pimp/doctor, multiple writers, a filmmaker, Keith's pals, friends of Mick's from the jet set. It became a source of tension.

KEITH RICHARDS: Personally I just don't want to know about 'em. I mean, how they get in there and why they're there in the first place, I don't really know. It's a difficult thing to handle anyway, because it starts with things like, Oh, Truman Capote is going to come along and write something on the Stones and he comes along and brings along Princess Lee Radziwill and some other socialites from New York and you're surrounded by those people. I mean, all those jet setters must be loud or something. They seem to be on this massive ego trip anyway, which I just don't want to know about. All I can say is those people will not be around a second time. There's no way they're going to be in our company ever again.

MICK JAGGER: The whole business was very exaggerated. After all, there were only two people on the tour, and they were only there for a couple of days. I mean, REALLY.

By the tour's end, the Stones were at another level in multiple senses of the word. The tour culminated on July 26, 1972, Mick's twenty-ninth birthday, with one of the band's greatest ever performances (the Birthday Show), followed by a celebration of the Stones courtesy of Ahmet Ertegun.

ROBERT GREENFIELD: The other iconic moment would have been the party on the roof of the St. Regis hotel where Ahmet Ertegun introduced the Stones to another level of social life in America. The entertainment was Muddy Waters and Count Basie . . . What you saw on the '72 tour was a weird mixture. The counterculture is still dying, but by the time they get to New York and they go to that party on the St. Regis roof, they are now enshrined as full-on superstar show business celebrities who play rock 'n' roll, which is no longer an outlaw form of music, but by the end of the Stones' '72 tour is now hip for the wealthy and the famous and the powerful.

The St. Regis roof party was the talk of the town, described by Bob Dylan as "encompassing. It's the beginning of cosmic consciousness. A Felliniesque finale to the Stones tour."

ROBERT GREENFIELD: That party makes Truman Capote's Black and White Ball look like small potatoes. That is the ultimate New York party.

The party was arranged by Ahmet Ertegun, the founder and president of Atlantic Records.

PETER RUDGE: It was a match made in heaven, the Stones and Ahmet, the son of an ambassador and aristocrat, a culturally sophisticated man with an unbelievable love of blues and jazz. Those characteristics were manifested individually in Mick and Keith. He was kind of that person who could sit with Keith for hours talking about music, could sit for hours with Mick talking about music. It was a magical run, the Rolling Stones and Atlantic Records. It's where the Stones wanted to be because they loved the soul and DNA of the label. They were with someone that could help build their social profile, to introduce Mick to a world he was fascinated with socially. And Ahmet knew how to play Charlie with all the jazz stuff. He knew how to play Bill Wyman with all of the football stuff. He was masterful.

He had a tremendous effect on the Stones—musically and individually. He genuinely loved being with them . . . It was fun . . . It was a team and Ahmet was very much a part of that team, and Ahmet respected the Stones agenda.

When they signed to Atlantic Records, they went to finishing school almost. They graduated. By the time they came out of Atlantic Records, they were institutionalized. They lost the street edge. Ahmet was a tremendous influence in the Stones' life.

ROBERT GREENFIELD: The heavy hitter on the tour was Ahmet. When Ahmet showed up at a gig, everybody stood at attention. He must have spent as much money on them in New York as they made at the Garden that night. Ahmet and Mick socially were parallel figures. Even Mick knew he was with someone of equal weight.

Greenfield was impressed with the Stones' work ethic. They were always trying to get better.

ROBERT GREENFIELD: Bill Graham said, "If they weren't great, nobody would want to buy tickets to come and see them." They always left it all on stage. I saw Keith furious angry screaming at Charlie at shows in England because he wasn't on the beat. That's somebody who gives a shit. I saw them after shows—they would record everything on little recorders—sort of disconsolate. Jagger sitting in a hotel room with his head in his hands, "Fuck, we were shit! So fucking bad." They always wanted to walk out and do great shows.

And usually, they did. It's interesting to note that Greenfield hasn't seen the Stones since.

ROBERT GREENFIELD: Once you're off the bus, you can't get back on.

CHAPTER 30

ON WITH THE SHOW

ONE OF THE Stones' most memorable run-ins with the law happened on the '72 tour.

ROBERT GREENFIELD: Boston is under siege. It has undergone three days of race riots and the entire police department is deployed in the ghetto.

STEVE NAZRO: My boss, Eddie Powers, who was president of the Garden, wanted to see me in the office. He said, "The Stones, because of the fog, could not land in Boston, and they were diverted to Green Airport in Rhode Island."

ROBERT GREENFIELD: The photographer for the local rag is there taking pictures. Mick and Keith are standing there waiting for their bags. The photographer's too close, snapping photos. Keith said, "Get the fuck out of here, man." For whatever reason Keith doesn't take kindly to the photographer's response and he smashes the camera. The photographer called the police, and they come and they put the grip on Keith. Now Mick, he's not going to let Keith get arrested without him getting arrested. So Mick makes enough trouble that they have to arrest him too.

PETER RUDGE: One minute I'm going through the Yellow Pages of the Rhode Island airport trying to look for a bail bondsman to get us out of there, then the next I remember the mayor calling me saying, "Peter, I have a city on fire. The Stones have got to get here or there's going to be a full-scale riot." I said, "Do what you can to help us. We can't get Keith out. We can't move. We're trapped here."

ROBERT GREENFIELD: Mick and Keith are fucking delighted because they have immunity. They know that they're supposed to be in Boston Garden starting a show at eight o'clock at night and everything these cops do to fuck this up is going to come back to them. Now we get the Stones' lawyers. One thing about the Stones, they are lawyered-up with guys that are so powerful they only have to make two phone calls. Peter Rudge is having a mental breakdown.

DON LAW: At that point, I got a call from Peter Rudge, who said, "We really screwed up this time. Keith kicked a photographer. The police hauled him off to jail." I said, "You should sit tight. We're going to see if we can get you out of there because we're not going to give up the show." So we got on the phone and we started calling people.

MIKE MARTINEK: I was standing fairly close up to the stage. It was stiflingly hot and very humid. The smell of sweat, sandalwood, and marijuana just permeated the place.

STEVE NAZRO: Stevie Wonder had already played. There was a break and people hadn't been notified yet. They asked Stevie Wonder to play again, and he did.

ROBERT GREENFIELD: We now have eighteen thousand stoned, angry, long-haired white kids, who can't get home because all public transportation has already shut down for the night. And some of them would probably like to break a few windows and set fire to a few buildings in downtown Boston . . .

DON LAW: One of the people we called was Kevin White, who then was able to call the governor of Rhode Island, who reached back to the police station and said, "We have a public safety issue. You have to release these guys." And that got them out and they sent them up with an escort to the Garden.

ROBERT GREENFIELD: Kevin White, in what I still believe to be an extraordinary act of personal courage, walked out on stage. The initial crowd reaction was, "Fuck you!"

DON LAW: Kevin White, who still had serious national political aspirations, came out said, "My city is in turmoil tonight and I need to pull the police out of here. But I have bad news: the Rolling Stones were fogged out of Boston, had to land in Rhode Island, and were arrested." The whole place boos. Then Kevin White said, "But I called and we've gotten them out and they are on their way." There was so much cheering it was like the Bruins won the Stanley Cup. The problem of course was we then had a couple hours to waste while they made the trip up.

ROBERT GREENFIELD: The Stones are famous for being late; they never go on stage on time. Everybody knows this. For a while Chip Monck is stalling, reading *Jonathan Livingston Seagull* to the crowd.

DON LAW: We wound up getting things to throw around: Frisbees, footballs, beach balls. Nobody got thrown out.

PETER RUDGE: We got into the old Boston Garden and they announced, "The Stones are here." Everybody just went crazy. It was just something amazing.

STEVE NAZRO: I was most impressed by the fact that we had no arrests. Everybody had paid to see the Rolling Stones and by God they were going to see the Rolling Stones. It took close to an act of God, but things worked out. Watching the show, you'd never know there was something wrong. They were magnificent; they were energetic; they played to the crowd; they gave a wonderful repartee back and forth. I was never a big Stones fan before then but I became a Stones fan that night.

MIKE MARTINEK: They released an atomic bomb of a show. One of the highlights was an incandescent rendition of "All Down the Line." To bring the whole thing full circle, many years later I was at the Museum of Fine Arts in Boston and I happened to notice . . . Kevin White. I said, "Mr. Mayor, you don't know me, but years ago I was at the Rolling Stones show when you got them out of jail. You made that show happen."

DON LAW: Kevin White was in his glory and I remember the next night, the Stones sent Kevin a personally signed poster, which he prized and had prominently displayed.

The Stones in all their glory on the 1972 tour

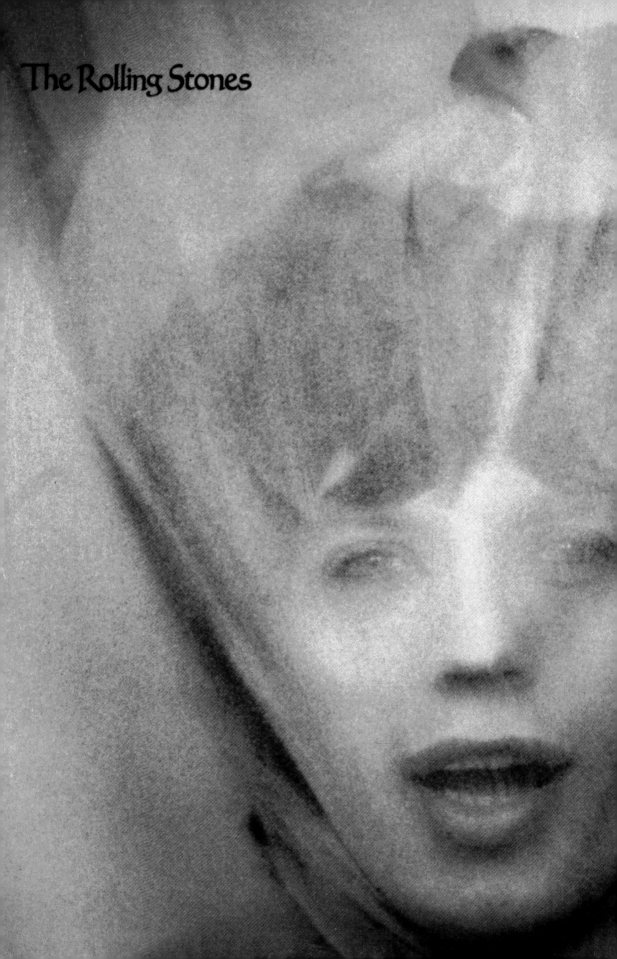
The Rolling Stones

CHAPTER 31

DANCING WITH MR. D

THE STONES' NEXT album, *Goats Head Soup*, was principally recorded in Jamaica and while it represents a step back artistically, it was a huge commercial success. An amusing quote from Mick at the time of the album's release suggests the Stones were maybe just a little complacent and bored.

MICK JAGGER: It was recorded all over the place, over about two or three months. I think you'll like the album. The tracks are much more varied than the last one, and all that crap.

ANDY JOHNS: Because of drug habits, those sessions weren't quite as much fun. And there are a couple of examples on there where just the basic tracks we kept weren't really up to standard. People were accepting things perhaps that weren't up to standard because they were a little higher than normal. But there still are some fantastic things on there.

Another issue was the continuing deterioration of Jimmy Miller.

ANDY JOHNS: He was somewhat of a frail individual and they got to him like they got to everybody. Sooner or later you lose your mind. Jimmy was mad keen and sort of halfway in control of *Sticky Fingers* but his grip was slipping a bit. On *Exile* they sort of stopped listening to him and by the time we got to *Goats Head Soup* it was like he wasn't there. That was a very tough record to make.

You know, Mick and Keith back then could be pretty fuckin' ruthless. It's a defense mechanism because people forget how big a deal they were. So everybody and their uncle is trying to grab the hem of their coat. They always want something, you know. "Listen to this song. You should really do this song. I've got this great idea for a hotel. Give me the money." Constantly. And the dope dealers and the groupies. So I guess that hardens you to a certain extent. I know it has to me a little bit.

KEITH RICHARDS: Jimmy Miller went in a lion and came out a lamb. We wore him out completely . . . Jimmy was great, but the more successful he became the more he got like Brian . . . He ended up carving swastikas into the wooden console at Island Studios. It took him three months to carve a swastika. Meanwhile, Mick and I finished up *Goats Head Soup*.

Miller was not invited for the recording sessions in Germany for *It's Only Rock 'n' Roll* (subsequently Mick and Keith assumed production credit under the name the Glimmer Twins).

ROBERT GREENFIELD: Although Jimmy Miller certainly deserves to be remembered as one of the greatest rock producers who ever lived, virtually no one who listens to his music now on various greatest hits compilations has any idea who he was. Nameless and faceless, he has become just another name on the back of a repackaged CD case. Perhaps that is the way he would have wanted it. To be remembered for the music and nothing else.

CHAPTER 32

ANGIE

THE STONES' SEVENTH trip to the top of the charts came on October 20, 1973. Of the eight singles that rose to that pinnacle, only one other could even remotely be considered a ballad—"Ruby Tuesday"—and that was only because of the uproar caused by the original A side—"Let's Spend the Night Together" (see chapter 14). "Angie," however, was a hard-core power ballad. Recorded for the *Goats Head Soup* album, it was released as a single on August 20, over a week before the official album release, and once again started tongues wagging (no pun intended). But first, let's take a look at the nuts-and-bolts process of the writing and recording.

KEITH RICHARDS: Sometimes you have a hook, a phrase or a word or a name or something which maybe you don't even intend to keep. A classic example is "Angie," it was just a working title, like who's gonna call a song "Angie," how boring another chick's name you know? But when you come around to actually writing the song and you sing "Angie, Angie," eventually you have to live with it and say, "This song's 'Angie.'" Whether you intended it to be or not, that's what it is. Sometimes you cannot get out of it, it's meant to be there and you have to accept it. Other times, maybe the way somebody's playing something will suggest a word or a phrase that nobody's thought of before. Songs just come about in so many different ways.

So *that's* how "Angie" got her name. Then what about all the wild speculation concerning who or what the *real* Angie was? Here are just a few of the names that have been floated over the years: Marianne Faithfull, Anita Pallenberg, Mick Taylor, Angie Bowie, Angie Dickinson, Dandelion Angela Richards.

MARSHALL CHESS QUITS IN 1977

MARSHALL CHESS: At the end of my time with the Stones I had major problems with various addictions. At the end of *Black and Blue* I decided to quit. I woke up in a five-star hotel in Montreux and I felt like shit. I walked into the bathroom, looked in the mirror, and I could see the shape I was in—black circles around my eyes, painfully thin, horrible to look at. That night I told Mick I wanted out. It was like telling a girlfriend I'd been dating for eight years that I was leaving because it wasn't working anymore. If I hadn't got out I wouldn't have survived. Quite simply, I'd have died. After I left the Stones it was a tough job coping with the change. My phone calls dropped from seventy a day to two a day. I had a million friends who loved me because I was a part of the Stones. Soon as I left, they didn't want to know. I had to get used to some kind of normality.

And how long did it take him to get clean?

MARSHALL CHESS: It took me years to get straight, properly straight. You stop taking drugs but it takes forever for your brain to start working normally again. I still smoke marijuana but I think of that as like having a beer. I haven't touched anything harder since 1978. It's really difficult to come off all that stuff. It's like climbing Everest. When you get to the top you get a tremendous sense of well-being.

Jagger has stated definitively that the song isn't about Angela Bowie, pointing out that they hadn't met when it was recorded. He has speculated in some places that the song is named after Keith's daughter. Keith solves the mystery—sort of. He was in Switzerland receiving treatment for heroin addiction.

KEITH RICHARDS: When I was in the clinic, Anita was down the road having our daughter, Angela. Once I came out of the usual trauma, I had a guitar with me and I wrote "Angie" in an afternoon, sitting in bed, because I could finally move my fingers and put them in the right place again, and I didn't feel like I had to shit the bed or climb the walls or feel manic anymore. I just went Angie, Angie. It was not about any particular person; I didn't know Angela was going to be called Angela when I wrote "Angie." In those days, you didn't know what sex the thing was going to be until it popped out. In fact, Anita named her Dandelion. She was only given the added name Angela because she was born in a Catholic hospital where they insisted a "proper" name be added.

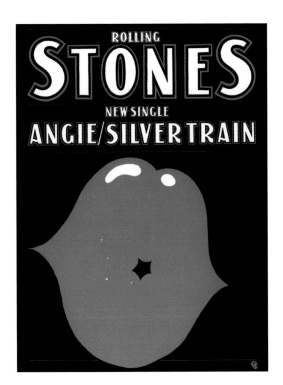

What can you make out of all this? It's up to all of us, really. Once a work of art is thrown out into the world, it no longer belongs to the artist. It doesn't matter what Robert Frost meant by "The Road Not Taken." What matters is what YOU think it means. The same goes for "Angie." Personally, I like this post on the Internet from Angie in Schnecksville, Pennsylvania, who wrote on a thread about "Angie": "I think the song is about me!"

One final postscript: "Angie" is the biggest-selling single in the whole Rolling Stones catalog. Keith's perceptive observation?

KEITH RICHARDS: When you get the middle of the road market, sales are amazing!

KEITH GETS A BLOOD CHANGE...OR DOES HE?

One of the most famous Stones' urban legends is that when Keith went to rehab in Switzerland in 1973, he had all his blood transfused as a way of beating his addiction. Keith himself was the source of the rumor as he claims he told a journalist he was having his blood changed to mess with him. In Tony Sanchez's highly unreliable account of being Keith's bodyguard, he does add some rich detail to the story, which has no doubt helped to propagate it, but according to both Keith and medical sources, the rumor is false. You can't cure addiction by merely detoxifying the blood. The problem—as Keith has proved over and over again—is staying clean afterward.

CHAPTER 33

TIME WAITS FOR NO ONE

THE TIME BETWEEN the recording and release of *It's Only Rock 'n' Roll* in 1974 and the recording and release of *Black and Blue* in 1976 marked another critical and volatile juncture for the Rolling Stones, and much of the turmoil revolved around the newest Stone—Mick Taylor. Mick's arrival in 1969 reenergized the group and put them back out on the road. The first three albums he contributed to—*Let It Bleed*, *Sticky Fingers*, and *Exile on Main St.*—are regarded as a trilogy of the group's finest work.

So why did this partnership last only a little over five years? Multiple reasons, of course. Some combination of drugs, interpersonal jealousies, recording studio squabbles, and, most important of all, an unhappy lead guitarist.

Taylor recalled the period in a 2010 interview with Gibson Guitars:

MICK TAYLOR: Most of 1974, I took a long holiday in Brazil, which was wonderful, and then I came back and we started doing recording on *It's Only Rock 'n' Roll* fairly quickly. The very track we recorded, that I remember anyway, at Musicland Studios in Munich was "Time Waits for No One." And it was done very quickly, so that was a song where most of the song must have been written before we even got into the studio, by Mick. 'Cause although it always says "Jagger/Richards," that doesn't necessarily mean that they both always write the songs. You know, there are some songs, maybe, that Keith had written on his own, like "Happy," but by and large most of the songs, especially when it comes to lyrics, are written by Mick.

That's a much gentler and more diplomatic recollection than the one he gave to Gary James in 1974:

Time waited for Mick Jagger, but not Mick Taylor, who officially left the band in December of 1974

MICK TAYLOR: I was a bit peeved about not getting credit for a couple of songs, but that wasn't the whole reason [I left the band], I guess I just felt like I had enough. I decided to leave and start a group with Jack Bruce.

Then even more telling:

MICK TAYLOR: I never really felt, and I don't know why, but I never felt I was gonna stay with the Stones forever, even right from the beginning.

And in an interview with *Mojo* magazine in 1997:

MICK TAYLOR: We used to fight and argue all the time. And one of the things I got angry about was that Mick had promised to give me some credit for some of the songs—and he didn't. I believed I'd contributed enough. Let's put it this way—without my contribution those songs would not have existed.

An eyewitness backs up this assertion:

ANDY JOHNS: Mick Taylor became discontent with his situation. On the 1973 tour of Europe I spent quite a lot of time with him and he would say, "They won't let me write any songs. Any time I have an idea I'm blocked out."

Mick made a fateful, tactical mistake when he neglected to inform the Stones of his thinking until December of 1974. The group was due to start recording a new album and was in the planning stages of another US tour when Taylor announced his decision. Our best storyteller about these events is the man who had the most to gain from Mick's departure:

RON WOOD: I remember the night. There was a party going on for Eric Clapton and unknowing to me, I was in the backseat with Mick. And Marshall Chess and Mick Taylor were in the front seat, whispering and very heavy and all this. I wondered what was going on. And apparently that night he told them he was leaving and I knew nothing about it. The Stones didn't want to break up the Faces. They didn't want to say, "Hey Woody, leave that lot, come with us," which was very nice of them really, because they could have been cutthroat about it.

Even when we arrived at the party I had no idea what was going on. And later on in the evening, Mick Taylor split. And I asked Mick, "Where's he going?" And he said, "I don't know." And I thought, "That's very unusual. He's only been here an hour. The whole party's just about to happen." So I just ruled it out that he wasn't feeling well or something. Mick was giving me these kind of tester questions, saying if it was possible that you could join, would you? And I said, sure, yeah. I definitely would but I still got the thing going with the Faces and Rod, blah blah blah. I don't want to mess that up because they're too good friends of mine. So Mick said, "What do I do?" I said, "If you really get desperate and you need me, find me wherever I am in the world and tell me you want me to do it and I'll do it."

The official news came out in two bland "Put on a Happy Face" press releases on December 12 and December 16: "Mick Jagger in Munich, where the Rolling Stones are engaged in the initial stages of recording their next album, confirmed that guitarist Mick Taylor would be leaving the group.

"He said, 'After five and a half years Mick wishes a change of scene—wants the opportunity to try out new ventures, new endeavors. While we are all most sorry that he is going, we wish him great success and much happiness.'

"Asked about the possible replacement Mick Jagger smiled: 'No doubt we can find a brilliant six foot, three inch blond guitarist who can do his own makeup.'"

Then four days later from Mick Taylor: "The last five and a half years with the Stones have been very exciting, and proved to be most inspiring. And as far as my attitude to the other four members is concerned, it is one of respect for them, both as musicians and as people. I have nothing but admiration for the group, but I feel now is the time to move on and do something new."

Then, just five days after that, Mick Jagger asserted:

MICK JAGGER: I suppose it was a bit inconsiderate of him to inform us a day before we were about to enter the studios . . . but maybe he hadn't made up his mind until that point . . . I received a call from the office that Mick Taylor wasn't coming to the Munich sessions. Then I received a call saying Mick Taylor wasn't going anywhere anymore with the Stones.

My favorite version of Mick leaving is the one given to me by Bill Wyman:

BILL WYMAN: I think he was resentful about not being able to contribute songs, or getting credits on things that he thought he had contributed to. He was trying to assert his strength a bit more than it really was. He was a new member and therefore obliged to accept things in a certain way because they had been like that for ten years. And I think he was being pushed by some people to be a stronger member of the band, rather than laid back like Charlie and I are. It was like a poker game, where you only have a pair, and you bluffed. And the bluff was called, and that was the end of it, because once someone says, "I'm leaving," you don't reinstate them again when *they* feel like it. It was a very inconvenient time he did it, and I didn't think he did it very politely.

The timing was definitely an issue for him.

BILL WYMAN: It was the day before we went in to cut an album, yeah. We finished up that album [*Black and Blue*] using all kinds of people that just dropped by; it was very inconvenient for us. We all really liked him a lot, but he did tend to get very, very moody and frustrated. It's the frustration that he didn't deal with outside the band, you see. Like I was saying before, I had many frustrations, but I dealt with them by doing other things outside the band. You have to do that. He didn't, and in the end he had to leave to do some of the things he wanted to do . . . which he could have done within the band, with no effort at all. And it shows, because it took him three, four years to cut an album, which was the first thing he was gonna do as soon as he left the band. And then it wasn't a success, so I'm sure he wished he hadn't left, I dunno . . . Maybe. It was a great period in our history because he brought something fresh and new—some brilliant playing—to the band.

As Kenny Rogers put it: "You gotta know when to hold 'em, know when to fold 'em . . ."

CHAPTER 34
IT'S ONLY ROCK 'N' ROLL

IN A SENSE, the *Black and Blue* sessions became the Great Rolling Stones Lead Guitar Search. Just think if Simon Cowell had been making shows in 1975 . . .

To no one's surprise, Ron Wood was high on the list.

Ron Wood (right) left Rod Stewart and the Faces to become a Rolling Stone in 1975

KEITH RICHARDS: *Black and Blue* was auditions for guitar players. That's why you've got three or four tracks with Wayne Perkins and two or three tracks with Harvey Mandel. And at the end, it was one of those weird coincidences that seem to happen with us all the time, that just as we were desperately looking for another guitar player, an English player, because that's what we are—Wayne Perkins is a lovely guitar player, but we're an English rock 'n' roll band and we just had to own up that there's something about having an American guy, that we're just not common in our upbringing and our culture that would eventually widen. And Woody came in and the Faces just happened to break up at that very moment.

RON WOOD: At the time they were also recording *Black and Blue* with Harvey Mandel and Wayne Perkins, and Jeff Beck had come and gone, and Eric Clapton had been approached. All kinds of things were going on. I still get ribbed by Eric Clapton. He says to me, "I could have had that job, you know." I say, "Ah no, sorry Eric, you haven't got the personality." I just rib him about it. Basically, the Stones wanted to remain an English rock 'n' roll band. Eric was already successful in his own right. All the other lovely English guitarists like Jimmy Page, they were doing their own things. When I finally did join, they all expressed that they were really rooting for me and they said that they were really pleased that I did it.

So when did it all happen?

RON WOOD: I had said to Mick, "Only ring me if you get desperate." They'd been trying all these guitarists, Stevie Marriott, all the ones I said—even more . . . When I was ill after one of the Faces tours, I was bedridden in LA. I was really feeling down. The phone rings and it's Mick. And he says, "Woody, remember what you said about getting desperate?" And I said, "Well, I see. I'm going back to England when I get better so I'll call by and see you in Munich." And he says, "OK then," and then I went there and I cut "Hey Negrita" and a couple of other tracks for *Black and Blue*. And they checked me into the hotel in Munich sandwiched between Harvey Mandel on the left and Wayne Perkins on the right. So it was like a whole string of guitarists. I walked in the studio and Charlie says to me, "Christ, out of all these guitarists who've walked in here, Woody walks in he starts bossing everybody around, we'll do this that and the other." It was no surprise to him that I did get the job just because I was a man after their own heart. Another silly Englishman.

There was still one last obstacle to hurdle before total commitment to the Stones became possible.

RON WOOD: At the time, Rod still hadn't folded up the Faces. So I still didn't say that I was joining. I said, "I'll do your '75 American tour, I'd love to, but before that I have to do a Faces tour and straight after it, I've got to do another one." So that year I played like three horrendously big tours. I said to Peter Rudge, "If you don't get me in the *Guinness Book of World Records* for the most overlooked person who has played in front of more people than anyone in one year . . ."

The definitive word about the transition from Mick to Woody came from Keith, in a 1977 interview with my longtime colleague and friend Dave Herman. Of course it does.

KEITH RICHARDS: I'll tell you the difference between playing with them two. The roles were much more fixed. With Mick, either I was going to play lead on one number and that was accepted as that, or Mick would which is what he was good at. And when somebody is as good as Mick Taylor, they tend to not realize how good they are and they tend to desperately want to get into other things, they want to sing, write songs, produce. Which is what Mick wanted to do, wants to do, and probably eventually will do. At the moment he hasn't done anything. Everything that he's done since, he still could have done and stayed with us. I'm sure it will eventually, in perspective, it will fall into place and probably a period to turn things over to do what he wants to do next.

While he was with the Stones, he very much got into playing drums, playing piano, playing bass. Almost like Brian did. Once they got to a point with an instrument, very much didn't even realize how good they were at what they were doing and rather would learn all those other things. Whereas with Ronnie there seems to be more of a knowledge of what we can do, what we're good at, and how we can play together. It's super-sympathetic, whereas with Mick it was sympathetic. It was quite a rigid role to play, much more so than with Ronnie where we can cross lead to rhythm backwards to forwards in a number.

ROBERT GREENFIELD: Mick Taylor was the sweetest guy who ever lived. Mick was a pure musician and such a pure soul, one of the great players of all time. Keith needs somebody like Ronnie Wood he can smack in the head and is a little scared of him. You can't say Mick Taylor didn't belong with the band, because his contribution to the band was immense, because he made them better. And he took them places they would never have gone. But they're not a solo lead-guitar band. That's the problem. It goes back to Keith and Brian: they play two guitars as one. You couldn't tell which was the lead and which was the rhythm. That's what Keith does as well as anyone except maybe Pete Townshend, he plays rhythm and he plays lead. It's crazy.

Just as they'd done in Hyde Park for Mick Taylor in 1969, the Stones needed another attention-grabbing way to introduce Ronnie and announce the Tour of the Americas (TOTA, for short) in 1975.

CHAPTER 35

ALL DOWN THE LINE

ALL I KNEW when I went to work on Thursday, May 1, 1975, was that sometime during the lunch hour of my ten A.M. to two P.M. radio show, I would be handing the baton to DJ Scott Muni for remote coverage of a press conference announcing the upcoming Tour of the Americas by the Rolling Stones. As always, rumors and anticipation of a forthcoming Stones sighting were generating a lot of buzz (was that term in use in 1975?) and rabid fan interest. A press event to address the facts about all of this was scheduled for noontime at the Fifth Avenue Hotel. At the appointed hour, I turned on the mic after playing "It's Only Rock 'n' Roll," and informed the audience that we would be switching over to our live, remote coverage of the event.

To my surprise, and I'm sure to the surprise of my listeners and most of the people in attendance at the actual press conference, noted comedian Professor Irwin Corey (who billed himself as "The World's Foremost Authority") strolled to the podium and proceeded to deliver one of his patented, incomprehensible monologues. His shtick was familiar enough to generate some laughs, but it did leave the roomful of hard-nosed journalists scratching their heads, wondering what the hell was going on. Until a voice from the back of the room announced that everyone there should spill out onto Fifth Avenue for a "surprise."

Scott Muni took to the air outside the hotel and sputtered (from an actual air check of the event):

SCOTT MUNI: Dave Herman is here . . . and here comes the truck now into view . . . and they're going to be . . . Yep, they are! There's Mick Jagger . . . and the Stones . . . They're all here! Now YOU hear the sound! Let's pick it up!

Photographer Bob Gruen ran alongside the flatbed truck on Fifth Avenue as the Stones played "Brown Sugar"

The music had already started in the background, but now it was coming through loud and clear. The Rolling Stones were playing live on a flatbed truck rolling slowly south on Fifth Avenue in New York City! They performed an elongated version of "Brown Sugar" with Billy Preston on electric piano and a new face (no pun intended) playing guitar. As the song ended, Muni returned to the air.

SCOTT MUNI: Alright, the truck is pulling away. And we're being crushed! Literally crushed! Mick Jagger has just thrown out the announcement of the tour . . .

DAVE HERMAN: The New York dates will be on . . . Five days in New York . . .

SCOTT MUNI: We're out on the street now, and it is raining, and has been . . .

DAVE HERMAN: [*incredulous*] The Rolling Stones playing on Fifth Avenue . . . on Fifth Avenue!

SCOTT MUNI: The Rolling Stones playing on Fifth Avenue . . . and did you notice who the new member was? I think that's most significant. Ron Wood was on guitar . . . Now let's go back to Pete in the studio.

I was flabbergasted. I'm sure people actually there couldn't believe their eyes, and I know people listening to the radio couldn't believe their ears—because I was one of them! They say radio is theater of the mind—what could be a better example? I could "see" and hear Mick Jagger and the Stones in my imagination, and it was all quite special and wonderful.

But here's another perspective from the eye of the hurricane:

BILL WYMAN: The truck, yeah (*laughs*). I don't know whose idea it was. Probably Mick's—he always comes up with these bad ideas that work. But it was quite fun to do. The sad thing was, when it came on TV they said we *obviously* weren't playing live— we were miming to a record. Now that was very annoying because we *were* playing live! It was raining and we were taking the risk of being electrocuted to death!

After all was said and done, Mick gave full credit for the stunt to Charlie Watts.

Promotional display for *It's Only Rock 'n' Roll*

MICK JAGGER: I think it was actually Charlie's idea. Jazz in the old days in Harlem . . . they used to do promotions for their gigs on flatbed trucks.

PERSONAL ESSAY: ROCK 'N' ROLL HIGH SCHOOL

While I was on the radio on May 1, 1975, my coauthor Bernie Corbett was stuck at Stoneham Junior High School outside Boston. Here's his story from that day:

A life worth living has a soundtrack. And from the moment I opened my ears, the Rolling Stones have provided the background to my mortal journey. Nineteen seventy-five was to be my year to roll with the Stones in concert. The rumor mill was rife with Stones tour speculation. And then, it happened. The same day the Stones took their trip on a flatbed truck down Fifth Avenue in New York, an article appeared in the *Boston Globe*.

I grabbed the paper and learned the Stones would be at the Garden on June 11 and 12. The last line of the story proclaimed, "Tickets go on sale today." That line encored in my head: TODAY!?!? There was no way I could get tickets. All was lost. I ran to the pay phone and I called my father's law office. My late father, God bless him, sensed the extreme urgency of the situation. I nervously repeated the Ticketron on-sale locations. Soon after, he immediately dropped the Foley divorce or whatever mundane case he was supposed to be working on and proceeded to address *my* case. Off he went to a couple of Sears stores. No luck. I got the news that evening. My teenage life was ruined.

Later that evening, he vowed he would find tickets. A friend at a local ad agency owed him a favor. Weeks passed with no resolution. And then one day after school, while I was occupying the third base coach's box during a Stoneham-Melrose freshman baseball game, I heard a voice. I looked over my shoulder and saw my dad. "We got two for the Stones!" By the end of the inning, my score—not the game score—was the talk of the dugout.

On June 11 my father and I witnessed the spectacle of the Greatest Rock 'n' Roll Band in the World in all their glory from Loge 11, up close and personal. I can still close my eyes and hear the strains of Aaron Copland's "Fanfare for the Common Man" giving way to the signature opening chords of "Honky Tonk Women." At the end of the two-and-a-half-hour performance, I was exhilarated. In my state of rock 'n' roll ecstasy I turned to my father and asked him what he thought. "It was underpriced," he observed, clearly pleased. It would not be the last time we got to experience the pure adrenaline of the Stones in concert together.

To my father, attorney Mitchell B. Corbett, may you rest in peace. You delivered and shared the greatest night of your eldest son's young life.

CHAPTER 36

AROUND AND AROUND

Most of the Stones' *Love You Live* album was recorded during the 1975 Tour of the Americas and the 1976 tour of Europe. But what really makes the record interesting is the side recorded at a small club in Toronto, the El Mocambo.

BILL WYMAN: We wanted to do some live music of a really different nature, in a club where we could get a really good atmosphere and a bit of audience reaction, just basic blues stuff like we did in the early days, on our live album.

How would it be to play a club after fifteen years away?

KEITH RICHARDS: That was what we were all wondering before we went on, "Gosh it's been so long since we did this." And the amazing thing was that two bars into the first number it just felt so natural, as if those years in between didn't exist. It didn't make any difference anymore. We could have been playing at the Crawdads next weekend. It just felt so natural that it just reinforced my belief that every band has got to make some sort of effort to break out of the circuit that we're all put on and we just sort of accept. For instance, I hate to say it, an American tour. If they tell us that the Stones are doing an American tour, we can probably name you 97 percent of the cities that we're going to hit. There just seems to be this circuit build up that gets more and more entrenched every time. There are theaters and auditoriums all over the place. They don't hold fifteen thousand, twenty thousand people but I don't see why you can't do them both.

Yet it's very different playing small venues, as the Stones well knew.

BILL WYMAN: First of all, you know that three-quarters of the kids are using binoculars in a big stadium, and you're just dots on the horizon. So you have to wear clothes not because they look good but because they stand out—a *brilliant* red jacket—so they can make out you're not an amplifier or something. When you're in a club it's smoky, and it's intense, and very personal. Like, in the El Mocambo, the girls were grabbing our legs and crotches, while we're playing, which adds a little bit to the show from our side (*chuckles*).

This was among the challenges of being superstars—the more success the Stones had, the more pressure there was to focus on the business rather than the music.

KEITH RICHARDS: I think it's true, there is that conflict. Individually it depends upon the band and its members. But for instance, the business side of it is how come the Stones aren't living in England together, which would be so much easier for us to organize things and get things together instead of everybody being three thousand miles apart. Half the time, Mick's in New York and I'm in Switzerland. Or I'm here and he's in New York and Bill's in France. That's the business side of it and that's the effect it has and it slows us down so much and it just . . . To get everybody into one place to even decide what to do next is a major operation.

The Stones at MSG in June of 1975

Why had it been so long since the Stones played a club? The answer came down to dollars and sense.

CHARLIE WATTS: If you're going to spend a quarter of a million dollars to build a stage for Madison Square Garden, how can you do a club the next day? You've got to earn back that money to make the whole trip worthwhile. We spend a million dollars, or a million and a half dollars, to set up a tour before we even come here. Just to organize a tour, from there to there, people going around checking out ceilings, how much weight the roof will stand, before you even sell one ticket. You've got to think financially, unfortunately, you can't play little clubs.

BILL WYMAN: It was an idea we'd had for some years, but we found it very uneconomical. In the old days, when you traveled in a van and you lived in tiny hotels, two in a room, you could afford to do small clubs. But touring America and staying in suites at the Plaza, and having the best food and good wine and restaurants means your expenses can reach five hundred thousand dollars—and you lose one hundred thousand dollars or two hundred thousand dollars each. But it's the only place in the world where you can actually make some money from touring. Europe you can't. England you can't. Australia's really hard, and . . . we have to make some money, especially Charlie and me, because we don't write songs. So the only money we physically earn is from record royalties, which I can't complain about, but if you only do one record every two years, that cuts it down. It sounds very mercenary, but it's the facts of life.

Fortunately for the Stones, they did eventually find a way to break out of the stadium touring rut, but amazingly, it wouldn't happen for another quarter century! The Stones' visit to Toronto wasn't only known for those El Mocambo shows, it was also the site for one of the more infamous episodes in Rolling Stones history. And that's the story you'll read as soon as you turn the page.

CHAPTER 37

BEFORE THEY MAKE ME RUN

ONE OF THE most significant Rolling Stones arrests happened in Toronto on February 27, 1977. It must be acknowledged that this incident really did represent the possibility of the end of the Stones. Keith was found with twenty-two grams of heroin, a large enough amount that he was initially charged with "possession of heroin for the purpose of trafficking."

The tabloid story got kicked to another level when the Canadian prime minister's young wife, Margaret Trudeau, was seen both at a Stones show at the El Mocambo and also partying with the band after. The press assumed she was having an affair with Mick, though Ron Wood implies he was the man cuckolding the PM in his book. Of course, knowing the Stones, it could have been both.

EDDIE KRAMER: There was a lot of political bullshit going on—as you can imagine—with Margaret Trudeau and Mick Jagger. Whether or not that actually happened I don't know. Certainly she was there that night. She introduced herself to me in the club. "I'm Margaret Trudeau. Who are you?"

KEITH RICHARDS: Maybe it's not bad Margaret Trudeau was involved because it took it out to a completely different level. Instead of everything just being centered on me and the Stones, it involved the prime minister of the fucking country . . . (laughs). The things they were fishing for: Was Margaret Trudeau fed up? Was she going to leave her husband to run off with a rock 'n' roll band? That's what they were really trying to get around, but the way Pierre [Trudeau] handled it made more out of less, unfortunately. Obviously he didn't know what was going on, because if he did he would have tried to cool things out.

The threat of a seven-year prison term haunted Keith for more than a year. He was allowed to leave Canada to enter treatment at a clinic near Philadelphia, where he cleaned up—or at least tried to. According to his memoir *Life*, Keith was on heroin during the *Some Girls* sessions in France and even once shot up in the bathroom on a plane from New York to Toronto, with a Mountie's spurs clinking outside the door!

Keith was overwhelmed by the support he received from Stones fans throughout his troubles in Toronto.

Keith Richards
in Court / Oct 23

He was wearing a 3-piece tan colored suit, a dark brown tie with a white shirt. The court room was filled to capacity.

A court sketch from October 23, 1978, by Laurie McGaw that appeared in the *Toronto Star*

KEITH RICHARDS: I know lots and lots of people dig the Stones but frankly, I was knocked out by the personal care and attention that people were paying just to me. I'd just like them to know that everything's fine and don't expect any major fractures in the future. I think we can keep it all together. And I hope we can get round their way soon. I like to be able to play everywhere once a year if it's possible. Sometimes by the time we get back to America it's three years. But this year, once we do this album and that's in the can, then we're on the road.

After multiple delays, Keith's trial was finally heard on October 23, 1978. Keith pleaded guilty to possession but not guilty to trafficking. The judge found him guilty but said, "I will not incarcerate him for addiction and wealth."

Keith was sentenced to just one-year probation. There were two conditions. One was that Keith was ordered to continue treatment for heroin addiction (which he clearly needed to do anyway). The other (of course!) was that he must perform a benefit performance for the Canadian National Institute for the Blind.

KEITH RICHARDS: This was to do with a blind girl who had followed the Stones everywhere on the road. Rita, my blind angel. Despite her blindness, she hitchhiked to our shows. The chick was absolutely fearless, I'd heard about her backstage, and the idea of her thumbing in the darkness was too much for me. I hooked her up with the truck drivers, made sure she got a safe lift, and made sure she got fed. And when I was busted, she actually found her way to the judge's house and told him this story.

WE PISS ANYWHERE, MAN

Ironically, considering Keith's reputation as an outlaw, Bill Wyman was the first Stone to be arrested, in 1963.

BILL WYMAN: We were coming back from a gig and I wanted to have a wee-wee, so we stopped at a garage—and they refused to let me so I went back to the car and Mick said, "Come on, Bill, we'll find one" and Brian Jones as well. So the three of us went over there and they still wouldn't let us use it, so we just did it there and got arrested. And we had to pay about twenty pounds, which was about thirty dollars then. We got publicity for about a year on that one. It was then we realized what we had to do to get publicity, you see.

Keith was free. And he finally beat his heroin addiction not long after that. Mick Jagger offers his perspective on the idea that the Stones became identified with drug use in the '70s.

MICK JAGGER: Yeah, I think it's very bad. I don't remember ever proselytizing for it myself. But I think it became a tremendous bore to everyone in the Rolling Stones who ever got either arrested or involved with drugs. So it was tremendously regrettable—especially the damage it did by persuading people how glamorous it all was. You might get different answers from different people in the band, but if I remember right, it was not the intention of the Rolling Stones to become drug-user outlaws. It was a real drawback as far as creativity went. And it went on until 1977, with Keith's bust in Toronto. All those things affected the band and gave us this image of being like a real bunch of outlaw dope fiends—which was to a certain extent, I suppose, true. But it was also imposed, somewhat. Because I think the original intent was just to do what one did and not make an issue of it.

CHAPTER 38

SOME GIRLS

KEITH RICHARDS: First of all those mid-'70s LPs remind me of being a junkie (*laughs*). What happened was I'd been through the bust in Canada, which was a real watershed—or WaterGATE—for me. I'd gone to jail, been cleaned up, done my cure, and I'd wanted to come back and prove there was some difference . . . some . . . some reason for this kind of suffering. So *Some Girls* was the first record I'd been able to get back into and view from a totally different state than I'd been in for most of the '70s.

The Rolling Stones haven't lasted for fifty years by standing still or staying static. As the times have changed, the Stones have changed: from an R&B cover band to a rock 'n' roll powerhouse; from playing small clubs to playing huge stadiums, then back to playing small clubs; from the music world's most outrageous young punks to its esteemed elder statesmen.

This ability to adapt, reinvent, and transform was never more apparent than it was in 1978. First of all, there were a couple of lean years and misfires after *Exile on Main St. Goats Head Soup*, *It's Only Rock 'n' Roll*, and *Black and Blue* weren't bad albums—you could make a great compilation taking the best of those three—but none had the power of the Stones' best work.

Then too, the music business itself was in the midst of its greatest changes since . . . well, probably since the changes that the Beatles, Dylan, and the Stones themselves had wrought in the '60s.

Punk and new wave were beginning to rock rock 'n' roll. Disco was inexplicably (to me anyway) pushing rock music out of the spotlight. There were even rumblings of a new kind of laser technology that could eventually supplant vinyl and long-playing records as the main delivery system for music. Against this backdrop, the Stones came roaring back with *Some Girls*.

KEITH RICHARDS: I think a lot of [the reasons for the quality of *Some Girls*] was Chris Kimsey. We were at a point where we asked ourselves, "Are we just going to do another boring Stones-in-the-doldrums sort of album?"

Kimsey had worked with the Stones as far back as *Sticky Fingers*, and while his credit on *Some Girls* is as an engineer, it certainly sounds like he functioned as a producer as well.

CHRIS KIMSEY: If I had any plan at all regarding sound, it was simply to get more of a live sound. Before I began working with them, their last few albums like *Black and Blue* and *Goats Head Soup* had sounded too clean in places, almost clinical. When I first went to Paris to set up the room at Pathé Marconi, it was intended for rehearsals only. But the room had such a good sound even though the disc was only sixteen-track, they began to feel comfortable. It made for a more relaxed atmosphere which led to a certain spontaneity in the music.

We'll talk about the influence of disco in the next chapter but start with the influence of punk rock on *Some Girls*. While the Stones were clearly a major influence for many punk rock bands, their rock-god status by the late 1970s also made the Stones an object of derision for many in that crowd. But Keith saw the similarities more than the differences.

Homemade Rolling Stones cartoon by Justin Melkmann originally drawn in 1987

KEITH RICHARDS: There's always new bands. I've seen them come and go, most of them. And the same probably occurs to the bands who are around now. I don't know if they're trying a little too hard to make something new out of something that really isn't but there again, we didn't consider what we were doing particularly new when we did it. We were really rehashing old stuff. It's just that people had missed out on it the first time around. Maybe that's what it's all about and what the Sex Pistols and the Clash and the Stranglers, etc., are doing now in England is rehashing what we did for people who missed out on it then. I see a lot of similarities in terms of images, PR-wise, sound-wise, of what they're doing to what we did. Some of the press stuff, you could just delete "Rolling Stones" and put in "Sex Pistols."

Record store display for *Some Girls*

I was in England a year ago for a month or so when the whole hype thing started with punk rock. This was at the time the Sex Pistols appeared on TV and let a few Victorian curses go and everybody was shocked. That's England, you know. It was real adolescent stuff. But it was no worse than us when we appeared on *Juke Box Jury* for the first time and everybody thought we were absolute morons. It was same old thing. They sound more like we did fifteen years ago than we could possibly do. I couldn't re-create that sound now. Some of those records sound like they came out of the same studio as our first album.

RON WOOD: Those punk songs [on *Some Girls*] were our message to those boys. We never sat around talking about punk, but you couldn't avoid it.

Though the album was recorded in Paris, one of the biggest inspirations for Mick's lyrics was New York City, where he was living and beginning his two-decade relationship with Texas-born model Jerry Hall.

MICK JAGGER: Obviously it was all influenced by New York feeling. More obviously I'd say in "Shattered," when I was writing that I was thinking, "God, I'm really nowhere near there but I'm just reliving it all." I'd been living there for the two years previously on and off, and it was a big interesting time for the city: the place falling to bits, going broke and Son of Sam and all that. It loomed large as an object in your imagination.

ANTHONY DECURTIS: There was a sense in which the Stones became a New York band, and that's reflected on the record. There were New York references throughout *Some Girls*. In "Just My Imagination" where Jagger sings, "Of all the girls in New York, she loves me true." That's not in the Temptations' version of that song. Of course, "Shattered" and "Miss You": "Walk in Central Park/Singing after dark/People think I'm crazy." These references are so specific and so much a part of the texture of New York. They were alert to what was going on in New York. That sense of New York kind of falling apart had all of the social tensions that were developing there.

The Stones just sucked that up, man. They just really thrived on it. It's part of that energy they have . . . Part of a job of an artist is to channel the complicated energy of the times, and that's what the Rolling Stones do. That's what they do in *Some Girls*. That was an album that was a survival statement of a city in crisis. It's framed by two songs about New York: "Miss You" and "Shattered."

Keith suggested a final reason the album was special: the growing rapport between him and the Stones' new guitarist.

KEITH RICHARDS: And you gotta remember it was Ronnie's first full album, first real album with the Stones. *Some Girls* was kind of like *Beggars Banquet*. Like we'd been away for a bit, and we came back with a bang.

THE STONES' PROCESS

In this never-before-published interview from 1977, Keith talked with our friend Dave Herman about the beginning of the album that would become *Some Girls*.

KEITH RICHARDS: While we were working on the live album, we were together quite a lot and we wrote quite a fair number of songs, considering the amount of time; probably we've got another three, four each that we've worked on alone; and then there's other things that Woody and I have had riffs of, which I think we've deliberately not worked on too much. A lot of rock 'n' roll tracks, I'm always scared of overworking them before we get to the studio because a lot of a good rock 'n' roll tracks depend so much on spontaneity, enthusiasm, and not being too familiar with the thing. I'd rather just have a riff and as long as I know this one, basic, interesting riff to hang something on, I know that we can tot it up in the studio and still get something of that first-take feel about it as well.

By this time, Keith had earned a reputation as the Stones' music director.

KEITH RICHARDS: Let's put it this way, at the beginning when we're cutting tracks, you could say I'm the director as far as the actual studio is concerned, which leaves Mick a free hand to be in the control room with the engineer and/or producer if we happen to be using one, so that I don't have to think too much about what's going down on tape but I can just concentrate on what we're all playing, and leave the sound of the actual track up to Mick to a certain extent.

So it's kind of a split thing. I'm only director on one side of the glass. That piece of glass is a brick wall in a way. It's a very effective block to communication. The fact that you have to communicate just through microphones and headphones, you block a lot of contact with everybody when you're normally writing songs, eye contact and things like that, that you have when you know somebody well. That's all cut off.

So what does a Rolling Stones recording session feel like?

KEITH RICHARDS: Usually starts with no more than two or three of us. Very rarely will the whole band start off on a track at once. There will always be Charlie, there will always be some rhythm, drums. Maybe one of us on guitar, maybe Ronnie, sometimes Mick plays good rhythm guitar, sometimes me. And then maybe after a bit, Ronnie or Bill might join in on bass or another guitar and then slowly maybe Mick will start to find a top line, without lyrics but maybe just chanting, just sounds, phonetics. It helps a lot to have a lead vocal line to go with, so you know that everybody's following at least one thing. And also because that is going to be the top line when you eventually do the vocals. Usually we have a bit of shouting going and everybody gets into that. It slowly builds up. Some songs will start off with the weirdest lineups. Like "Happy" started with one guitar, baritone sax, and that was the beginning of that track. Bobby Keys was with us at that time and it just so happened that we were the first ones at the session and we started going and then drums came and slowly we started adding more. Generally, especially with fast tracks, rock 'n' roll tracks, quite often they'll start with two, three people at the most, to get into a groove, to get a thing going, and then I guess the criterion is if everybody else starts going and picking up on it and playing it, then you know you've got something going. And if they don't, eventually it just pieces out and you find something else and start again on another riff.

By the time *Some Girls* came around, Keith was no longer trying to write singles, and hadn't been for some time. As he reflected in that same 1977 interview:

KEITH RICHARDS: Not since 1966. Ever since albums have become bigger than singles, we haven't because the pressure isn't there to do it. You don't need singles now. Yeah, it's nice to have them but it isn't an absolute necessity. In the early and mid-'60s it was an absolute necessity to have a new number one hit song every three months and because it had to be there, you did it.

I think it would be a shame if that art was lost completely because one of the things that rock 'n' roll is suffering from is overindulgence. Musicians are bound to do it if given the situation. The great thing about the single was the limitations that it set. You've got to say it all in two minutes thirty seconds, three minutes at the most, and you know when you've done it right; and it was a little form in itself which has disappeared now because the necessity of it has disappeared. I think now if people still want singles and still go in to make a single as such, as opposed to just a track and choosing after, "Oh this one would make a good single," and just editing it down. But if you make a single, if that's becoming more of a trend then that's a good thing because limitation is what rock 'n' roll is all about. It's a very limited form of music and the great thing about it is how many variations you can get within those very strict confines. Although it's just a label, like anything else, rock 'n' roll these days can cover everything from the Sex Pistols to Weather Report. It's a universal term for popular music now.

Keith Richards

CHAPTER 39

MISS YOU

ONE OF THE highlights of *Some Girls* became yet another number one hit single (their eighth!). The beat drew from another musical influence: disco.

RON WOOD: Mick has a history of checking out what the kids are listening to, whether it was during the disco era or funk, or whatever. He always keeps one eye and one ear on what they're listening to and how we might be able to apply it to what we do and how we might put our stamp on it.

MICK JAGGER: We didn't intentionally set out to make a disco record. To me, it's just like . . . that bass drum beat and my falsettos just fit nicely around the bass part. Vocally, it's more gospel, because nowadays disco records are much more repetitive . . . "You know, I wanna dance and shake my booty," repeated eighty-nine times!

BILL WYMAN: The idea for those [bass] lines came from Billy Preston, actually. We'd cut a rough demo a year or so earlier after a recording session. I'd already gone home, and Billy picked up my old bass when they started running through that song. He started doing that bit because it seemed to be the style of his left hand. So when we finally came to do the tune, the boys said, "Why don't you work around Billy's idea?" So I listened to it once and heard that basic run and took it from there. It took some changing and polishing, but the basic idea was Billy's.

CHARLIE WATTS: A lot of those songs like "Miss You" on *Some Girls* . . . were heavily influenced by going to the discos. You can hear it in a lot of those four-on-the-

THIS SIDE

MISS YOU

PRODUCED BY THE GLIMMER TWINS

THE ROLLING STONES

 NEW SINGLE ON ROLLING STONES RECORDS

floor rhythms and the Philadelphia-style drumming. Mick and I used to go to discos a lot . . . It was a great period. I remember being in Munich and coming back from a club with Mick singing one of the Village People songs—"YMCA," I think it was—and Keith went mad, but it sounded great on the dance floor.

The song is also highlighted by the harmonica playing of Sugar Blue, who the Stones first heard when he was busking in Paris.

SUGAR BLUE: The Paris subway, the Metro, they're clean, they're large, they're well lit. It's a beautiful space to play. I had met some people from playing around. Quite a lot of people from the "upper crust" that would hang out with the Stones. And I met this cat who said, "Hey man, we really like the way you play. Why don't you come over and play with the Stones?" And that's the way it fell out.

"Miss You," the eighth and final (for now) Rolling Stones number one single danced its way to the top of the charts on August 5, 1978. While they haven't had a number one since then, you can never rule out a return to form for this band. As Elvis Presley has proved over and over since his death in 1977, gems from such a vast catalog can still make a run at the charts when reintroduced and promoted properly to a new generation of rock fans. Would you expect anything less from the Rolling Stones?

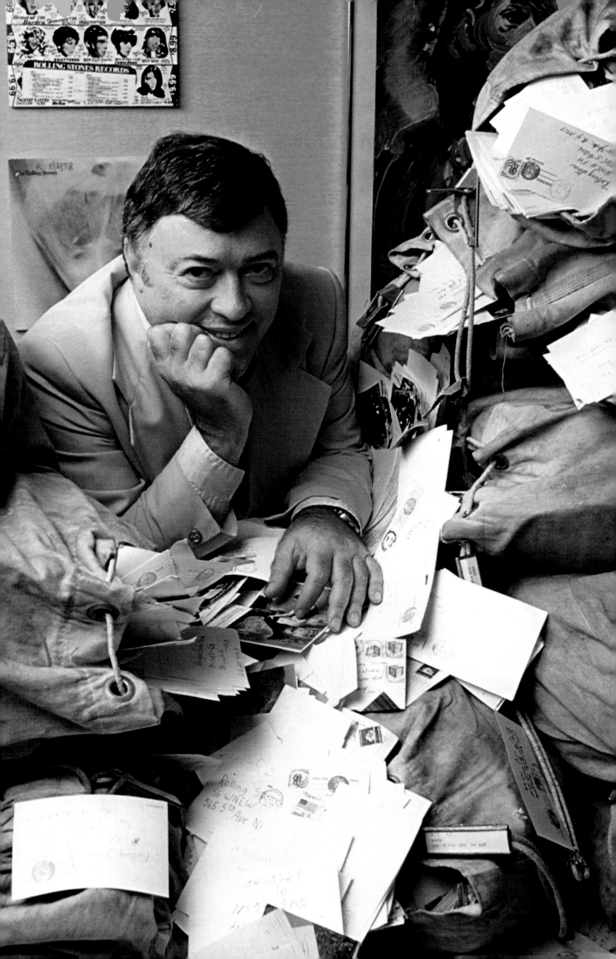

CHAPTER 40

SEND IT TO ME

Look at this picture. Take a good long look at it.

If it reminds you of the climactic scene in the 1947 Christmas movie classic *Miracle on 34th Street*, then we are on the same page. The United States Postal Service proves the existence of Santa Claus by delivering canvas bags full of mail to a man named Kris Kringle who is on trial at a courthouse in New York City for claiming to be the real, true, genuine, one and only Saint Nicholas himself!

Thirty-one years later, the Rolling Stones could have used the same defense in court to prove their continuing status as the Greatest Rock 'n' Roll Band in the World!

Excitement was at fever pitch when the group announced plans to tour the United States to support their very well-received June 1978 release *Some Girls*. It was the band's first time on the road here since their spectacular Tour of the Americas in 1975, on which they sold out Madison Square Garden six times (one hundred and fifty thousand–plus fans!). It was going to be a little bit different in 1978 and, dare I say, a lot more special and exclusive in the Big Apple.

At a time when ticket scalping for top-draw rock concerts had grown to epidemic proportions, a unique strategy was chosen for their one and only New York date at the thirty-three-hundred-seat Palladium Theater on Fourteenth Street between Irving Place and Third Avenue. Tickets were made available *only* by lottery through the most credible, influential FM progressive rock radio station in the country—WNEW-FM. Take a peek at those mailbags engulfing program director Scott Muni in his office. Over four hundred thousand postcards were received in three days for those thirty-three hundred seats!

Winners were selected at random and notified by telephone where to purchase their prized tickets. The ducats themselves were undated and details about the show were not revealed until the day before the actual concert.

The conclusions you could draw from all of this? Yes, Virginia, there IS a Santa Claus!

STONES CONTROVERSIES IN THE '70S

ANTHONY DECURTIS: I think the whole thing with the Stones and women—I find their depiction of the relationships between men and women realistic. It's not sentimental. That doesn't mean that they don't like women. It's about the kind of power plays that come into play in a relationship. It's not prudified. But it's not negative. It's just honest. It's not the usual view of love you get in pop music. It allows for the darker elements . . .

It seems like with every Stones album, there was another controversy. The feminist group WAVAW (Women Against Violence Against Women) was outraged over the promotional poster for *Black and Blue* (right). Keith and Mick's attitude was: "It's a joke, get over it."

For *Some Girls*, the main flap had to do with a throwaway lyric about black girls and what, to his mind, they wanted to do all night. Jesse Jackson got involved, protesting the song.

MICK JAGGER: I think [the races] are all well covered—everyone's represented (*laughs*). Most of the girls I've played the song to LIKE "Some Girls." They think it's funny; black girlfriends of mine just laughed. And I think it's very complimentary about Chinese girls, I think they come off better than English girls. I really like girls an awful lot, and I don't think I'd say anything really nasty about any of them . . . (*laughs*). The song's supposed to be funny.

As for his take on Jesse Jackson, here's a quote from 1985:

MICK JAGGER: I haven't seen him since. That's an example of an ad-lib getting you into a lot of trouble. No Italians complained. There's a line about French girls. I don't know if anyone was really upset apart from him.

On *Saturday Night Live*, Garrett Morris gave a mock editorial where after acting offended, he quoted the line and said, "I have one thing to say to you, Mr. Mick Jagger . . . Where are these women?!?"

Controversial promo poster for *Black and Blue* featuring Anita Russell

CHAPTER 41

HANG FIRE

NINETEEN EIGHTY-ONE was an interesting year for the Stones on a number of fronts: a new album; a new tour; a new technology; and a new single destined to take its place among the greatest and most memorable Stones songs of all time.

Let's tackle that last one first. "Start Me Up" was just another one of those instant Stones classics solidifying Keith Richards's nickname: "The Human Riff."

BILLY ALTMAN: On "Start Me Up," I think the Chuck Berry riffs that Keith had teethed on as a kid, they have just become a part of his DNA as well. It's all just a Chuck Berry riff turned a little bit sideways but now they don't sound like Keith doing a Chuck Berry riff, they just sound like Keith Richards. At that point, it had become his own.

Charlie Watts's work stands out as well.

BILLY ALTMAN: Charlie is just tremendous on "Start Me Up." He uses space so well, which is something you don't think of a rock drummer using much. They're always trying to fill space. But Charlie is one of these drummers who understands the room between on his drum kit, especially on the later albums. I think it goes back to his being a jazz drummer. If you listen to the end when the song slows down and then starts to wind back up again, he becomes almost the center of the song as they use him to build everything up throughout the choruses.

The funny thing is that "Start Me Up" is a song that had been lying around for a long while before it ever made it out into the world on the *Tattoo You* album. Keith explains:

This photo was taken in 1980. Ronnie, Mick, and Keith had an interesting year ahead of them in 1981

KEITH RICHARDS: That was in the can for ages, and mostly we'd forgotten about it. We had about thirty takes of it reggae and there was just one or two other takes where we did it with a backbeat, just straight rock 'n' roll. So to us it was that interminable reggae track we did way back then. And then—right at the end of the reel—was this rock 'n' roll version, you know.

While the song seemed like a sure thing to be the Stones' ninth number one single, it never quite made it. It was stalled at number two for a couple of weeks by the likes of (get this!) "Arthur's Theme (Best That You Can Do)" by Christopher Cross, "Private Eyes" by Daryl Hall and John Oates, and worst of all, "Physical" by Olivia Newton-John, which stayed at the top of the American charts for a "physically" sickening ten weeks! Though denied number one status during its initial run, "Start Me Up" has more than earned its weight in gold in a number of high-profile ways in the years since. It was the show opener at many future Stones concerts; Microsoft paid millions for it to use for their Windows 95 advertising campaign; it has become a staple at sporting events of every conceivable kind; and it was one of the three songs that the Stones performed at halftime during the 2006 Super Bowl (chapter 48).

And if all of this wasn't enough, "Start Me Up" served the very important purpose of introducing or reintroducing the Rolling Stones to generations of fans in America and globally as well. On August 1, 1981, MTV made its debut on cable television systems all across the United States. Stephen Davis explained the new wrinkle this way:

STEPHEN DAVIS: Traditionally musicians had always traveled to their audiences to sell their music. Now, with a video in heavy rotation to a select audience, a band could appear before several million fans several times per day. For rich bands like the Stones, video obviated the ancient need to keep moving or die. MTV also became a major launching pad for solo stars: Madonna, Bruce Springsteen, Prince, and—in epic fashion—Michael Jackson, whose *Thriller* album became the biggest seller in recording history on the strength of short- and long-form videos. Among the video audience, bands became almost passé. The video revolution's cameras loved a face more than a band, a fact not lost on ever-ambitious Mick Jagger . . .

Longtime collaborator Michael Lindsay-Hogg was given the assignment to shoot the video for "Start Me Up." He recalled:

MICHAEL LINDSAY-HOGG: In '81 we talk about doing "Start Me Up" and "Waiting on a Friend" and "Neighbors." This was the beginning of MTV. Mick and Charlie and I went out for lunch one day and Mick said, "Have you seen anything from MTV yet? Because that's the future." So we did "Start Me Up" very down and dirty. I've always thought with the Rolling Stones, to do their performance is a gift to the director—you don't want to get in their way too much.

Screen capture from 1981's ubiquitous *Start Me Up* video

In the early days of MTV, "Start Me Up" was one of the most programmed videos on the upstart channel. And, true to Stephen Davis's observation, the TV screen just loved Mick Jagger's face. Yes, the rest of the band was there, but when you look at that video over thirty years later, you can't help but notice that it's mostly Mick, Mick, and Mick! His well-toned body; his bare arms flailing about; his face; but, more than any of those features, it's his lips! As true as it was in the '60s when we first noticed them, it's those lips that hypnotize and mesmerize. Here's what noted author Tom Wolfe had to say about them back in the day:

TOM WOLFE: In the center of the stage a short thin boy with a sweatshirt on, the neck of the sweatshirt almost falling off his shoulders, they are so narrow, all surmounted by this enormous head . . . with the hair puffing down over the forehead and ears, this boy has exceptional lips. He has two peculiarly gross and extraordinary red lips. They hang off his face like giblets. Slowly his eyes pour over the flaming bud horde (see chapter 11!), soft as Karo syrup, and close, and then the lips start spreading into the most languid, most confidential, the wettest, most labial, most concupiscent grin imaginable. Nirvana! The buds start shrieking, pawing toward the stage.

Fueled by MTV, *Tattoo You* would go on to become the Stones' most successful selling album to date.

BILLY ALTMAN: *Tattoo You* as an album sounds a bit disjointed. A lot of the songs sound better out of context as opposed to sitting down and listening to the whole thing as an entire album. "Start Me Up," "Hang Fire," "Waiting on a Friend" are all really good songs that I think sounded better on the radio than they did on the album when listened to as a whole. I think that's probably a function of it getting recorded over an amount of time.

Tattoo You itself was a patchwork quilt of outtakes and leftovers from *Some Girls*, *Emotional Rescue*, *Black and Blue*, even as far back as *Goats Head Soup*. But an album was needed to tour behind, and this is the one that came off the Stones' assembly line. It put the group back on the radio and, even more important, back on the road to start the '80s.

CHAPTER 42

BLACK LIMOUSINE

Rɛʜᴇᴀʀsᴀʟs ғᴏʀ ᴛʜᴇ Stones' 1981 tour took place on Long View Farm in Massachusetts.

STEVE MORSE: They rehearsed for that '81 tour at Long View Farm. And that was in central Mass. in farm country. And they would be up all night, they had a soundstage, and they would perform, and they wouldn't start until after midnight. So they were a bit of a nuisance to the farmers in the surrounding valleys out there.

GREG PERLOFF: Bill Graham and I showed up at Long View Farm to meet with the band and no one was there. We found the caretaker and he told us that Mick went out for a ride. So we took a football out of the car and started throwing it around. For like an hour. We had nothing to do. No idea where we were staying or anything. And all of a sudden, galloping up on horseback, comes Mick Jagger. It was like a scene out of a movie.

That was when Chuck Leavell first started playing with the Stones.

CHUCK LEAVELL: My connection was through Bill Graham. One day I'm at home and I get a call from his office saying, "Would you be interested in auditioning for the Rolling Stones?" I was very interested because at the time, I didn't have anything going on . . . Ian Stewart called me. We had a great talk; I was very surprised and very pleased, obviously. This was on a Thursday and I actually had a gig Friday and Saturday of that weekend and I asked him if it would be OK if I come up Sunday or Monday and his response was, "Well, we'd really like to have you there tomorrow."

So the next day I was on a plane to Long View Farm. Stu picked me up; we had a nice talk. We got there to the farm. I saw Mick jogging out with the security guys.

One person was notably absent at Long View Farm, at least at first.

Keith Richards rocks the stage once again at Madison Square Garden in 1981

GREG PERLOFF: All of a sudden people start showing up. And there's no Keith Richards. Later on we sit down for dinner at this long table, it's the whole band and some crew guys, and Bill says, "Where's Keith?" And they were all like, "Oh," like no one had noticed he was missing. And then, about twenty feet away, you see this arm flop over the sofa, and someone says, "There's Keith." He had been out on the sofa for the entire time we had been there.

We get to the next day and we're really ready to get to work—still no Keith. You've got the barn, which is also a recording studio but from the outside it could be a horse barn. And then outside you've got this pond, and while we're waiting for something to happen, Bill and I start throwing the football around again. And at that point, Keith Richards walks out, boots on, blue jeans on, no shirt, telecaster strapped over his shoulder, and he starts walking out of the barn and towards the lake. And there was a cord on the guitar, the longest cord you've ever seen in your life, like a two-hundred-foot cord. And Keith stares at the lake and starts in on the opening riff to "Under My Thumb." We stopped and went, "Yeah. That's why we're here." It was magic. And that was the beginning of the '81 tour.

The tour grossed over thirty-six million dollars over fifty shows. But that doesn't mean there wasn't tension between the two notoriously difficult personalities who were in charge, Bill Graham and Mick Jagger.

GREG PERLOFF: There were interesting ego things. Bill was a very famous promoter and producer at that time. And early in the tour there was this wonderful article about Bill. And Mick asked to see Bill and Bill went to his suite and Mick had the newspaper laid out and said, "Bill, what's the name of this tour?" The answer being the Rolling Stones. It was one of the few times I ever saw Bill shook up. The message was, there is one star on this tour, and it's not Bill Graham.

Greg didn't let his ability to book the Stones go to his head.

GREG PERLOFF: I was doing all the deals for the tour as Bill was actually out on the tour. I was twenty-nine years old and feeling a bit full of myself. And an agent friend said, "You know, Greg, anybody can book the Rolling Stones. Let's see you book Dr. Hook on a rainy Tuesday in Des Moines." There's no band in the business even close to how big the Rolling Stones are. If you want to understand the power of the Rolling Stones from a different perspective, for six months of my life, everybody took my phone call.

The Stones made an unusual gesture at the end of their time at Long View Farm, a special thank you to any of their neighbors they might have bothered.

STEVE MORSE: I saw the sneak concert at Sir Morgan's Cove in Worcester. But the Stones made sure that they gave free tickets to the Sir Morgan's Cove show to the farmers. The Stones took care of their neighbors.

Bill Graham was the tour manager at the time. And I recall how he kicked all the media out, away from the door. As the day evolved, there were about fifteen hundred to two thousand kids trying to get in unsuccessfully. And the tickets had been given away on WAAF, the Worcester rock station. Literally handed out on the streets. If you were wearing an AAF shirt, you'd get a ticket. It became a great promotion for the radio station.

Bill Graham would get in shouting matches with the media. There was a photographer I brought with me named Stan Grossfeld. And Stan later won two Pulitzer Prizes. At the time, he was making a name for himself and he and Bill got in an unbelievable shouting match because Bill would not let Stan in. So Stan somehow got in and he ends up coming out on a balcony overlooking the front door, getting these incredible photos of the crowd. And here's Bill Graham down on the sidewalk waving his fist, "You get down off of there!" And Stan happily took his picture.

It was just an eleven-song set. Just a tune-up for the tour. They arrived and left in a thirty-five-foot-long Winnebago. And as they were leaving, Jagger opened the blinds and started mugging for the cameras.

A still from Hal Ashby's *Let's Spend the Night Together*, a concert film about the 1981 tour

One of the notable aspects of the Stones' 1981 tour is that it was the first time a rock band had a corporate sponsor. In the Stones' case: Jōvan Musk men's cologne.

STEVE MORSE: The American rockers at the time wouldn't have considered corporate sponsorship. They thought it was cheesy to get involved with it. The British acts were out in front with that. A lot of the American bands and music critics didn't like it at all. But as time went on and people saw how expensive it was to tour and how the tickets would have to be raised astronomically to compensate, then all of a sudden it became OK to do.

GREG PERLOFF: At that point we were totally against corporate sponsorship. Bands didn't charge as much as they could for tickets because it was unseemly. The Stones actually came to us with Jōvan. It was groundbreaking at the time.

Graham wasn't assured of getting the '81 tour but in the end, he won out.

GREG PERLOFF: There were a number of companies competing for the '81 tour and we were fortunate enough to get it. When we did the Stones in '78, we did some special effects. We had some helicopters flying overhead dropping plastic blow-up girls down and Ping-Pong balls, and at the same time we had helium balloons coming up from the front of the stage. This was for *Some Girls*. In those days, the local promoter could actually do some of these special promotion items and this was the first tour that they really went out and did some really good business. That had a lot to do with getting the '81 tour.

SUMMIT AT BUDDY'S PLACE

One of the most memorable nights on the '81 tour was on November 22, when the Stones played Buddy Guy's club in Chicago, the Checkerboard Lounge. Muddy Waters joined them on the bill.

BUDDY GUY: First of all, they had promised to do that seven times before they finally did it. They wanted it to be a surprise. They shocked everybody, including me. They came up in one of the raggediest vans that ever rode. I think the door was cracked; the windshield was cracked. And they was all disguised.

They was trying to do it and keep the media away. But you couldn't keep the media away from there. This particular night, Junior Wells and I was coming out of Vancouver through Seattle and we almost missed the plane. When I got almost to the Checkerboard—and I owned the Checkerboard at that time— they had the road blocked off. One of the policemen said, "You can't go up there because the Rolling Stones is there." Thank God there was a sergeant recognized me and said, "Well, you can't stop him, because he's the one that owns the club."

When I got to the front door there was people on top of the building, and I thought it was going to crash in because it wasn't real good construction. They was hanging off the roof . . . and some of them recognized me and one guy screamed, "Buddy, I'll give a thousand dollars to get in there." The place didn't hold but sixty-four people. And the Stones had fifty-four. I started crying out of one eye. That night I didn't make anything off the bar; nobody was drinking. I had the Rolling Stones in my place and I didn't make a nickel.

In the end I was so happy because it put the club on the map . . . I saw Charlie Watts a year, two years later and he said, "I got to apologize Buddy, 'cause I don't even remember being in your club." When I walked in the door he was laying out on the bar . . . There was so many people out of it that night, so I say, "Everybody's high but me. Give me a shot of Jack Daniel's."

Muddy started singing his song about champagne and reefer. And there was at least twenty policemen in there when Muddy started singing and Mick Jagger threw a bag of weed up there. I said, "Oh shit, they're going to get arrested." The police didn't do nothing but laugh. They didn't give a damn what they did.

Back then, I didn't have any kind of awards or anything. And every time I got to play with Muddy and the Rolling Stones on the stage that was up there with my Grammy and my induction into the Hall of Fame. I was sitting on top of the world. How high can you go?

The shows featured a mix of indoor and outdoor venues.

GREG PERLOFF: The outdoor tour had these beautiful scrims in front of the stage, and the indoor shows had a stage that was in the shape of a flower that opened up and it was a spectacular stage. The Stones have gone on to become one of the real leaders in concert production. There was resistance at the time, Keith saying, "I want to play on a stage, I don't want to play on a fucking toy." Bill and Mick convinced him. At that point he said, "Well, I'll do it. But if this stage doesn't hold up, you're fucking paying for it."

Were there any incidents?

GREG PERLOFF: And we get through the entire tour and we're in Hampton, Virginia, filming the last two shows of the tour and we do the second-to-last show and everything's great and someone on the crew decides we need a photograph of the entire crew. So we all go on the stage to take this picture and the stage collapses. Thank God no one was injured but there went a lot of the profits from the tour. We had to rebuild the stage for the show and the filming the next night.

From a business point of view, the Stones debuted a couple of other advanced concepts in '81.

GREG PERLOFF: The idea of not paying to sell our merchandise. The other thing on the US tour is we only advertised in one market. We started out with a press conference to introduce the shows. And every show just blew out. This was the beginning of the Stones really becoming a professional organization.

Part of the way the Stones compensated for a lack of traditional promotion was radio (see chapter 39).

GREG PERLOFF: In those days, FM radio ruled. We did a lot of press conferences. Radio had to cover the tour. They had to be the first to announce it, all of the information. There were no presales back then. The tickets went on sale and if you were first in line, you got the front row. We realized that radio was going to sell it for us. All we had to do was whisper, "The Rolling Stones are coming."

CHAPTER 43

HAD IT WITH YOU

KEITH RICHARDS: I would say that (in the early '70s) you've got the seeds of why we're not together right now. I mean, Mick and I have different attitudes, and throughout most of the '70s, I was living in another world from him. I didn't blame him—he'd earned the right to do what he wanted. It was just that I couldn't RELATE to [his lifestyle]. And even if I could've related to it, I was too busy being busted—which, I mean, is equally as dumb, you know?

Mick and I are incredibly diverse people. We've known each other forty years—ever since we were three or four years old. But while a certain part of our personalities is incredibly close, there's an awful lot which is very, very different. And so, yeah, it kind of got up my nose a bit, that jet-set shit and, like, the flaunting of it.

Put it down to the law of unintended consequences. One unpredictable effect of Keith Richards getting straight was that there was suddenly a lot more tension between him and Mick. When Keith was in a fog, Mick got his way all the time in terms of music and business decisions. Sober Keith—well, sober compared to himself—understandably wanted to be more involved.

KEITH RICHARDS: This situation was a culmination of things that had been going on for several years. The immediate problem was that Mick had developed an overriding desire to control everything. As far as he was concerned, it was Mick Jagger and *them*.

Conflict defined Mick and Keith's relationship through most of the 1980s

To make matters worse, both Ron Wood and even Charlie Watts developed drug problems of their own. Put all this in the hopper and you have another crisis that threatened the band's very existence.

Musically speaking, after *Some Girls* the band quickly resorted to rehashing. Mick described 1980's *Emotional Rescue* as "a lot of leftovers." As enjoyable as *Tattoo You* was, it wasn't new material. *Undercover* represented more of an effort from the band—it was composed of all new material but can't be called one of the Stones' better albums. *Undercover* was the Stones' last record for Atlantic in the USA and they needed a new deal. Unbeknownst to the rest of the band, Mick also piggybacked a solo deal on the Stones' new agreement with CBS and their president, Walter Yetnikoff. Things were getting ugly.

KEITH RICHARDS: It was total disregard for the band. We didn't build this band up to stab each other in the back.

Of course, from Mick's perspective, it's understandable that Keith's sudden interest in the band after years of being out of it must have seemed a little odd. Another incident from around this time involved Charlie throwing a punch at Mick.

BRENDA JAGGER

In addition to writing songs about Mick, Keith had a code name for him during the World War III period.

BILL GERMAN: It was during the sessions in Paris when Keith went into a bookstore and saw a book by Brenda Jagger. At the time, he wanted to stab Mick in the eyeballs, so referring to his prima donna lead singer as Brenda was a much healthier way to vent. Mick didn't know about the nickname, it was all behind his back. But Keith told me to stop by the studio anytime—as long as Brenda wasn't there.

KEITH RICHARDS: Charlie biffed Mick once in Holland. Mick had a couple of drinks and he can get a bit silly. So, about five in the morning, he calls up Charlie and says, "Is my drummer there?" There was this ominous silence at the other end of the phone and I'm like, "Mick, I don't think that was a very clever thing to say." Twenty minutes later, Charlie knocks on my door—Savile Row suit, tie, polished brogues—and says to Mick, "Don't ever call me your drummer." Smack! And there's this long table with a platter of smoked salmon on it and the window's open and there's a canal outside and Mick falls on the platter and starts sliding down the table towards the open window.

For the next album, *Dirty Work*, Mick and Keith were at each other's throats.

BILL GERMAN: The Stones were obligated to deliver an album, but Mick's head was already inside his solo-album stuff. Mick didn't really contribute that much to *Dirty Work*. So they start recording *Dirty Work* in Paris at Pathé Marconi, and Mick was busy doing interviews with MTV. And Keith was not pleased with that. So a lot of the work fell on Keith's shoulders. Keith and Woody were the ones that wound up writing a lot of the Stones' songs on the fly. They would come up with stuff they were feeling at the moment. Woody told me, "It was a good thing we were able to play guitar or otherwise we would have killed people." It was a great outlet for them.

Keith wrote barely disguised songs about Mick with titles like "Fight," and "Had It with You." Mick didn't have many songs of his own to contribute, and delayed the sessions themselves, busy simultaneously working on his solo album, the forgettable *She's the Boss*, a title which Richards has said "says it all."

Mick didn't want to tour *Dirty Work*. Keith thinks this was because he wanted to tour solo but it certainly also seems plausible that Mick thought going out on the road with Charlie and Ron Wood abusing drugs, and he and Keith hating each other, was just a bad idea.

Mick didn't choose the best way of telling his bandmates he didn't want to go on the road.

BILL GERMAN: He sent them all the same telegram. Something to the effect that he was going to pursue other interests in 1986. And that's how they learned about it.

Then the tabloid battle between Mick and Keith began. Mick got things off to a rollicking start when he said in an interview that the Rolling Stones were a millstone around his neck. Keith says in *Life* that this was the moment that World War III was officially declared. Keith had a lot of great nasty lines about Mick from that period but this one representative sample will suffice for our purposes. A reporter asked him when he and Mick were going to stop bitching about each other in the tabloids.

KEITH RICHARDS: I don't know. Ask the bitch.

Keith got involved in other projects, including the film *Hail! Hail! Rock 'n' Roll* and starting his own band, the X-Pensive Winos.

BILL GERMAN: The first Winos album, *Talk Is Cheap*, is a masterpiece. One critic called it the best Stones album in years. And it taught Keith something about himself, that he could be a leader and a lead singer.

By the start of 1989, Mick and Keith were starting to mend fences. In January, they met in Barbados to see if they could work together "without killing each other." In *Life*, Keith sums up their relationship:

KEITH RICHARDS: Mick and I may not be friends—too much wear and tear for that—but we're the closest of brothers and that cannot be severed.

Indeed, big things lay ahead for the Stones in '89, starting with their induction into the Rock and Roll Hall of Fame on January 18.

HAIL! HAIL! ROCK 'N' ROLL

One of Keith's main projects during the mid-'80s was a movie called *Hail! Hail! Rock 'n' Roll*, which reunited Chuck Berry with his old piano player/collaborator Johnnie Johnson (who had given up music and was driving a bus at the time). Berry was a very up-and-down performer as Bill Wyman explained to me in 1977.

BILL WYMAN: I haven't really bought his records in the last ten years, because they always seemed like lazy attempts to rehash, unfortunately. But he's still great on stage. And I do hear he uses good musicians these days to back him sometimes. That was always the failing with him; he was always so fantastic, and yet he wouldn't pay that extra little bit of cash to get some good musicians behind him so that he could have a great show. He'd just grab somebody for ten bucks a night. It focused everybody's attention on him, because the rest of the band was no good. I've always found that top people have always wanted to produce the best show that they could and not just knock it off like that.

Berry, like many rock legends, had his own set of personality issues.

BILL WYMAN: He's very hard to talk to. One day he'll be very nice; the next day he won't even speak to you. We must have earned him a few dollars . . . as he probably earned us a few, I'm sure (*laughs*). I mean, he's always been an idol and a god of ours, and sometimes he's not polite enough even to say hello. And when Keith wanted to play with him—when he went on stage with Ian Stewart and a few people in California to back him—Chuck Berry threw 'em all off . . . because they were playing better than he was, probably. Physically, he told them to leave the stage. What a downer that must have been. I think he was a bit resentful of the applause that Keith was getting.

Being booted off stage wasn't the only incident Keith had with Berry.

BILL GERMAN: I got a phone call from a friend of mine who told me, "You won't believe this, but Chuck Berry punched Keith last night in the eye at the Ritz." They were backstage after Chuck played and Keith tapped Chuck on the shoulder. You don't touch Chuck Berry; he doesn't like being touched. Then Chuck, claiming that he didn't know it was Keith, just turned around and just punched Keith. Keith said to a few people that were in the room, "Chuck Berry is the only person in the room who could get away with that without being killed."

Chuck Berry duckwalks across the stage in St. Louis during the filming of *Hail! Hail! Rock 'n' Roll*

Keith told me another story: He was in LA having just finished taping a TV show for Dick Clark. He's waiting at LAX to fly back to New York and he bumps into Chuck at the airport and Chuck is sitting on his guitar case. Keith goes up to him and they start exchanging phone numbers and as they're doing it Chuck accidentally drops a cigarette down Keith's shirt. The way Keith put it to me was, "Every time I see Chuck Berry I end up wounded."

Keith didn't hold a grudge, but the filming of *Hail! Hail! Rock 'n' Roll* didn't end up being much easier. There's a great scene in the movie of Chuck arguing with Keith about how to play the bends in "Carol."

KEITH RICHARDS: The rest of the band behind me, the guys that are with me, if you look at their faces, are going, "He ain't gonna take much more of this, watch out or you're going to get stabbed or that guitar's gonna go round your chops." I was willing to take all of that. I ate the bullets and chewed lead. If I could show the rest of the guys that I'm willing to take any amount of crap to do this gig, then I've got that much of a better band. Also, it's gonna fox Chuck. He's trying to provoke me, and I ain't gonna go for it.

TAYLOR HACKFORD: When you're making a documentary, if everything is sweetness and light and everyone is patting each other on the back, you're kind of doomed to having an uninteresting film. I knew going into this project that it was going to be difficult. There were going to be fireworks. And if I made the film and rode that bucking bronco, there'd be conflict. There'd have to be with Chuck Berry.

Part of the issue was that Chuck didn't like to practice.

KEITH RICHARDS: He's never rehearsed in his life. He thought the rehearsals were for the band. He didn't realize they were for him. He needed rehearsing. The band knew their shit. There were some bits a week earlier where Joey Spampinato [of NRBQ] is showing Chuck how to play, and what really happens, in "Around and Around." Chuck would go back and listen and—to give him his due—would come back and say, "You're right." After playing for twenty-odd years with pickup bands, he didn't know how to play live anymore. It was bugging him that this band was really kicking him up the butt and suddenly he realizes he's not really cutting the mustard.

I interviewed Johnnie Johnson and asked him about the film.

JOHNNIE JOHNSON: Yeah, I look back at that and I hear a lot of mistakes I made while I was playing, but who noticed the mistakes then? You know, I'm just making this movie. I was just so excited about it, and I was making a nice piece of change out of it also. What else could you ask for? Plus getting the recognition that I had been denied before then. And people see you on the street and know who you are. I was in San Francisco after the movie was made, and my wife and I were walking down the street and a fellow—you know the streets are very wide in San Francisco—and this fellow comes running across the street and I didn't know if he was coming to stick me up or whatever—but he runs across the street and he says, "You're Johnnie Johnson! Johnnie Johnson! Can I have your autograph?" I didn't know what he was up to, but I mean after that people began to recognize me, and would probably never have recognized me before that because they had never seen me.

I asked him to tell me about his relationship with Keith.

JOHNNIE JOHNSON: Well, the first time I ever met him was during the making of the picture, but naturally everybody knew of the Rolling Stones. And when I first met him, I mean, we just hit it off as very good friends.

Matter of fact, his secretary had me come to New York to play by myself at one of his parties. And I'm sitting up there as nervous as I could be 'cause I never played no big party for a star like Keith Richards before, and I'm playing for him at this party, and Keith is sitting on this side, and Eric Clapton on this side, and I'm trembling like I'm frozen.

In the end, though, Keith made the right decision to work with Berry.

KEITH RICHARDS: If I'd turned the gig down, somebody else would have done it and I would have been kicking myself. It would have been a sore point with me for the rest of my life.

The experience was also a real turning point for Keith.

Keith went formal as the musical director for *Hail! Hail! Rock 'n' Roll*

TAYLOR HACKFORD: Keith knew he wouldn't be there if not for Chuck Berry. Up to that point, Keith was a dark figure in the Rolling Stones. Mick was the brilliant front man. Keith was in the back. It was his junkie days, he was very clearly self-destructive and everybody knew it.

Hail! Hail! Rock 'n' Roll was Keith's coming out party. He loved the Rolling Stones. He wanted the Rolling Stones to go on forever. Mick decided to leave and do a solo project which was an insult. I think Keith for the first time stood up and defined himself outside of the Rolling Stones. It was the first major project he did outside the Rolling Stones.

CHAPTER 44

NOT FADE AWAY

I⸱T WAS INEVITABLE that there would one day be a Rock 'n' Roll Hall of Fame. Surely this uniquely American art form deserved to stand shoulder to shoulder with all of the other major cultural and financial "leisure-time-activity" institutions in the country. It happened in the mid-'80s. By virtue of my associations with WNEW-FM and K-ROCK, I was pleased and honored to attend the first six Rock 'n' Roll Hall of Fame induction ceremonies, which were all held in New York City. Every one of them had touching and memorable moments and that certainly includes the January 1989 event in the Grand Ballroom of the Waldorf-Astoria Hotel. Why?

Here are nine good reasons: Dion, the Ink Spots, Otis Redding, the Rolling Stones, Bessie Smith, the Soul Stirrers, Phil Spector, the Temptations, and Stevie Wonder.

Those were the newest additions to the Hall, and I was thrilled to be there to watch the spectacle unfold. I took great personal pride in Dion's selection because we were both Italian-Americans from the same Bronx neighborhood and had become quite friendly over the course of my years on the radio. He was always an inspiration to me and certainly deserved this recognition as one of the finest male vocalists that rock 'n' roll has ever produced.

Then there were the Rolling Stones—as close to a sure thing for this honor as you could imagine. Right up there with Elvis and Chuck Berry and the Beach Boys and the Beatles. The only question left to be answered was how would these titans of irreverence handle this potentially solemn elevation to sainthood?

Not to worry. Another rock legend set the proper tone in his induction speech.

PETE TOWNSHEND: Rock 'n' roll has quite obviously been around for a lot longer than I thought . . . Keith Richards once told me that I think too much. The truth is that I think, generally, that I talk too much. But I don't think first. And faced with injecting the Rolling Stones this evening, I realized that thinking isn't going to help me very much . . . I can't analyze what I feel about the Stones, because I'm really an absolute stone fan of the Stones, and always have been. Their early shows were just shocking, and absolutely riveting and stunning and moving, and they changed my life completely. The Beatles were fun . . . I'm not demeaning them in any way. But the Stones were really what made me wake up. At the Beatles' shows, there were lots of screaming girls, and at the Stones'—I think the Stones were the first to have a screaming boy. And the sheer force of the Stones on stage, and that perfectly balanced audience—a thousand girls, and me—it kind of singled them out. They're the only group I've ever really been unashamed about idolizing . . . and each of them in their own way has given me something as an artist, as a person, and as a fan. And it would be crazy to suggest that any of the things they gave me were wholesome, practical, or useful.

Then Pete went into full-on roast mode:

PETE TOWNSHEND: Even Bill Wyman hurt me—and not really because I'm jealous of the female company he keeps, no. He got such a big advance for this book he's doing about the Stones' life that the book is obviously expected to sell more copies than the last couple of Stones albums. You've heard how much he got? You've heard how much they sold. It's a wonder Ahmet even bothered, really. Charlie wounded me in the last year by having a much more dramatic drug problem than mine. Keith had a much more dramatic cure.

Then he went back to serious mode . . . briefly.

PETE TOWNSHEND: And Brian Jones hurt me by not bothering to take a cure. Because I loved him a lot. He was very, very important to me. He was the first real star who befriended me in a real way . . . I've missed him terribly, and I always felt that when he finally did collapse, that the Stones were a very different group. Mick gave me something too. A bad case of VD. Sorry, that's wrong. Mick's mix CD had a bad case . . . And Ronnie Wood of course is now a Rolling Stone; I can't help but think of him as the new boy. And it's wonderful to note that, due to his tender age, he still has his own teeth. But I did notice that tonight, they've been set into what looks like someone else's face.

Townshend's speech wouldn't have been complete without a comment about the problems the various band members were having with Mick:

PETE TOWNSHEND: Will the Stones ever work again? On an early British TV show the producer took Andrew Loog Oldham . . . and advised him to sack the singer

. . . I'm glad that after all these years, the lads in the group have finally seen fit to take his advice.

His close was terrific:

PETE TOWNSHEND: The Stones will always be the greatest for me. They epitomize British rock for me, and even though they're all now my friends, I'm still a fan. Guys, whatever you do, don't try and grow old gracefully; it wouldn't suit you.

Mick and Keith were completely gracious and true to themselves in their respective acceptance speeches:

MICK JAGGER: It's slightly ironic that tonight you see us on our best behavior, but we're being rewarded for twenty-five years of bad behavior . . . I'd like to pay tribute to two people who can't be here tonight. One, Ian Stewart, a great friend, a great blues pianist, whose odd but invaluable musical advice kept us on a steady, bluesy course most of the time. And to Brian Jones, whose individuality and musicianship often took us off the bluesy course, with often marvelous results. Jean Cocteau said that "Americans are funny people. First you shock them, then they put you in a museum." We'll we're not quite ready to hang up the number yet, so on behalf of the Stones, I'd like to thank you very much for this evening.

KEITH RICHARDS: Yeah, my turn. I'd like to say thank you to Leo Fender, for making the goddamn things we've gotta play, right? I'd like to say thank you . . . to Ahmet especially, for putting up with us for sixteen years. And also, of course, Ian Stewart, because it's his band, I work for him, you know? I'd like to thank you all.

Later that year, Mick summed up his feelings about the event:

MICK JAGGER: I don't like award shows. I only went last year under pressure. I hope it was grace under pressure.

With Townshend and the Who slated to be inducted in 1990, was Mick plotting revenge?

MICK JAGGER: No, I won't be going. I've had my fill of the Hall of Fame. I told them last year, I'll be somewhere else.

CHAPTER 45

MIXED EMOTIONS

CHUCK LEAVELL: This was kind of the rebirth, if you will, of the Rolling Stones. They had not toured in seven years. I think it was do or die. "Either we're going to go out here or we're going to make it work." There was a lot of tension in *Undercover* and in *Dirty Work* and those sessions. Not the best of times for relationships between Mick and Keith, but the fact is that they did find a way to work with each other rather than break up the band, which I think is remarkable. When *Steel Wheels* came around, I think everybody realized the whole is greater than the sum of its parts.

The *Steel Wheels* album was recorded in March 1989 on the island of Montserrat. With Mick, Keith, and Ronnie all fresh off the road, the sessions were smooth and fast and the album got good reviews.

One cool footnote saw the Stones go back to Morocco to record the musicians of Joujouka, the tribe Brian Jones had worked with twenty years earlier on his last musical project. Then it was time for the *Steel Wheels* and Urban Jungle tours.

CHUCK LEAVELL: *Steel Wheels* was a real turning point for the band—an opportunity to reinvent themselves to a degree, to go out and do a major tour. And, obviously, that is what happened. We had a long rehearsal period prior to that tour; at that point Mick had found Matt Clifford who was more on the technical side of keyboard and synthesizers and sampling. They looked to me to carry on Stu's parts . . . That's the way it worked on *Steel Wheels*. It was one of the most extraordinary production sets in rock 'n' roll . . . It was tight; that was a great tour. Everything really went well.

STEEL WHEELS (TO SHEA STADIUM)

How appropriate it was that I took the Long Island Railroad for my long-coveted interview with Mick Jagger at Shea Stadium in October of 1989. It was my own mood-setting version of "steel wheels" on my way to speak with Mick and check out the show. It was a trip I had taken many times since my oldest son (and a co-author of this book!) had become a Mets fan in the '70s. But this was going to be different. This was going to be some face-to-face time with the man whose records I had been playing on the radio since 1964—Jumpin' Jack Flash himself! Lucifer! Mick the Magic Jagger!

By 1989, WNEW-FM had given up any pretense of being a progressive rock radio station. It had abandoned its freeform roots in favor of a slick, commercial, lowest common denominator format generated by a computer program called DJ Select. (Ugh!) What was responsible for this abomination? The usual suspects—greed, homogenization, and slavish devotion to commerce over art. Add to the mix a series of bad owners, bad general managers, and, worst of all, bad program directors who put the station on the path to its eventual demise in the late '90s.

I had come from an era in which athletes played their entire careers for one team. Even as the world and the media and the business were changing all around me, I naïvely assumed that I would play out my career at WNEW-FM.

Not so fast, Mr. Fornatale!

After twenty years at 102.7 FM in New York, I accepted an offer that I couldn't refuse from our fiercest competitor down the dial—92.3 K-ROCK. I made the move in September of 1989, thanks to Mark Chernoff, one of the *best* program directors I ever worked for. My new employers wanted to make the most of my defection. They promoted the hell out of my arrival and made it quite clear that knocking WNEW-FM from its lofty perch was a main priority. They searched tirelessly and relentlessly for weaknesses and vulnerabilities—cracks in the foundation of the once mighty 102.7.

One golden opportunity presented itself less than three weeks after my arrival at K-ROCK. The Rolling Stones were coming to New York to play six concerts at Shea Stadium. Was there any way the new upstart "classic rock" station could undermine "the place where rock lives," as the sloganeers called it. Turns out, there was.

Another new wrinkle in the marketing of rock 'n' roll was spearheaded by the Stones on this tour. They had developed their own line of official clothing—way beyond the standard T-shirt sales—that was going to be sold not only at the concerts, but also at mainstream consumer outlets such as Macy's. The promotion director at K-ROCK came up with a brilliant idea. The station would fully promote the new line of Rolling Stones clothing on the air in exchange for an exclusive interview with Mick. All parties agreed to the terms and a rendezvous was set up to take place in Mick's dressing room prior to one of the shows at Shea. NEW had been caught napping, and the fact that a former DJ of theirs got the assignment added to the embarrassment of the situation. Needless to say, I was thrilled and grateful to rub their noses in it after witnessing the decay of a great radio station that I had loved for so long as a listener and as a performer.

I was at the press gate right on time with my equipment-bearing engineer. We were led through the bowels of Shea to the Mets clubhouse that I had been to a couple of times before—but was shocked to see that it was unrecognizable as a Major League team's locker room. The whole area had been redone in the ambience of a desert oasis! There were floating curtains everywhere, beautiful women dressed in harem outfits, tables full of food and fruit and beverages—even real palm trees, for God's sake! (Maybe even a hookah or two, but perhaps that was just my imagination running away with me!)

We were setting up our equipment in Davey Johnson's office—also not looking anything like a baseball manager's lair—when in strolled Mick Jagger looking feisty, fit, and friendly. I was nervous, but focused. After all, here was a man quite used to handling "the press," quite used to fielding questions that were very often stupid, prurient, repetitive, and banal—and, only sometimes, profound and thought provoking. But this was Shea Stadium, and with my opportunity to meet Mick, I was determined to swing for the fences.

Mick reached out his hand, greeted me warmly, and said, "I've enjoyed listening to you on the radio." He was going out of his way to make me feel comfortable! What a trip. And it worked. I decided to start our conversation with a question that I thought would break the ice in a favorable fashion, and show him right away that this wasn't going to be one of those banal interviews:

"Hello again everyone, this is Pete Fornatale back with you on 92.3 K-ROCK on location at Shea Stadium with my special guest, renowned fashion designer—Mick Jagger!"

He got the joke right away.

MICK JAGGER: Well, that's a first! (*laughter*) That's a first, I must say!!

PETE FORNATALE: You've been described many, many ways over the years. How does this one feel?

MICK JAGGER: Well, it's quite good really, something I'm quite comfortable with. I've been interested in fashion for a long time and I know lots of designers and I've watched how they work and I've watched how they promote and I've

The triumphant *Steel Wheels* tour: the beginning of the second half

seen, you know, a lot of clothes and fashions come and go and seen them come around again . . . And I always took a bit of [offense] to a lot of rock 'n' roll merchandising, just basically 'cause it was the same thing over and over . . . And, um, it really just came about from an accident of being shown black T-shirts again, with tongues on them.

And I said, "Well, that's very nice—black T-shirts with tongues on them. We have no real objections to them. It's just perhaps we should do something as well as that." And they said, "Oh, no. What people really want, Mick, is black T-shirts with tongues on them; they don't really want anything else." Well, I said, "Let's try." Don't underestimate people, you know, they read fashion and they see people and what they're wearing and everything else. It's not only in New York and LA that they wear fashionable clothes.

PETE FORNATALE: What is your hope for the rock wear, Mick? Is it something just for the tour or do you see it having a life after?

Mick the businessman takes over.

MICK JAGGER: Well, we talked very early on, we said that—you know, this is the first time we got into retail. It seemed to me common sense to go into retail . . . If you didn't come to the show; you didn't have the money to buy whatever you wanted to see at the show—you could buy it in the store afterwards or why don't you buy it next month or buy some more for your kids or something. So I figured it would be good to go into retail and there was quite a lot of resistance—I don't think that rock 'n' roll merchandise has been sold extensively in retail before. There was a little bit of resistance in the beginning, but I think, now—we think it's been successful enough that we can—we want to carry on, so we're gonna design some more stuff for spring and so on.

PETE FORNATALE: If the clothes have half the life of the music they'll be around a very long time.

MICK JAGGER: We'll see.

Obligatory fashion talk aside, it was time to home in on the things that I really wanted to know.

PETE FORNATALE: Did you expect that at this point? Did you expect the music to have the longevity and the meaning in people's lives that it seems to have—that it's obvious that it has?

MICK JAGGER: No, I'd never thought about it in that way; I don't think that most artists do. I think it's very dangerous to start thinking about your work as far as posterity is concerned. Pop music's a very much thing of the moment—and it lasts a moment, and if people pick it up later on and still enjoy it, that's wonderful; and if they don't, then they don't. It's very ephemeral.

PETE FORNATALE: But you have such a body of work, at this point, to draw from.

MICK JAGGER: Well, that's the thing, if you do enough, then you got a better chance because the good things will stand up, hopefully.

PETE FORNATALE: A friend of mine gave me a video tape of the Stones' six appearances on *The Ed Sullivan Show*, and I watched it knowing we were going to do this interview as much to see what you were wearing as what you were [singing], and it was a really interesting evolution from '64 to '69. Do things like that have any interest for you?

MICK JAGGER: We're gonna put out a retrospective video; I mean, that's one of the fun things about looking at these old things . . . So, "What is he wearing, and what—what's Keith wearing, is he really wearing that jacket?" (*laughter*) I mean, some of them stand out really well and some of them are terrible and you can laugh at them and some of them are good, and some of them are just laughs. There is a good military jacket I was wearing on *The Ed*

Sullivan Show which you could still wear now; and then there's some other stuff that you just wouldn't be seen dead in.

PETE FORNATALE: Now, it seemed to me from watching the tape that Brian was the most fashion conscious. Is that a fair statement? Do you agree?

MICK JAGGER: Umm—I don't think that's really fair. No, I think everyone was pretty fashion conscious. Maybe he was just more outrageous.

PETE FORNATALE: You seemed genuinely surprised at the press conference in July when someone pointed out that it was the twenty-seventh anniversary of the Stones' first gig together. Are those milestones just unimportant to you or are there some that are?

MICK JAGGER: None—none of them are important to me.

PETE FORNATALE: Because?

MICK JAGGER: I just don't take notice of them. I'm really not interested in the past very much. That's for other people to get involved. I'm only interested in what's going on at the moment.

PETE FORNATALE: To do what I saw you do on that stage a couple of weeks ago, you really have to be in shape for it though—correct or not?

MICK JAGGER: I've always been very lucky, I've always been in very good shape—and I've never had to work very hard at it, and I see people struggling . . . But you know, I don't smoke and stuff like that. Those kinds of things really slow you down. The trouble with us being on the tour, though, is that you do have to be disciplined to a certain amount—more than you'd want. I mean, you can't really go and get drunk every night; I can't have a hangover and do what I do. It's impossible. So it's a bit like being on the tennis circuit, you know, and I see friends I know, a little bit, that are tennis players, and they want to go out and have a good time, but they just CAN'T because they have a match tomorrow. Well, it's like that almost every day for me. And so, I can't go and party every night. I can only do it occasionally.

PETE FORNATALE: By the way, it's very obvious to me that you feel the responsibility to those sixty thousand people every night of delivering the absolute best that you can be . . .

Mick Jagger, modeling the Rolling Stones fashion line

MICK JAGGER: Well, they've paid money, and they—not only that, they've got high expectations. They don't want to see sort of second-rate stuff, and if you're in any way under the weather, you're letting them down. I mean, sometimes you get a cold or something, but you try not to let that show.

PETE FORNATALE: That brings to mind as well, the ability of the Stones to relate to audiences of every age. When you look around that stadium, you must, at this point, see everything from toddlers to senior citizens. What do you attribute that to?

MICK JAGGER: I bet it's just really that the Stones have been around so long (*laughter*).

Yeah—we've got a very, very large age range. In 1981 it was large and now it's even larger, so that's because you've kept some of the people that came in the '60s and you've added on the '70s and added on the early '80s, and here we are almost in the '90s and you get very large disparate age groups. So, I don't know how they actually—I don't, I'm in the worst position to judge, but—I don't know how they actually get on, side by side. That's the thing that interests me. You know, someone you don't know. You find yourself in this, and there's four of you, and you're partying, and you're eighteen years old and you've had a lot of beer and you're sitting next to a family of rather staid, middle-aged people.

PETE FORNATALE: But, you know, it's not the same as being with four people on a subway car . . . They might not have anything in common, but those other four know that they have love of the Stones in common.

MICK JAGGER: I know what you're saying, but I—I'm kind of—anyway it interests me, but I can't see it (*laughter*).

I knew we were clicking at this point so it was real easy to stick to questions about the group and the music.

PETE FORNATALE: The show covers such a wide spectrum of your music; have you rediscovered some songs from the group's past that you're really enjoying performing this time around?

MICK JAGGER: I think "Ruby Tuesday," which we haven't done for a while. And, I did that when I went to Japan to do solo things. I found that the audience loved that one, and they still like it here; and then "Two Thousand Light Years from Home," which we've never done before, ever; and that goes down well. It's hard, breathing life into them every night; that's more of a problem to keep the performance to the point where it still retains your interest. If you get bored with it, then the audience will feel that. So, we have to try and change the set a little bit and bring in some more new numbers from the new album and alternate it.

PETE FORNATALE: Mick, you have been a celebrity for so long now. What aspects of it do you like and which ones do you absolutely hate?

MICK JAGGER: Well, it's hard—even when I'm working on the road I don't like to be photographed the whole time. And that's the whole thing; you have to look good the whole time. It's a nightmare, really. I don't like that part. You know, they always have to wear something that looks good and you don't want to look all crumpled and asleep. When you're on the road you're expected to be on twenty-four hours a day almost.

PETE FORNATALE: Yeah.

MICK JAGGER: And I don't like that. And when I'm off the road and when I'm not working I don't want anyone to bug me; but you can't really expect them not to. They still want you to sign bits of paper and be nice to them and so on. Sometimes you don't always want to be nice; you know, you want to get on with your own life. And when you're with people you don't always want to have to be nice to the people at the next table and be gracious and you want to turn your back and say "go away," (*laughter*) but then you count to five and you say, "HELLO, and how interesting that your son is also at the concert. The End."

PETE FORNATALE: (*laughter*)

MICK JAGGER: It doesn't sound very difficult, but after a while it just gets a bit monotonous, you know, to be like that and that's when you see these stories of celebrities standing off and getting annoyed with camera people . . . It's kind of natural 'cause they do bug you. You know, they stand outside your house, or whatever.

PETE FORNATALE: I've always thought that one of the good things about celebrity is that it probably gives you access to meeting people of stature or creativity that you might not have had the opportunity to do otherwise.

MICK JAGGER: Sure.

PETE FORNATALE: Is there anyone left in that category for you?

MICK JAGGER: Who I'd like to meet? Well, there's loads of people. I mean, I just like watching people work in other fields to see how they handle themselves. It is interesting, you get to meet people. I like talking to the sort of people who were in power at one time or in power now; about how they handle their particular problems and so on. And, you know, they do sometimes give you the best seats at the restaurant as opposed to sitting next to the kitchen.

PETE FORNATALE: (*laughter*)

MICK JAGGER: I'm not denigrating being famous—it has its fun moments.

PETE FORNATALE: That's great. Let's see if we can bring it full circle. I'm just going to ask you—design is not something new to the Stones. Obviously, there have been images portrayed of the group, throughout the group's career. Now I'm just guessing, but when you look back at old pictures of yourself, some you're going to want to put back in the drawer and never look at again, and others you're gonna want to keep out there because you still think it says something relevant about you at that time of your life. Either through album covers or photos, can you do that for me; and pick a couple of lasting images of the Stones that still say something today?

MICK JAGGER: Well, I think the early pictures that David Bailey did of the Rolling Stones from the first album covers and so were very formative for the band's image . . . I can't imagine how many photographs there are. I mean, things are very important in the beginning. [As for later images,] I suppose the *Sticky Fingers* cover that wasn't a photograph of the Stones was also a very good piece that Andy Warhol did. It's always good to have something that's a bit groundbreaking, and that causes a bit of a stir, as well.

PETE FORNATALE: The tour has just been fabulous and the future of the Stones seems limitless. What's left? What's left to achieve from your perspective?

MICK JAGGER: Well, I enjoy doing other projects, I enjoy doing stage design and clothes design. I enjoy doing music, obviously it's what I like, but I like to stretch myself in other areas. And I'm interested in other things as well. And I think the Stones will always be an important part of my life, but I'm interested in doing different things outside the Stones. And, for instance, the thing we were starting to talk about, the fashion thing, and other things, too. But, I think the Stones will keep going for a while yet.

PETE FORNATALE: It's almost the '90s. What'll you do right after the tour?

MICK JAGGER: It's in the hands of the gods. I know I can't predict the future (*laughter*). But '89's been pretty good so far.

PETE FORNATALE: It's been great.

MICK JAGGER: Thank you.

And that was it. Almost a half hour with Mick that felt more like two minutes. As we were packing up our gear and getting ready to leave, I thought about the question I had asked him concerning his celebrity and how it gave him the opportunity to talk to talented and interesting people that he might otherwise have never had the chance to meet and hang out with. I knew exactly what his answer meant. Even though I was on a much smaller and lower rung of the "celebrity" ladder, I got the chance to meet and hang out with Mick Jagger and it was priceless.

CHAPTER 46

IN ANOTHER LAND

BACK IN THE '80s, I wrote, co-produced, and voiced a syndicated radio feature called *Rock Calendar*. Its purpose was to highlight a specific rock 'n' roll event that took place on every calendar day of the year (365 shows; 366 in leap years). Knowing that a number of those dates would involve the Rolling Stones, I set my sights on talking to the group member who would most enjoy the task of sifting through the band's history. After a little research, by process of elimination, I knew that it wasn't going to be Mick or Charlie, and for a whole set of *different* reasons, probably not Keith or Ron either. It became a no-brainer to choose Bill Wyman. He had even described himself as the group historian, so that is exactly where we began the conversation:

BILL WYMAN: Yeah, I am, because I'm the only one who really cares about it; no one else gives a damn, really. Charlie Watts gives his gold records away to his chauffeur or to the taxi driver who brings him to the airport; he doesn't care about those things. So I've compiled this whole mass of stuff which I store in various places and refer to occasionally because it really pisses me off every time a book or article comes out the dates are wrong . . . the facts . . . everything's wrong! And one of these days I'm going to put the record straight. [He did in his 1990 book *Stone Alone*.]

PETE FORNATALE: You had a solo hit in 1981—"(Si, Si) Je Suis un Rock Star"—tell me about that experience.

BILL WYMAN: It's really exciting—it's like the first time we as a group had a hit; everything feels new again. We all have our insecurities and doubts about whether we as individuals are as good alone as our position in a famous band implies we should be. We all feel this way—Mick, Keith, Charlie, Ron—so you always try to do something outside the band to build your confidence and assuage those doubts. I'd attempted that before with two solo albums, but they were done much more for the fun of it, and to learn a bit about producing and arranging.

PETE FORNATALE: Both of which got a lukewarm reception.

BILL WYMAN: Yeah, after that I said, "Let's just forget about this. I'm not meant to be doing solo stuff." I didn't want to face that same non-response again. But then this song came up and I did a demo and everybody said, "You've got to record that." So I did . . . reluctantly I might add!

PETE FORNATALE: Why have you not written more for the Stones?

BILL WYMAN: Firstly, I don't think I write songs that are appropriate for the band. And secondly, we record once every eighteen months or so; and Mick and Keith have such a tremendous amount of material that there really isn't room left over. Woody gets a bit in here and there, but he lives in the same country as they do, so he hangs out a bit more; I live in the south of France.

PETE FORNATALE: What about the rumors about Mick and Keith erasing each other's tracks on various albums?

BILL WYMAN: The story is that Mick and Keith are the producers. They work together on the basic tracks but from then on they work separately and form their own opinions. So you end up with various mixes that Keith's done as well as alternate mixes that Mick has done of the same material. At that point they haggle out which versions of each tune are best. I've never heard of them erasing each other's tapes (*laughs*)—it's more a question of fighting it out over which version of any given song will appear on an album.

PETE FORNATALE: Let me ask you some impressions about your fellow Stones. Mick?

BILL WYMAN: Alright, Mick. It's difficult because I know both the public image and the real person and they both merge into his character for me—the sublime and the ridiculous! (*laughs*) He is totally different in public than he is in private life. Unfortunately, he seems to think—as most of us probably do—that there's a way you react in public and a way you react at home. Sometimes he carries his public persona over into his private life, which gets to be a real pain in the ass because you know he's full of shit. So you have to remind him and bring him down . . . Come on, Mick! And then he comes back to normal.

PETE FORNATALE: How does it manifest?

BILL WYMAN: His voice changes, for one thing, and he starts talking with that pseudo-Southern accent. And sometimes in private he starts using a very rough, Cockney accent, which is also not his real voice. It's actually more like the way Charlie and I talk, dropping the *H*s and all that. He never talked like that before, because he came from a middle-class family and went to middle-class schools. I've got interviews with him on radio and television from the '60s where he's talking like the Queen does—"Oh, well, it's quite interesting to . . ." He's getting a bit like Peter Sellers: I don't think he knows which one is the real Mick Jagger (*laughs*). It keeps the mystery going.

PETE FORNATALE: Keith?

BILL WYMAN: Shy, introverted. He's very nice, really. He can be a real bust, though (*laughs*). If he's in his regular mood, he's great. But if he's in a bad mood you can't be in a good mood with him, because he kind of dominates the mood of the room. Maybe he had a hard couple of hours at home or his car broke down, or he lost his favorite cassette and he doesn't really want to talk, so you just leave it for a few hours and then he's alright. As I say, he's very introverted and to overcome that he makes the appearance of being very carefree and brash, flailing his arms and rubbing his hair when he comes into the room. He's a bit insecure I think.

Except for the first three years of the band he's always been a little bit difficult to relate to. Maybe because we're totally different people. For instance, Keith will come into a hotel room and in fifteen minutes it looks like it's been a gypsy camp for the last twenty years. He just makes things look like that. He throws things around. I couldn't live like that. I could stay in a hotel room twenty years and it would still look like it did the first day I got there. And Woody's exactly the same as Keith!

PETE FORNATALE: Well, Woody then?

BILL WYMAN: I think he's getting too much like Keith. And one Keith's enough. To have a Keith in the band is great, but to have a Keith and a Keith Mach Two gets a little strange for me. Musically, he's fine. But it's like Keith and the shadow, in a way. Woody wasn't quite like that when he joined.

He was just all fun and games and laughing. He united the band much more when we were kind of drifting apart personality-wise. It's very frustrating to be in the same band that long because what you liked in 1963 you don't necessarily like in 1981. So there's a lot of things that get left out, that you can't deal with in the same band. That's

Bill Wyman, backstage at Sullivan in 1965

why Woody does solo albums, and Mick Taylor probably got really frustrated, and Brian Jones, too. So Charlie has to play with a jazz band, and I had to do some solo albums and some producing, and Mick did movies. You do have other things that you want to do. When we all came into this band, we probably never thought it would last more than two or three years and suddenly it's a third of your life. That's the whole thing about leaving after twenty years, because it's enough for me. No matter how great it is. Wonderful to do, and be in that band, but I've got so many other things that I want to do in my life, I don't want to still be going out on a stage in a wheelchair in ten years' time.

PETE FORNATALE: Charlie said once that he hated rock 'n' roll. Do you buy that?

BILL WYMAN: He probably said something like "I don't like rock 'n' roll" but he didn't mean he didn't like rock 'n' roll music. He meant he didn't like all the things that go with rock 'n' roll—living in a hotel, constant traveling, etc. He much prefers to play jazz, where he can just get dropped off at a club and jam with some people and then go home. That's a lot of what he does now. But I know he does like rock 'n' roll music as well because he listens to a lot of it, a lot of new wave stuff and everything. English papers are terrible that way. They abbreviate what you say and précis it down to such little pieces that it becomes totally different from what you intended.

PETE FORNATALE: As far back as 1969, there were rumors that Bill Wyman was leaving the band or being forced out of the band or fired by Mick. Do you have any comments on those stories?

BILL WYMAN: The thing I said about retiring? Yeah it escalated into something amazing. What actually happened was the guy said, "How long do you think the band is gonna last?" And I said, "Well, probably a couple of years." We've been saying that since '62. So he says, "How long do you think you're gonna go on?" And I answered, "Well, if we do last a few more years we'll be at our twentieth anniversary in December of 1982 and if the band is still functioning then—which it may or may not, I don't know—then I think that would be a good time to stop, while we're still up there, and then start to do something else. Because you can't play rock 'n' roll

THE MVP OF THE SECOND HALF

The Rolling Stones new promoter for the 1989 tour was Torontonian Michael Cohl, who had worked with the Stones on a local level going back many years but never for a prolonged period. Cohl had figured out a way, through what he called package touring, to eliminate all the various middlemen and expand the concert business. He guaranteed the Stones a reported sum of 70 million dollars. All along, Cohl suspected he might just be setting the price for Bill Graham, but in the end the band chose Cohl, and a string of sellouts later proved that Cohl and the Stones were a match made in heaven.

One of the hallmarks of the Stones' tours in the last quarter century has been their ability to take something that should be impersonal—the stadium concert—and turn it into something intimate and memorable, an intergenerational concert experience that is truly one of a kind. They've done this not only through the energy of their performances but also through creative staging, lighting, superior sound, special effects, and the use of video. Michael Cohl has played a big role in all of this.

In a famous 1989 interview, Keith famously said the Stones were at the beginning of the second half. Michael Cohl just might be the MVP of the second half.

forever." Then that escalated into how I was quitting the band on that day in '82 and I didn't like Mick and Keith and so on. I felt a bit rotten, you know, the way it was put, it looked like I was being bitchy . . . and we're not like that.

I can only add two addenda to this. The first is that following the afternoon I spent with him gathering facts and stories for *Rock Calendar*, I could never, ever think of him again as "the quiet Stone." And secondly, something he said to me as we were wrapping things up has only become more poignant in the years since:

BILL WYMAN: See, I can never buy a Stones album, put it on, and just listen and say, "Wow! That's good" or "That's bad," because before it even goes in the shops I know the whole thing by heart . . . It's like I've never seen a Rolling Stones concert, which might be a good kick one day . . . (After I leave) I just might do that!

The actual self-imposed end of Bill Wyman's tenure with the Stones came about twelve years after our conversation. He was quoted as saying he left because he had developed a fear of flying and because he didn't see anything new happening in the future. Richards seemed in denial about Wyman's departure, at least jokingly so, "No one leaves this band except in a coffin," he opined.

CHAPTER 47

NEW FACES

THE FIRST POST-WYMAN effort was 1994's *Voodoo Lounge*. The process of replacing half of their rhythm section wasn't easy. The Stones interviewed dozens of bassists to fill Wyman's shoes.

INTRODUCING DARRYL JONES

When did you first hear that the Stones were hiring?

DARRYL JONES: A friend of mine called me on the phone and said, "Bill Wyman is leaving the Stones." He found Mick's management's number and I called. Whoever I spoke to said nothing was going to happen immediately, but they'd add my name to the list. Then I spoke to someone in the camp after I got the gig who told me, "You know, your name was already on the list." I had met Mick very briefly when I played with Sting.

Darryl's choice of beverages may have helped him land the gig. Darryl told us that when he was playing with Miles Davis in New York, he spent a lot of time hanging out in Irish pubs, drinking Guinness. By coincidence, all the bassists who auditioned for the Stones were offered a Guinness by Ronnie Wood, as a kind of icebreaker, maybe even a test. Most declined.

DARRYL JONES: Ronnie said, "Great to meet you. Do you want a Guinness?" I said, "Sure, I dig Guinness."

Darryl's time with the Stones was off to a great start! As for the audition itself?

DARRYL JONES: I was happy to be there and was looking forward to playing, no matter what the outcome. I walked in and saw Keith and Mick. Then Mick said, "Listen Darryl. If you don't know the songs, we'll teach you the songs, and then we'll have you audition. From the beginning they created a really relaxed atmosphere. That they were that loose and that willing to really give me a chance made a real difference.

The final call about the band's new bassist would belong to Charlie—an unprecedented position of power within the band for him. But Charlie and Darryl were a natural fit, both personality-wise, and musically.

DARRYL JONES: I think my work with Miles Davis didn't hurt that.

Darryl told a funny story about how after the decision had been made to hire him for the tour, no one bothered to tell him at first.

DARRYL JONES: Charlie told Keith, "Don't you think it would be a good idea to tell him he's hired?" That's when Keith told me. It was January of '94.

How is it playing with Keith?

DARRYL JONES: I love standing next to him. Nobody plays guitar that way. He is a rhythm motherfucker. He's one of the most improvisational guitarists I've worked with. He's always trying new things. It's always exciting. He's always trying to fit a square peg into a round hole. That irreverence is a big part of the Stones' sound.

Darryl brought his own fluid and funky style of bass playing to the Stones, not easy when replacing a legend like Bill Wyman, who was known for anchoring the Stones' sound.

DARRYL JONES: If it was a case that the bass line that Bill played was really the song, then I cut it close to what Bill played. There are certain things on "Miss You" that have to be done for it to be "Miss You." But I listened to the feeling of the songs and tried to re-create the feeling from what I do naturally.

Chicago-born bassist Darryl Jones

Jones seemed the perfect man for the job, as he was friendly with Keith's colleagues in the X-Pensive Winos, and had played with acts as diverse as Eric Clapton, Madonna, and Miles Davis, the latter gig no doubt endearing him to Charlie Watts in particular.

CHUCK LEAVELL: I was not a part of that process . . . There was something like eighteen, twenty guys that auditioned for the gig. The word that I got through the band was that they were all good. Any one of them would work fine. "Charlie it's up to you."

Darryl's such a versatile player; he's well versed in many styles. He knows when to pump it and he knows when to lay back. He has a great sensibility of music. He's a superb musician.

Voodoo Lounge also featured a new producer. Detroit-born Don Was saw his first Stones show in 1964 on the band's very first trip to the Motor City. He has famously stated that hearing *Exile on Main Street* helped him decide to drop out of the University of Michigan in 1972.

DON WAS: I knew Mick a bit but I'd never met Keith before. I went to an audition in New York, where they were trying out bass players. My interview for the job was listening to Keith tell me why he doesn't need a producer.

Like Jimmy Miller before him, a fine bass player in his own right, Was became an active participant in the studio.

KEITH RICHARDS: To me, [Don Was is] very much like working with Jimmy Miller, who's a producer but also a musician. To the Stones, it's a real extra plus to have a guy that knows how things are played, what's done. And Don's real contribution was, "You've got a hundred songs here. We have to choose!" (*laughs*) You know, "Let's cut this list down by half to start with, and then eliminate," because there was just songs coming up. We had more and more stuff and we were in danger of just being buried in an avalanche of material. And it was his job to hone down that. Also I had Don Smith engineering, the guy that did the two Winos records, as well. So I had a team going there that was very well used to working with each other. Don Was, the new guy, slotted in beautifully and handled the personal stuff really well. Just keep your mind on what you're doing, you know? The atmosphere was very much *Exile on Main St.*, actually. I can't think of sessions since where things were quite that loose and free, and ideas were popping up.

Was would go on to be the band's producer for eighteen years and counting, even getting the job of remastering *Exile on Main St.* (much to our friend Andy Johns's chagrin) and also *Some Girls*, the most recent Rolling Stones reissue as of this writing.

There's no doubt *Voodoo Lounge* has a retro feel that connected with Stones fans and the resulting tour showed that the Stones still had major drawing power—they played to over eight million people and racked up half a *billion* dollars.

The Rolling Stones with Pete Fornatale and Dave Herman from the *Voodoo Lounge* tour

The Stones at the Meadowlands on the *Bridges to Babylon* tour

Chuck Leavell's role expanded for the *Voodoo Lounge* tour. He became a de facto stage manager for the band and also it was one of his responsibilities to create the set lists.

CHUCK LEAVELL: The next tour that came around was *Voodoo Lounge* . . . I think there were some in the band that felt we really didn't need the extra keyboard; there really wasn't a whole lot of call for orchestral sounds with the band. There were some songs: "Angie," for instance, had strings on the record. So I suggested, "Why don't we get a horn section that has a fellow that can play keyboards. If we have two or three songs that need a string part or some other keyboard part, then he could come down and do that . . ." That seemed to go down well with everybody.

Another album followed in 1997, *Bridges to Babylon*. Though to be fair, that record is more like a mash-up of a Richards solo album and a Jagger solo album.

KEITH RICHARDS: A long way from Andrew Loog Oldham's kitchen—a collaboration without actually being together.

Despite the unusual process of getting the album made, the Stones would go on to tour it for the better part of two years. This was emblematic of who the Stones had become by the second half of their existence: road warriors intent on making money and spreading the gospel of rock 'n' roll.

KEITH RICHARDS: Being on the road is the life of the band, it's the essence of it. Without that, the band wouldn't be capable of doing anything else. If we stopped doing everything else, and could still be able to play live, it would be fine. But if the band couldn't play live anymore, you can't just do recording sessions and playing for yourself, the only way you're going to get the full experience of the band, the band needs to be able to improve all the time, is to have an audience to play to.

I enjoy the whole thing about being on the road, I enjoy the pace of it, and anything that would normally be a drag maybe is really insignificant because you do have those two and a half hours on stage. I sometimes feel sorry for the people that come round on tours and I don't know how they make it because they don't have those two and a half hours on stage. They just have been watching the band each night and saying yeah, that was a good show, living it through us, that would be murder for me. I enjoy watching the band improve, tighten up, all the time. The more it plays, the better it gets, which is always very sad that last week when you know you've got three more gigs left . . .

For two or three months it's total energy output and then everybody's gone, there's nothing to do. You're ready to go but there's nothing that requires that amount of energy that you've still built up.

BRIDGES TO BABYLON

Mick Jagger famously studied for two years at the London School of Economics. He never did graduate, and instead had to learn many lessons the hard way. Like so many of the seminal blues artists they admired, the Stones in their early years were ripped off, exploited, taken advantage of, and advised improperly about management contracts, record deals, royalties, and even performance fees.

But a lot has changed.

In the beginning, the measure of the Stones' success was taken by the teen magazines and fanzines; then it was by the more serious rock periodicals such as *Rolling Stone*, *Crawdaddy*, *Fusion*, and *Creem*; the once-mighty general-interest magazines like *Life*, *Look*, and the *Saturday Evening Post* all got in on the act too; but these days you're more likely to find accurate information about the Stones juggernaut in *Fortune* magazine or the *Wall Street Journal*.

The Stones began to take control of their finances as early as the free Hyde Park concert in 1969, and the formation of Rolling Stones Records a year or so later. Since then, they have made very few errors in their quest to maximize earnings and profit potential. They have been in the vanguard of every financial growth spurt in the evolution of rock 'n' roll. Even leaving out recording and publishing royalties,

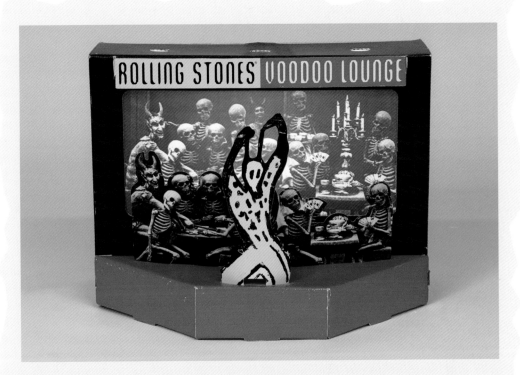

here is a litany of ways in which the Rolling Stones have paved the way for all the others who followed in their wake. Here are ten of the Stones' ingenious marketing ploys:

1. Partnering with Granada Productions to make a documentary about the Hyde Park concert.

2. Commissioning a film about the '69 US tour (that captured all of the drama and turmoil of Altamont).

3. The Jōvan sponsorship of the 1981 tour, notably the first major rock tour sponsorship. (Total investment for name on posters and tickets: one million dollars)

4. Also in '81, and also a first, using a concert as a pay-per-view event.

5. During the *Steel Wheels* tour in '89, launching a Stones-themed clothing line sold not only at the concerts but also in retail outlets. This too was a first.

6. In 1991, they became the first rock band to release an IMAX concert film, *The Rolling Stones at the Max*.

7. In 1995, the Stones made an unprecedented deal linking one of their songs to the ad campaign of a major consumer product. Here's the story Pop-History

Dig chronicled: "In the annals of advertising history, one of the great coups in the use of rock 'n' roll music to help sell things came in the summer of 1995 when Bill Gates of the Microsoft Corporation used the Rolling Stones' "Start Me Up" song to help launch his company's Windows 95 computer software. As the story goes, it was Gates's idea to use the song, as the tune dovetailed nicely with the prominent "start button" feature that appeared on the Windows computer screen. Initially it was rumored that Gates paid something in the neighborhood of ten to fourteen million dollars to the Stones to use their song. The actual figure may have been lower than that. But as the story goes, Gates reportedly asked Jagger personally how much it would cost to use the song. Jagger, being the naughty boy he is, threw out what he thought would be a very high number, something in the millions; a number that would surely dissuade Gates in his quest. But Jagger's ploy didn't faze Gates—at least according to legend. Whatever amount Jagger had suggested, Gates agreed to it on the spot.

8. In September of 2002, the Stones did their first live television concert ever, for HBO subscribers only from Madison Square Garden in New York.

9. Brilliant repackaging/remastering of classic albums, like *Exile on Main Street* in 2010 and *Some Girls* in 2011. Don Was told *Rolling Stone*, "There's so much material if they never went in the studio again, you could have a new Stones album every year for the next fifty years, and it would all be good."

10. *Bridges to Babylon* on PBS in 1998. The Stones took their act to public television, a savvy move that helped PBS gin up donations and also made money for the band. As a certain lucky DJ said on the radio, "Mick and Keith have been on public television more this week than Bert and Ernie."

CHAPTER 48

DON'T STOP

BEHOLD SIR MICK JAGGER. In June of 2002, Mick was knighted and this honor brought to the fore once again the difference between him and Keith Richards. Keith was horrified that Mick accepted. It's the rock 'n' roll version of "You Make the Call."

KEITH RICHARDS: I thought it was ludicrous to take one of those gongs from the Establishment when they did their very best to throw us in jail.

MICK JAGGER: It's a great recognition of what the band's achievements have been over the years we've been together.

For their fortieth anniversary, also in 2002, the Stones released an album and did a tour. True to the Stones' nature, neither was conventional. The album was called *Forty Licks*, and due to a settlement with Allen Klein, it was the first time the Stones' entire catalog was able to be represented on one compilation. They also bravely included four new songs along with the classics, and while none of them are going to make you forget about "Brown Sugar," it is notable that the Stones were still trying.

The tour was unique in that it featured three separate shows for three separate-sized venues: stadiums, arenas, and theaters.

CHUCK LEAVELL: It did present some challenges. But with challenges come opportunities. I think we began to look at what songs would work well in those venues. Keith called it the "Fruit of the Loom Tour": small, medium, and large . . . It gave the band an opportunity to dig even deeper into that incredible catalog and pull out songs that made sense to do in any particular setting whether it's a club, arena, or big stage . . . Doing the set list was really fun for that . . .

STEVE MORSE: They had learned many of the songs from the early days to play at the smaller venues on that tour, the Orpheum in Boston for example. Digging out some of the old blues stuff. Buddy Guy came out. They scaled the shows. When they played a stadium, they did mostly the hits. It was groundbreaking in that sense. How many bands can play three separate venues in one city? They also played the Fleet Center and it was a cross between the Orpheum show and the stadium show. Some hits with some obscurities. I give them a lot of a credit for the vision of doing that.

Mick, Keith, and Charlie on the *40 Licks* fortieth anniversary tour

PARENTING KEITH RICHARDS-STYLE

Keith and Anita's relationship finally dissolved for good in 1979. By 1983, Keith had married Patti Hansen and they moved to Connecticut and had two daughters, Theodora (born 1985) and Alexandra (born 1986).

At some point circa 2001, male visitors who came to call on Keith Richards's daughters at his house in Connecticut were greeted by an odd sight: the rock 'n' roll legend himself pacing around the area where the kids were hanging out with a bowie knife, sharpened, in his hands. He had one phrase of advice for his kids' friends: "You will respect my daughters; you will respect my house," was all he said.

The Stones' 2005 tour, A Bigger Bang, kicked off at venerable Fenway Park in Boston.

LARRY CANCRO: We had only done two concerts before the Stones approached us. And we didn't understand what it would mean to be the first show in a worldwide tour. When you're the very first stop, there are no answers to your questions. They had an idea for a stage. And the idea for the stage kept growing and growing and growing. They sent us drawings and we saw the elevator shafts and the private suites in the stage. The more we looked at it the more daunting it became, the more outfield it took up, the less seating area there was left on the field. Stage size matters when you have to have a game two days after they leave.

Of all the concerts we've ever done, this was the only time we ever had rain during the installation. We had to replace over a third of our outfield grass when we got this stage out.

A BIGGER BANG

In 2005, the Rolling Stones were back in the studio as a band who actually worked together. Perhaps part of the reason Mick and Keith were able to work together so well again is they gained some valuable perspective when they learned Charlie had cancer.

DON WAS: Mick and Keith are writing songs in a collaborative fashion that probably hasn't been seen since the late '60s.

The album's title was perhaps a wink at Bill Wyman, who was once quoted during the WW III period as saying, "It's a pity we didn't go out with a big bang. Instead we went out with a whimper."

Keith writes about the making of that album in *Life*:

KEITH RICHARDS: Only Mick still thinks you have to take things into "real" recording studios to make a real record. He got proved totally wrong on our latest album—at time of writing—*A Bigger Bang*, especially because we did it in his little chateau in France. We had got the stuff all worked up and he said, "Now we'll take it into a real recording studio." And Don Was and I looked at each other, and Charlie looked at me . . . Fuck this shit. We've already got it down right here. Why do you want to spring for all that bread. So you can say it was cut in so-and-so studio, the glass wall and the control room? We ain't going nowhere, pal. So finally he relented.

One of my favorite moments was when Ronnie Wood and Charlie Watts came out of the dugout from the clubhouse, which was their dressing room, and Ronnie Wood was telling Charlie, "I visited here as a kid. My uncle lived in Boston and he brought me to a game. We sat right over there. I can't believe we're about to play here." The Stones have kept that sense of wonder throughout their five decades together and it's one of the reasons they've been able to overcome all the obstacles and remain as relevant as they have.

CHAPTER 49

ROUGH JUSTICE

In February of 2006, the Stones played the Super Bowl halftime show in Detroit Michigan. This was second in a series of "sure thing" halftime shows after the Janet Jackson, Justin Timberlake "wardrobe malfunction" debacle in 2004. In 2005, Paul McCartney got the gig. Who better than the Stones to pick up the mantle?

LAURENCE RANDALL: We like to have a G-rated show. We think we've done a good job of that since 2005. The Rolling Stones are the Rolling Stones. One thing we have learned over time is that you can't tell an artist what to play or they will play the opposite. There were lyrics in the two songs not suitable to the NFL or their broadcast partners. In the conversations we had with them, we offered two alternatives a) if you would like to choose another song, you have a huge, vast catalog or b) if you're not going to choose another song, you have to drop those lyrics.

Of course, the Stones being the Stones, they chose the unoffered option c. They sang the lyrics and had them censored. The "dead man come" line in "Start Me Up" was bleeped, as was the word "cock" in "Rough Justice." Ironically, the third song in the set, "Satisfaction," which had caused the Stones some trouble on Ed Sullivan back in the day (see chapter 13) escaped censor free.

CHUCK LEAVELL: I'm from Alabama. I was born in Birmingham and wound up—we settled in Tuscaloosa when I was probably in the fourth or fifth grade. That's where I got my musical start. Hey, roll Tide!

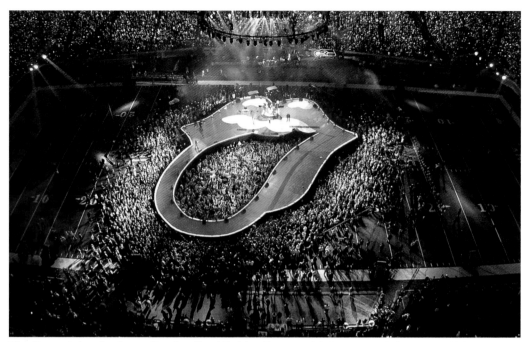

The Stones play the Super Bowl at Ford Field in Detroit, Michigan, on February 5, 2006

Chuck was not the only guy on tour who was a sports fan.

CHUCK LEAVELL: The guys are all interested in sports. Of course, it tends to be more about soccer for them. Mick and Charlie in particular love cricket and watch the cricket matches all the time when we're on tour. One of the things that fascinated me was, you got a lot of technical challenges to roll out this stage, throw it together, get all the equipment hooked up, be right on time for the television, do those songs to a particular time requirement, then break it apart and get the game back going. It was absolutely fascinating to do the rehearsals and see the precision all the people had to work with to make it come off right. It was a tremendous honor and so much fun being up there.

DARRYL JONES: That was pure joy, pure terror. Somebody said to me, "I heard a billion people are going to be watching." It was really special. I was hoping we got a good one and we did.

And here's an eyewitness account from a lucky Stones fan.

KURT SCHWARZ: The NFL championship game between the Pittsburgh Steelers and the Seattle Seahawks was played in front of sixty-five thousand rabid American football fans and was reportedly televised to over one hundred million people worldwide. I was there, not for the game, but FOR THE STONES!

First, a little background. A call went out about a month before the game for two thousand volunteers to "act" as an audience for the Don Mischer–produced extravaganza. Are you kidding me? My brother and I jumped at the opportunity to see the Stones for free in our hometown. The commitment was a serious one. We were subjected to a ton of downtime and waiting during over fourteen hours of rehearsal time spread out over two days. Believe me, it was worth it.

During the dress rehearsal in Ford Field, Friday night before the game, we got the Rolling Stones, live, for a sound check and complete run-through including lighting, cameras, and pyro. How cool. They worked effortlessly through "Start Me Up," "Rough Justice," and "Satisfaction" three times. Twice in front of all of us and once with us sequestered in the tunnel leading to the field. What an amazing vibe with two thousand people waiting in the wings all rocking and bouncing to a sing-along of "Satisfaction." Between takes, my brother and I got to meet a few of the very cool Stones crew (Thanks Shep!) and even got an autograph from Chuck Leavell.

Now, on with the show! On a tongue-shaped stage designed exclusively for this event, the Stones ripped through their set. We watched the show from the lower right side of the lips, not our designated mandatory prerehearsed show position. But hey, after all, I'm a fan not a prop. No surprises, no special guests. Just pure rock 'n' roll. Just the way it should be.

THE STONES' MUSIC POST *TATTOO YOU*

Rolling Stones fan Matt Blankman has an annual ritual: to listen to all of the Stones' albums in chronological order. We asked Matt to provide his perspective on the Stones' recordings post 1981. Take it away, Matt!

Tattoo You, the Stones' 1981 album release, was largely a hodgepodge of outtakes, leftovers, and neglected tracks from previous album sessions. Associate producer Chris Kimsey dug into can after can of tapes, some of which dated all the way back to the Mick Taylor era and *Goats Head Soup* sessions of late 1972, and compiled the worthy tracks. Mick Jagger did the bulk of the work bringing them into the present, writing lyrics and melodies, recording vocals, and helping Kimsey shape the unruly stew into a unified album that sounded up to date. The result was a huge financial and critical success. *Tattoo You* is fully in a classic Rolling Stones vein and yet was ready for 1980s radio. The last Stones album to hit number one on the Billboard album chart, it's also what is now generally thought of by critics and Stones fans alike as the last great Rolling Stones album.

In the years since *Tattoo You*, Rolling Stones albums have all met a similar fate: lots of hype and attention at release, followed by reviews that breathlessly suggest that either a) it's their best work since *Some Girls* or *Exile on Main St.* or b) it's an embarrassment and they need to retire. For most fans, after running out the day of release to purchase any new Stones album, the initial excitement wears off within a few weeks, and albums such as *Steel Wheels* and *Bridges to Babylon* wind up gathering dust on the shelf while *Sticky Fingers* and *Aftermath* never leave the stereo for very long. Their album output in the three decades since *Tattoo You* may not live up to the brilliant standard they had created in the '60s and '70s, but these records all have their moments where the genius of the Rolling Stones fully shines through.

The Stones would release two more albums without touring, *Undercover* (1983) and *Dirty Work* (1986). However neither has aged particularly well and very few of the tracks ever made their way to the band's live sets or classic rock radio. The lead single from *Undercover*, the politically charged "Undercover of the Night," stands out as one of their more successful attempts at updating their sound for the '80s, as does Mick's oddball "Too Much Blood." There's no new ground broken on the back-to-basics horny-schoolboy rock 'n 'roll romp "She Was Hot," but that doesn't stop it from working.

Dirty Work saw the Mick and Keith feud of the 1980s at its zenith—Mick was absent from most of the album sessions. Made with then-hot producer of the moment Steve Lillywhite, the record suffers greatly from a dearth of good new Jagger/Richards songs. Ronnie Wood coaxed fellow British guitar hero Jimmy Page into playing lead on "One Hit (to the Body)," the only track that sounds remotely like a classic Stones single, but the production sounds terribly dated, with its 1980s "big drums" and female background vocalists. "Had It with You" is a lively, nasty rocker (and seemingly echoes Mick and Keith's ongoing hostilities), but the lone track that truly transcends the album is Keith's haunting, piano-driven ballad "Sleep Tonight," with a guest appearance by Keith's friend and sometime collaborator Tom Waits.

Détente was in the air a few years later as Mick and Keith got back together, wrote a few dozen new songs, and the Stones reemerged in the summer of 1989 with *Steel Wheels*. *Steel Wheels* saw a little nostalgia in the mix, as "Blinded by Love" was an acoustic-based song that wouldn't have sounded out of place on a 1966 Stones platter. As for the singles from the album, "Mixed Emotions" (or as Keith reportedly called it, "Mick's Emotions") was an effective call to arms, the strident "Rock and a Hard Place" less so, but both seemed like a Rolling Stones simulation rather than the real thing. Far better was the lost love song "Almost Hear You Sigh," originally written by Richards and Steve Jordan for the former's solo debut album *Talk Is Cheap*, retooled slightly by Jagger for the Stones. However, the album's most memorable track may be the sublime and delicate Richards-sung ballad that closes the album, "Slipping Away." The band seems to agree, as it's been in the concert repertoire ever since and was re-recorded for the partly live *Stripped* album in 1995.

Bill Wyman decided to call it quits in 1993. But later that year they were back in the studio with producer Don Was working on *Voodoo Lounge*. The whiffs of nostalgia on *Steel Wheels* grew stronger on *Voodoo Lounge*, as Was tamped down Jagger's desires to sound current in favor of a more classic Stones sound.

Jagger groused about it afterward, but Was's instincts were in sync with Stones fans. The lead single, "Love Is Strong," seemingly owed a lot to Richards's work with his X-Pensive Winos, but Jagger delivered a slinky, sexy vocal and strong harmonica work. Despite several slashing guitar workouts, once again, they were at their best with the quieter songs. "New Faces" was a surprising delight—a harpsichord-driven acoustic song about jealousy of a young rival suitor that could have come from *Aftermath* or *Between the Buttons*. Ronnie Wood broke out his pedal steel guitar for "The Worst," featuring Keith's gravelly, lived-in lead vocal and a gentle Celtic-country-rock lilt. "Blinded by Rainbows" is a moving tale of a lost soul amid political and religious violence and strife made haunting by one of Jagger's best vocal performances in years. Keith scored again with his second lead vocal of the album, the spooky, gritty "Thru and Thru," seen by some as a message to the missing Wyman rather than to an errant lover. (Years later, the track was used on the seminal TV series *The Sopranos*, and the song quickly found its way back into the set list.) *Voodoo Lounge* lacks only a truly great rocker to join the pantheon of classic Stones albums.

Jagger would get his wish to let the Stones experiment with more contemporary sounds a few years later with *Bridges to Babylon*. Don Was returned, but Jagger brought in the Dust Brothers (riding high after working with Beck on his breakthrough album *Odelay*) to give some tracks a more current sheen. The resulting album is a bit scattershot, despite some strong material. Jagger's attempts to incorporate hip hop and electronic elements to the blues workouts and ballads he and Keith had written seem gimmicky and have not aged as well as the more straightforward tracks. The lead single "Anybody Seen My Baby?" cringe inducing fifteen years later, with the sample of rapper Biz Markie sticking out like a sore thumb.

Nevertheless, the Stones still knew how to construct and execute a great track, as the terrific "Already Over Me" illustrates, featuring an expressive, sensitive vocal by Mick and beautiful guitar textures from Keith. "Flip the Switch" rocked at an absurdly fast clip and "Too Tight" was an unjustly neglected, driving barn burner buried near the end of the album. Other strong material, like "Saint of Me" and "Might as Well Get Juiced," sound gummed up from the Dust Brothers overactive production. Keith protested that the more traditional takes of the bluesy "Juiced" blew the doors off the album version, and perhaps to reward his acceptance of Mick's experiments, he was given three lead vocals on the album: including the gorgeous jazz ballad "How Can I Stop," featuring jazz legend Wayne Shorter on soprano saxophone.

The band got back together in 2002 to record some new tracks for a greatest hits collection (*Forty Licks*) and tour. The tour was excellent, the new songs adequate but forgettable. (Quick—when was the last time you heard "Don't Stop"?) It took until 2005 to get a new full-length studio album out of the Stones, and it was worth the wait. *A Bigger Bang* was the most natural, least forced album the band had made in decades. Critics were again quick to suggest it was the best Stones record since *Tattoo You* but this time they were probably right. It neither sounded like the Stones pretending to replay their glory years or aping current pop trends, it simply sounded like the Rolling Stones. "Rough Justice" and "Oh No, Not You Again" were strong, driving rock 'n' roll tunes that showcased classic Stones swagger and "Back of My Hand" the best bit of pure blues they'd recorded in eons. "Biggest Mistake" is an enjoyable and darkly funny sadsack tale of lost love. "Let Me Down Slow" showed they could still write an exemplary pop song and "Streets of Love" was a lovely, shimmering ballad. Perhaps they were inspired by their friend Bob Dylan's late-career comeback, but *A Bigger Bang* found the Rolling Stones at peace with being the Rolling Stones, simply making strong music together, without pretense or affectation.

CHAPTER 50
SHINE A LIGHT

In 2006, Martin Scorsese and the Stones collaborated on the film *Shine a Light*. It was filmed at the Beacon Theatre in New York City.

KEITH RICHARDS: The Beacon Theatre is special for some reason anyway. Especially if you can play there for more than one night. The room sort of wraps its arms around you and every night gets warmer. It's a great-feeling room. And also, this band, it didn't start off in stadiums.

MICK JAGGER: Keith was saying how it's good to play there more than one night and I agree with him. Because the first night we played was more like a rehearsal for us in a way and by the time the second night came round we got more adjusted to playing in the small theater. We'd played a lot of small theaters in the past but we hadn't done it on this tour, so this was like quite different. By the second night, we knew this was going to be the night with all these people there, so I felt really good about that.

Why was Scorsese chosen to be the director?

MICK JAGGER: He's the best one around. And he's very painstaking on the editing to produce the movie that you see. It's not all in the shooting, it's obviously in the editing too.

MARTIN SCORSESE: For me, each song was like a narrative, a dramatic story. The whole sound of the band is like a character, one character for each song. And so, with the grace of these wonderful cinematographers, they were able to know exactly when to move that camera, like poets at times, to pick up when someone else was going down. We shot this in thirty-five millimeter, not video, so we were working with ten-minute loads, and cameras were going down all the time, running out of film. That's why there were so many cameras, to pick up the slack when one ran out of film. The key was to find the moments between the members of the band as they played together, how they work together; they work it like a machine, in a way, an engine in each song.

Promotional picture of the Stones with Martin Scorsese for *Shine a Light*

One of the special musical guests was Buddy Guy.

MICK JAGGER: We've done quite a few shows with Buddy Guy in the past. He's one of those continually wonderful blues performers that you admire. I think the thing that Marty captured in the duet thing we did was really one of the high points of the movie for me. The other guests [Jack White, Christina Aguilera] all in their own slightly different ways, all add to the movie and I like all the duets because they all really work. And they don't always work those duets.

BUDDY GUY: They called and invited me to mostly play. And I think Mick wanted me to not sing a whole verse. And we rehearsed it and come into record tonight and he looks at me and says, "I lost my voice. You got to do a whole verse."

I asked Keith for a guitar to go on the wall of my club. Every time I see him he said, "You don't have it?" I said, "Man, you know you haven't given me no guitar." He handed me a guitar right there. I didn't even know they was filming that.

There was a special guest on the other side of the camera as well.

ALBERT MAYSLES: I got a call from Martin the day before they started shooting and he said, "I've got eighteen thirty-five-millimeter cameras and I'd love to have you come with your video camera. Besides, both Mick and Keith have asked you to come."

"TRENDY, SEXY, AND HIP"

If there was ever a scintilla of doubt about whether or not the Stones will continue to attract newer and newer generations of rock 'n' roll fans, check out this piece written by my current twenty-something WFUV Mixed Bag engineer Jeremy Rainer. He cajoled his way into the filming of Shine a Light *and offered up this once-in-a-lifetime eyewitness account.*

My brother and I were hired as extras for the second Beacon concert. At five thirty P.M. on November 1, 2006, Alex and I reported to a school on West Seventieth Street, dressed "trendy, sexy, and hip" as we were instructed. We'd received an e-mail with instructions on how to dress, what to bring, and how to act. A special note at the bottom of the page said this:

You guys will be in the very front of the stage and will be the only people on camera for the documentary. We really need high energy. Dance, sing along, cheer on the band. They need your energy to play a really amazing show.

We checked in at the school, received wristbands and a debriefing, and waited. Everybody was really pumped, and was reminiscing about past shows they'd been to. I was extremely excited; the last four times I'd seen the Stones, I'd been sitting in the nosebleed seats at stadiums and arenas—nothing had prepared me for seeing them up close.

We were initially placed near the exit door on the side of the stage. Scorsese and his entourage walked past us; he was dressed in a long wool coat and scarf down to the floor. Keith's model daughters were standing a few feet in front of us. This definitely had the air of a movie shoot. There were film cameras on balconies, film cameras on dollies, film cameras on cranes: Scorsese and his team were ready to catch all angles of this performance. After a terrific opening set from Buddy Guy, my brother and I weighed the merits of sneaking down into the pit, which is where they'd said we'd be. Finally, Alex said, "C'mon. Let's take a walk." We walked through the crowd, past Alec Baldwin and Bruce Willis, flashed our wristbands, and entered the pit. Right away, a production guy yelled, "Hey YOU!" . . . I was certain we'd get kicked out . . . "I want you to stand right there," he said. "Right there" was ten feet away from the stage.

The houselights finally went down after what seemed like an hour, and the crowd erupted as Keith hit the opening chords of "Jumpin' Jack Flash." Even though this show was technically part of the *Bigger Bang* tour, the band didn't perform any songs from that album. Instead we were treated to a fantastic blend of big hits and rarely performed songs, like "She Was Hot," "All Down the Line," "Some Girls," and "I'm Free." There were special guests too: Jack White sang on "Loving

Cup," and Christina Aguilera sang on "Live With Me." Buddy Guy joined the band for a blistering version of Muddy Waters's "Champagne and Reefer" . . . I remember Keith being so impressed that he gave Buddy his guitar after the song!

But the most exciting moment for me came during "Sympathy for the Devil." Thirty seconds or so after the drum loop started, Mick entered from the back of the hall through a backlit doorway, which made for a spectacular visual display. During the song, he was working the runways as only Mick can, and he was moving and dancing like a man possessed.

Screen capture shining a light on our friend Jeremy Rainer

When you're that close to a band that great, it's impossible to take it all in. From the nosebleeds, you can clearly see the sum of all the parts; when you're ten feet away, the energy level is so high that you have to focus on a single musician at a time. But you can also watch what goes on between the musicians: the synergy, the interactions, the finger-pointing, the glances; the push and pull that keeps the show together. That is a thrill in itself.

Two hours after they hit the stage, after red-hot renditions of "Start Me Up," "Brown Sugar," and "Satisfaction," it was all over. The concert was finished, and the cameras were off. Alex and I slowly made our way home, neither one of us quite believing what had just happened. The next morning, there was no sleeping in. My brother had to catch a bus back to Binghamton to take a test—in rock 'n' roll history.

I told my dad that I never have to see the Stones again; the Beacon concert was one of the greatest experiences of my life, and it was worth all the pre-show anxiety and post-show exhaustion. It took me a week to get back into a normal state, both mentally and physically.

The big payoff is that I'm in the film! I distinctly remember where I was standing and what I was wearing, and can be clearly seen during "Brown Sugar." Not only that, but the album that was released, and actually all of the concert footage in the film, was recorded during the second night. What you have on the album is 99 percent of the concert I went to, with no overdubs and minimal editing. Both the film and the album are treasured keepsakes of an extraordinary, unforgettable experience.

EPILOGUE

MEMORY MOTEL

I AM WRITING THESE WORDS on Sunday, March 25, 2012, at 5:05 P.M. in the barroom of the Memory Motel in Montauk, Long Island (the place immortalized on one of the best songs from *Black and Blue*). I came here seeking inspiration for some final thoughts and wisdom to share with you about the fifty-year odyssey of the Rolling Stones.

Montauk has its annual St. Patrick's Day parade on the last Sunday in March, and the post-parade party is in full swing. The place is packed wall-to-wall with inebriated young people clad in every shade of green and the music blaring from multiple speakers is SO loud and SO un-Stones-like that I think I might have wasted a trip out here.

Then out of the corner of my eye in a hidden corner of the bar, I glimpse a wall seemingly festooned with Stones memorabilia. I inch my way toward that oasis, and sure enough there is a treasure trove of photos, newspaper articles, album covers, gold records, and, the pièce de résistance, a large framed print of the tongue logo autographed by Mick, Keith, and Ronnie. Here they are! These are the memories at the Memory Motel! The tangible ones, anyway. The mental ones are left to the imagination: the music created, the songs heard, the love made, are all in the eye and/or mind of the beholder.

Paul Simon once famously wrote, "Preserve your memories. They're all that's left you." Recordable media have raised the level of preserving memories to an art form in and of itself. All manner of books, films, albums, CDs, videos, and websites have chronicled almost every minute of the Stones' existence. I suppose these accounts (including this one, I hope) will be around for at least the next fifty years to answer any lingering questions about the twentieth/twenty-first century musical group called the Rolling Stones.

And, perhaps the biggest question of them all will be: Will the Stones still matter on their one hundredth anniversary in July of 2062? My answer is, "Unequivocally yes!" As long as there are humans on earth who are still interested in music, then so too will there be great curiosity about the Rolling Stones.

Fifty years ago, rock 'n' roll was still in its infancy. The '60s had barely begun. The Beatles were toiling away in relative obscurity. Dylan was still "Hammond's Folly" at Columbia Records. Bruce Springsteen was twelve years old! John F. Kennedy was the president of the United States. Television was still black and white. And Elvis was just out of the army making *G.I. Blues* in Hollywood instead of barnstorming the country state by state proclaiming, "Have you heard the news? There's good rockin' tonight!"

This was the pop cultural cauldron in which the Stones began to brew.

I'm astonished how quickly the 1963 headline WOULD YOU LET YOUR SISTER GO WITH A ROLLING STONE? turned into WOULD YOU LET YOUR GRANNY GO WITH A ROLLING STONE?

So let me wrap this up with some predictions and speculation about what is yet to come.

The Stones have set *the* standards and raised *the* bar at every level of their evolution. They will certainly *not* go out with a whimper. One final stab at proving to the world—and maybe even proving to themselves—that they were, still are, and always will be the Greatest Rock 'n' Roll Band in the World!

Totally in character, they will ignore the actual date of their own fiftieth anniversary. They will let the media nerds and fans (including you and me) do the celebrating for them. Then, when they are ready, they will seriously begin to put together that Farewell Tour (probably in 2013—the year in which both Mick and Keith will turn seventy years of age). They will invite Bill Wyman to join them—and he will. They will invite Mick Taylor to join them—and, of course, you know he will. They will hit the road and take this show to every corner of the earth, but particularly to the USA, where rock 'n' roll was born, and where the Rolling Stones have lived and reigned for most of their fifty years.

We started this book with July 12, 1962. To bring things full circle, let's give the final words to Keith Richards:

KEITH RICHARDS: I mean, for me, the beginning of the '60s was when I got to be eighteen and nineteen, so in a way, it was a magical time, because I actually managed to turn my little juvenile fantasies into a way of life. I mean, I never dreamt that I would be able to do it, so it was magical in that sense, in that I'm still here playin' rock 'n' roll, and makin' a livin' at it, which is what I wanted to do. And I thought that would be impossible—that that was something that happened to stars. Even when we got our first record out, we all looked at each other with a little bit of dismay, you know? Because there was no precedent at that time; nobody lasted. You shot up there, and you were gone. There was no possible way you could believe that it was gonna last for anything more than another two years. So for us, it was like, "Oh, man, this is great, makin' records—but that means it's the beginning of the end," you know?

I, for one, prefer to think that then (and even now!) it was just the end of the beginning.

The author at the Memory Motel in 2012

ACKNOWLEDGMENTS

Without the aid of my father, these are going to be tough to write without forgetting a lot of people. Apologies in advance but here goes.

Thanks most to Ben Adams. It's his book; we work for him. Thanks also to Mitch Corbett. This is the payoff for a life misspent in pursuit of all things Rolling Stones.

Thanks also to those who've helped us write and shape this book, especially Matt Blankman, Jeremy Rainer, and Chris Wertz.

To Cheryl Ceretti, Professor Victor Coelho, Paul Goldman, Dave Herman, Fred Mullen, and Diane Snow, for sharing your resources.

To Susan Van Metre, who has been a rock through all this.

Nate Knaebel and George Gibson from Bloomsbury have both gone above and beyond in their efforts to help with this book. Frank Scatoni has provided invaluable help and support.

Without the help of Giro DiBiase, Tim Kelly, Ira Korman, Laurie McGaw, and especially Larry Marion, the visuals in this book wouldn't be nearly as cool. Thanks also to our friends Ron and Howard Mandelbaum of Photofest.

Jon Wilde and Harvey Kubernik were both gracious in allowing us to "borrow" their work.

To Kevin Goldman, for being a friend.

To Paul Simpson, ever a clutch performer.

Others to thank: Bill Ayres, Tom Bensen, Patty Bernstein, the family of Sid Bernstein, Rob Bowman, Crissy Boylan, John DeChristopher, Tommi Degerman, Phil Doherty, Geoff Dorsett, Geoff Edgers, Brian Fadden, John Ferguson, Phil Fiumano, Jeffrey Foskett, Mark Gompertz, Sarah Karos, Paul Kurland, Annie Lawlor, Andrew Leach,

Brian McCarthy, Drew Marrochello, Leigh Montville, Brittany Morrongiello, Brian Netto, Archie Patterson, Neil Porter, Sandi Smith, Katherine Somova, Don Thiergard, Tony Traguardo, Richie Unterberger, Lissa Warren, Cristina Zizza, and Kathy Zuckerman.

CAST OF CHARACTERS

Keith Altham is an English rock journalist, publicist, and author.

Billy Altman is a rock critic and friend of the family.

Marty Balin was one of the lead singers for Jefferson Airplane.

Sonny Barger is a founding member of the Hells Angels Motorcycle Club.

Sid Bernstein promoted both the Beatles and the Stones on their first tours of America.

Steve Binder was a renowned director who worked on both the *T.A.M.I. Show* and Elvis Presley's '68 Comeback Special.

Bob Bonis was the Stones tour manager on their first tours of the US and was also an excellent amateur photographer. Many of his photos appear throughout this book. You can see more of his work in the books *The Lost Beatles Photographs* and *The Lost Rolling Stones Photographs*.

Craig Braun worked with Andy Warhol in the '60s and is best known for his work helping to design the *Sticky Fingers* jacket.

Larry Cancro works for the Boston Red Sox as senior vice president of Fenway affairs.

Marshall Chess is the son and nephew of the founders of Chess Records. He was also the first president of Rolling Stones Records.

Eric Clapton is a rock 'n' roll guitar god.

Alan Clayson is the frontman for Clayson and the Argonauts and the author of many rock books.

Merry Clayton is an accomplished American singer best known to Stones' fans for singing on "Gimme Shelter."

Sam Cutler, author of *You Can't Always Get What You Want: My Life with the Rolling Stones, the Grateful Dead, and Other Wonderful Reprobates,* is most famous for being the Rolling Stones' tour manager in 1969.

Joe D'Allesandro is an American actor and Warhol superstar, immortalized as "Little Joe" in Lou Reed's "Walk on the Wild Side."

Stephen Davis is an American music journalist.

Norman Dayron was a producer for Chess Records.

Anthony DeCurtis is an American author and rock critic.

Marianne Faithfull is an English singer and actress.

Mick Farren is an English journalist, author, and rock 'n' roll singer.

Robert Frank is a renowned photographer and filmmaker.

Bill German is the rock historian who ran the *Beggars Banquet* fanzine and authored the book *Under Their Thumb.*

Gary Pig Gold is a Canadian singer-songwriter, record producer, filmmaker, journalist, and author.

Bobby Goldsboro is an American musician who appeared with the Stones on their first US tour.

Bill Graham was a famous (and feared) rock promoter and impresario.

Robert Greenfield is an American journalist and author.

Peter Guralnick is an American author and music critic.

Buddy Guy is an acclaimed Chicago blues guitarist and friend to the Rolling Stones.

Taylor Hackford is an American director who worked with Keith Richards on *Hail! Hail! Rock 'n' Roll.*

George Harrison was the Beatles' secret weapon.

Dave Herman worked with my father for many years at WNEW-FM and K-ROCK. Several of the interviews that appear in this book were done by him.

Barney Hoskyns is an English rock critic and author and the editor of the website Rock's Back Pages (www.rocksbackpages.com).

Dartford-born **Rick Huxley** was the bassist for the Dave Clark Five.

Chrissie Hynde is the singer/songwriter/guitarist and all around frontwoman for the Pretenders.

Mick Jagger needs no introduction.

Andy Johns is an English record engineer and producer who worked extensively with the Stones and other rock luminaries.

That description also fits his elder brother, Rock and Roll Hall of Famer **Glyn Johns**.

Rock and Roll Hall of Famer **Johnnie Johnson** is a pianist best known for his work with Chuck Berry.

Darryl Jones is a Chicago-born guitarist who has played bass with the Stones since 1993.

Aki Kanamori is a Rolling Stones fan who attended Altamont.

Phil Kaufman was a rock 'n' roll road manager and friend of Gram Parsons.

Saxophonist **Bobby Keys,** who shares a birthday with Keith Richards, met the Stones on their first tour of the States and has played with them on and off ever since.

Engineer and producer **Chris Kimsey** worked with the Stones from *Sticky Fingers* through the *Steel Wheels* tour.

Al Kooper should be in the Rock and Roll Hall of Fame.

South African–born **Eddie Kramer** was an engineer and producer who worked with the Stones, the Beatles, Led Zeppelin, and Jimi Hendrix, among others.

John Landis is an American director and screenwriter.

Don Law's company, Tea Party Productions, promoted the Stones' Boston appearance on the 1972 tour.

Chuck Leavell is an American keyboardist who has played with Eric Clapton, the Allman Brothers, and, of course, the Rolling Stones.

Sometime Rolling Stones foil **John Lennon** was a member of the Beatles and remains one of the most important and influential musicians ever.

Michael Lindsay-Hogg is a filmmaker who has worked with the Stones many times, including on *The Rolling Stones Rock and Roll Circus.*

Paul McCartney was a member of the Beatles and is one of the most famous singers and songwriters of all time.

Ray Manzarek was the keyboardist for the Doors.

Mike Martinek is a Stones fan who attended the 1972 tour show in Boston on July 18.

John Mayall has been a blues musician for more than half a century. He founded John Mayall and the Bluesbreakers.

Joyce Maynard is an American journalist and author.

Albert Maysles is a documentary filmmaker.

Producer **Jimmy Miller** was the architect behind one of the most successful periods in Stones history.

Steve Morse is an American rock journalist.

Andrew Mosker is a Canadian musicologist and the world's foremost expert on the Rolling Stones' Mighty Mobile Unit.

Scott Muni was one of the great rock 'n' roll deejays of all time.

Steve Nazro is the director of events at Boston Garden.

Andrew Loog Oldham was a co-manager and producer of the Rolling Stones from 1963 to 1967.

Anita Pallenberg is an actress and model who was Keith Richards' partner from 1967 to 1979.

John Pasche is an art designer who designed the famous tongue logo.

Greg Perloff's company is Another Planet Entertainment; he was the tour coordinator on the '81 tour.

Laurence Randall is the director of programming for the National Football League.

Keith Richards is the illegitimate son of Chuck Berry and Jimmy Reed.

Peter Rudge is a rock 'n' roll tour manager who worked with the Stones from 1972 to 1977.

Kurt Schwarz is a Rolling Stones fan who blogs at www.reallifehusband.com.

Martin Scorsese is a legendary filmmaker.

Gloria Stavers, one of the first female rock journalists, was the editor in chief of *16* magazine throughout the 1960s.

Ian Stewart was a founding member of the Rolling Stones.

Sugar Blue is an American blues musician best known for playing the harmonica on "Miss You."

Ed Sullivan hosted a wildly popular variety show from 1948 to 1971.

Blues legend **Hubert Sumlin** played guitar for Howlin' Wolf.

Dick Taylor was the original bassist for the Rolling Stones, he later went on to found the Pretty Things.

Mick Taylor was the lead guitarist of the Rolling Stones from 1969 to 1974.

Dean Torrence, of the surf rock duo Jan and Dean, co-hosted the *T.A.M.I. Show*.

Irma Thomas is an American blues and soul singer who sang the original version of "Time Is on My Side."

Roast-meister **Pete Townshend** moonlights as the guitarist for the Who.

Kenny Vance was an original member of Jay and the Americans.

Klaus Voorman is a German-born artist and musician, most famous for his work with the Beatles.

Don Was is an American musician and producer who has worked with the Stones since *Voodoo Lounge*.

Charlie Watts is the greatest drummer in rock 'n' roll history.

Chris Welch is an English music journalist.

Mike White is a film critic and the author of *Impossibly Funky: A Cashiers du Cinemart Collection*.

Tom Wolfe is an American journalist and author.

Guitarist **Ron Wood** was a member of the Jeff Beck Group and the Faces and has been with the Stones since 1975.

Leslie Woodhead is an English filmmaker.

Bill Wyman was the longtime bassist for the Rolling Stones.

SOURCE NOTES

This book started based on interviews my father did with Mick Jagger and Bill Wyman. Then our friend Dave Herman graciously gave us access to never-before-published interviews with Keith Richards, Mick Jagger, Charlie Watts, Ron Wood, and Bill Wyman.

Most of the other interviews were either from my father's archives or done specifically for this book, including ones with: Billy Altman, Marty Balin, Sid Bernstein, Craig Braun, Larry Cancro, Alan Clayson, Sam Cutler, Norman Dayron, Anthony DeCurtis, Marianne Faithfull, Bill German, Bobby Goldsboro, Robert Greenfield, Buddy Guy, Taylor Hackford, Andy Johns, Johnnie Johnson, Darryl Jones, Aki Kanamori, Al Kooper, Eddie Kramer, Don Law, Chuck Leavell, Michael Lindsay-Hogg, Ray Manzarek, Mike Martinek, John Mayall, Albert Maysles, Steve Morse, Andrew Mosker, Steve Nazro, Andrew Loog Oldham, Greg Perloff, Laurence Randall, Peter Rudge, Hubert Sumlin, Dick Taylor, Irma Thomas, Dean Torrence, Kenny Vance, and Leslie Woodhead.

Because of my father's passing, compiling the source notes for this book has been a challenge. Every effort has been made to credit other writers whose research we've used. If we have missed anyone, we apologize and encourage accidentally neglected sources to contact us through the book's website (www.50Licksbook.com). Proper credit will be given both there and in future editions of this book.

BOOKS

Sid Bernstein (as told to Arthur Aaron), *Not Just the Beatles . . .* (Jacques & Flusster, 2000).
Richard Buskin, *Inside Tracks: A First-Hand History of Popular Music from the World's Greatest Record Producers and Engineers* (Quill, 1999).

Alan Clayson, *The Rolling Stones: The Origin of the Species: How, Why and Where It All Began* (Chrome Dreams, 2007).

Sam Cutler, *You Can't Always Get What You Want: My Life with the Rolling Stones, the Grateful Dead, and Other Wonderful Reprobates* (ECW Press, 2010).

Stephen Davis, *Old Gods Almost Dead: The 40-Year Odyssey of the Rolling Stones* (Broadway, 2001).

Sean Egan, *The Rough Guide to the Rolling Stones* (Rough Guides, 2006).

Marianne Faithfull with David Dalton, *Faithfull: An Autobiography* (Cooper Square Press, 2000).

Bill Flanagan, *Written In My Soul: Conversations With Rock's Greatest Songwriters* (Contemporary Books, 1987).

Bill German, *Under Their Thumb: How A Nice Boy from Brooklyn Got Mixed Up with the Rolling Stones (and Lived to Tell About It)* (Villard, 2009).

Bill Graham and Robert Greenfield, *Bill Graham Presents: My Life Inside Rock and Out* (Da Capo Press, 2004).

Jeff Greenfield, *No Peace, No Place: Excavations along the Generational Fault* (Doubleday, 1973).

Robert Greenfield, *Exile On Main Street: A Season In Hell with The Rolling Stones* (Da Capo, 2006).

———, *The Last Sultan: The Life and Times of Ahmet Ertegun* (Simon and Schuster, 2011).

———, *S.T.P.: A Journey Through America with the Rolling Stones* (Da Capo, 2002).

Mark Hoffman and James Segrest, *Moanin' at Midnight: The Life and Times of Howlin' Wolf* (Da Capo, 2005).

James Karnbach and Carol Bernson, *It's Only Rock 'n' Roll: The Ultimate Guide to the Rolling Stones* (Facts on File, 1997).

Phil Kaufman with Colin White, *Road Mangler Deluxe* (Colin White & Laurie Boucke, 2005).

Michael Lindsay-Hogg, *Luck and Circumstance: A Coming of Age in Hollywood, New York, and Points Beyond* (Knopf, 2011).

Dora Loewenstein and Philip Dodd (editors), *According to the Rolling Stones* (Chronicle Books, 2003).

Michael Lydon, *Rock Folk: Portraits from the Rock 'n Roll Pantheon* (Dial Press, 1971).

Alan Lysaght, *The Rolling Stones: An Oral History* (McCarthur and Company, 2003).

Larry Marion, *The Lost Rolling Stones Photographs: The Bob Bonis Archive 1964–1966* (It Books, 2011).

Keith Richards (with James Fox), *Life* (Little Brown, 2010).

Ethan A. Russell with Gerard Van der Leun, *Let It Bleed: The Rolling Stones, Altamont, and the End of the Sixties* (Springboard Press, 2009).

Harry Shapiro, *Alexis Korner: The Biography* (Bloomsbury, 1996).

Bill Wyman, *Stone Alone: The Story of a Rock 'n' Roll Band* (Da Capo, 1997).

Bill Wyman with Richard Havers, *Rolling with the Stones* (DK Publishing, 2002).

PERIODICALS

Keith Altham, "Rolling Stones: The Greatest Show On Earth," *NME*, December 21, 1968.

Francis J. Connolly (with research by Bernard M. Corbett), "A History of Boston Garden: A Diamond Jubilee," *Boston Phoenix*, 1988.

David Dalton, "Ladies and Gentlemen, Before Your Very Eyes, the Greatest Show on Earth," *Mojo*, October 2004.

Patrick Doyle, "Stones Go Back to Some Girls," *Rolling Stone*, November 24, 2011.

Mick Farren, "The Rolling Stones: *Sticky Fingers*," *Ink*, May 1, 1971.

Robert Greenfield, "The Rolling Stone Interview: Keith Richards," *Rolling Stone*, August 1971.

Barney Hoskyns, "The Rolling Stones: *Sticky Fingers* and *Exile On Main St.*," *The Observer*, June 2004.

Patti Smith, "Jag-arr of the Jungle," *Creem*, January 1973.

"Special Collectors' Edition: Rolling Stones 40th Anniversary," *Uncut*, 2002

"Special Edition: Inside the World's Greatest Rock and Roll Band," *Mojo*, 2002.

"The Ultimate Music Guide: The Rolling Stones," (special issue 4), *Uncut*, 2009.

Chris Welch, "The Rolling Stones: *Rock and Roll Circus*," *Melody Maker*, 1968.

Jann Wenner, "The Rolling Stone Interview: Jagger Remembers," *Rolling Stone*, December 14, 1995.

VIDEO

The Ed Sullivan Shows Starring the Rolling Stones (SOFA Entertainment, 2011), DVDs available at www.edsullivan.com.

Steve Binder, director, *T.A.M.I. Show: Teenage Awards Music International (Collector's Edition)* (Dick Clark Productions, 2009).

Taylor Hackford, director, *Chuck Berry Hail! Hail! Rock 'n' Roll* (Image Entertainment, 2006).

Stephen Kijak, director, *Stones in Exile* (Eagle Rock Entertainment, 2010).

Michael Lindsay-Hogg, director, *The Rolling Stones Rock and Roll Circus* (Abkco Films, 2004).

Albert Maysles, David Maysles, Charlotte Zwerin, directors, *Gimme Shelter* (Maysles Films, 2000).

Martin Scorsese, director, *Shine a Light* (Paramount, 2008).

WEBSITE RESOURCES (all accessed January 2012)

The amazing website www.timeisonourside.com run by the incomparable Ian McPherson was the source for many of the additional Stones' quotes you'll find herein. Check his site in the Sources section for further information if you're curious.

Rock's Back Pages (www.rocksbackpages.com) provided a lot of great background information and source material. If you don't already, you should really have a subscription.

Kurt Schwarz's account of seeing the Stones at the Super Bowl comes from the excellent It's Only Rock and Roll website (www.iorr.org). It can be found at www.iorr.org/tour05/sb.htm.

Joe D'Allesandro, "Album Cover Joe: Sticky Fingers" from www.joedallesandro.com/album.htm.

Paul DeRienzo, "Sonny Barger Interview" from pdr.autono.net/SonnyBarger.html.

Gary Pig Gold, "Skuawk! DVD Pick: *The Rolling Stones-Rock and Roll Circus*," skuawk.com, 11 February 2005.

Peter Guralnick quote from www.npr.org/templates/story/story.php?storyId=130276817.

Rick Huxley quote from www.thedc5.com/tvedsullivan.html.

Harvey Kubernik, "Engineer Andy Johns Discusses the making of the Rolling Stones' *Exile On Main Street*," from www.goldminemag.com/article/engineer-andy-johns-discusses-the-making-of-the-rolling-stones-exile-on-main-street (originally published in *Goldmine* magazine).

Harvey Kubernik, "Merry Clayton Interview" from Rock's Back Pages, 2009.

John Landis quotes from video accessed via www.trailersfromhell.com/trailers/9.

Pete Lewis, "Marshall Chess: All the Right Moves" from www.bluesandsoul.com/feature/576/marshall_chess_all_the_right_moves.

Not Fade Away Gallery, www.NFAgallery.com.

Jon Wilde, "Sex, Songs, and the Stones: An Interview with Marshall Chess," from www.sabotagetimes.com/music/sex-songs-and-the-stones-an-interview-with-marshall-chess-part-1/ and http://www.sabotagetimes.com/music/sex-songs-and-the-stones-an-interview-with-marshall-chess-part-2/, accessed January 2012.

Additional background information about the Redlands bust came from redlandsbust.blogspot.com and http://dietcokeandsympathy.blogspot.com/2009/11/drug-bust-at-redlands-stones.html.

IMAGE CREDITS

Chapter 1
Pg 7: Ira Korman Collection
Pg 8: Photofest

Chapter 2
Pg 13: Photo by Bob Bonis © NFAgallery.com
Pg 14: Leslie Woodhead, Manchester, 1965

Chapter 3
Pg 19: Photo by Bob Bonis © NFAgallery.com
Pg 20: Photofest

Chapter 4
Pg 24: Photofest
Pg 26: Tim Kelly Collection/Photofest

Chapter 5
Pg 30: Photo by Bob Bonis © NFAgallery.com
Pg 32: Photo by Bob Bonis © NFAgallery.com
Pg 35: Larry Marion Collection

Chapter 6
Pg 38: Photo by Bob Bonis © NFAgallery.com

Pg 39: Photo by Bob Bonis © NFAgallery.com
Pg 40: Michael Ochs Archives/Getty Collection

Chapter 7
Pg 44: Tim Kelly Collection/Photofest
Pg 45: Photo by Bob Bonis © NFAgallery.com

Chapter 8
Pg 46: Photo by Bob Bonis © NFAgallery.com

Chapter 9
Pg 50: Tim Kelly Collection/Photofest

Chapter 10
Pg 52: Photofest

Chapter 11
Pg 58: Tim Kelly Collection

Chapter 12
Pg 60: Photo by Bob Bonis © NFAgallery.com

Chapter 13
Pg 64: Screencap on left © SOFA Entertainment: The Ed Sullivan Shows Starring the Rolling Stones DVDs available at www.edsullivan.com; screencap on right courtesy of Photofest
Pg 65: Larry Marion Collection

Chapter 14
Pg 66: Tim Kelly Collection/Photofest

Chapter 15
Pg 70: Images courtesy Photofest
Pg 73: Photo by Bob Bonis © NFAgallery.com

Chapter 16
Pg 74: Ira Korman Collection

Chapter 17
Pg 79: Photofest
Pg 81: Tim Kelly Collection/Photofest
Pg 85: Photofest

Chapter 18
Pg 89: Photofest

Chapter 19
Pg 95: Photo by Bob Bonis © NFAgallery.com
Pg 96: Photo by Bob Bonis © NFAgallery.com
Pg 101: Photofest

Chapter 20
Pg 102: Photofest

Chapter 21
Pg 106: Tim Kelly Collection/Photofest

Chapter 22
Pg 109: Ira Korman Collection
Pg 113: Photofest

Chapter 23
Pg 116: Larry Marion Collection
Pg 119: Photofest

Chapter 24
Pg 122: Hulton Archive, photographed by David Montgomery, Getty Images

Chapter 25
Pg 126: Photofest

Chapter 27
Pg 137: Photo by Jo McDermand, courtesy Norman Dayron

Chapter 28
Pg 142: Copyright © 1969–2012 Phil Franks
Pg 143: Ira Korman Collection
Pg 146: Photofest
Pg 148: Tim Kelly Collection/Photofest
Pg 150: Photofest

Chapter 29
Pg 154: Mitch Corbett Collection, photographed by Giro Studio

Chapter 30
Pg 160 Mitch Corbett Collection, photographed by Giro Studio
Pg 163: © Bob Gruen/www.bobgruen.com

Chapter 31
Pg 164: Photofest

Chapter 32
Pg 169: Tim Kelly Collection/Photofest

Chapter 33
Pg 171: Photofest

Chapter 34
Pg 174: Photofest

Chapter 35
Pg 178: © Bob Gruen/www.bobgruen.com
Pg 179: Mitch Corbett Collection, photographed by Giro Studio

Chapter 36
Pg 182: © Bob Gruen/www.bobgruen.com

Chapter 37
Pg 185: © Laurie McGaw, 1978, for the *Toronto Star*

Chapter 38
Pg 188: Combative high school T-shirt design by Justin Melkmann
Pg 189: Mitch Corbett Collection, photographed by Giro Studio
Pg 192: © Bob Gruen/www.bobgruen.com

Chapter 39
Pg 194: Tim Kelly Collection/Photofest

Chapter 40
Pg 196: Courtesy of George Meredith
Pg 199: Larry Marion Collection

Chapter 41
Pg 201: Photofest
Pg 202: Screencap courtesy of Photofest

Chapter 42
Pg 205: © Bob Gruen/www.bobgruen.com
Pg 207: Photofest

Chapter 43
Pg 211: Photofest
Pg 215: Photofest
Pg 217: Photofest

Chapter 44
Pg 220: John Chiasson/Getty Images

Chapter 45
Pg 225: Photofest
Pg 228: Photofest

Chapter 46
Pg 235: Photo by Bob Bonis © NFAgallery.com

Chapter 47
Pg 239: Redferns Collection, Robert Knight Archive/Getty Images
Pg 240: Author's personal collection
Pg 241: Photofest
Pg 243: Mitch Corbett Collection, photographed by Giro Studio

Chapter 48
Pg 246: Photofest

Chapter 49
Pg 250: A. Messerschmidt/Getty Images

Chapter 50
Pg 256: Photofest
Pg 258: Screencap courtesy of Photofest

Epilogue
Pg 261: Author's personal collection

ABOUT THE COAUTHORS

Bernard M. Corbett (*left*) is the radio voice of Boston University hockey and Harvard University football. He is the author and coauthor of fifteen books. He lives in Stoneham, Massachusetts, and is a lifelong Rolling Stones fan.

Peter Thomas Fornatale (*right*) is a freelance writer and editor who lives in Brooklyn, New York. His favorite Rolling Stone is Charlie Watts.

For more, check out www.50Licksbook.com.